Perspectives on the Emergence of Scientific Disciplines

Maison des Sciences de l'Homme, Paris
Publications
4

MOUTON · THE HAGUE · PARIS

Perspectives
on the Emergence
of Scientific Disciplines

Edited for PAREX by

GERARD LEMAINE / ROY MACLEOD
MICHAEL MULKAY / PETER WEINGART

MOUTON · THE HAGUE · PARIS / ALDINE · CHICAGO

.Project PAREX (a contraction of Paris-Sussex) was created in 1970 to promote collaboration on an Anglo-French basis between scholars working on different aspects of the social studies of science. Within the last few years, it has become European in scope and broadly interdisciplinary in character. PAREX organises each year one general meeting and several working sessions on particular themes. The secretariat is provided by the Maison des Sciences de l'Homme (54 boulevard Raspail, 75270 Paris Cédex 06).

Contents

Preface

To historians and sociologists concerned with the growth of modern science, the study of disciplines and specialties has been particularly important. The structure and function of disciplines not only reveal essential social characteristics of scientific activity, and the mechanisms of communication, recognition and reward; they also provide access to cognitive features which distinguish one domain from another. In many ways, their study has given impetus to the understanding of scientific development, and to the consideration of social and economic circumstances which may have influenced the rate and direction of that development.

To a large extent, however, this study has proceeded in a fragmentary fashion. Work in the field reveals wide differences in assumptions, methods and explanations, in relation to quite different periods and cultures. Historians have often neglected the importance of analytical categories in describing similarities and differences among disciplines in given historical periods, while sociologists have tended to underestimate the importance of historical context, the vagaries of personal relations, and the pressures on individual scientists as 'actors' in the *arcana theatri* of specialized knowledge. These traditional disciplinary differences have, in practice, been magnified by differences between the scholarly traditions of different countries, which have tended to give different emphases to particular questions and forms of explanation. Perhaps unsurprisingly, generalizations have not been easily forthcoming. Looking to the future, many would agree that it is becoming important to consolidate what we know about the strategies of different disciplines, and the processes by which new ideas and techniques reproduce or alter accepted modes of thought. This task has acquired special urgency in recent years, as the possibility of locating mediations between the 'inner logic' of scientific thought and the external conditions which may advance, retard, or stimulate its application, has become a principal problem not only for scholars but for students of science policy as well.

The possibility that comparative studies, or at least the comparison of results, might lead in the direction of a more systematic approach to the study of disciplines on an interdisciplinary and European basis, prompted PAREX to organize a meeting on the 'Naissance des nouvelles disciplines: conditions cognitives et sociales' in Paris in December 1973. The relative success of this meeting in airing conflicting viewpoints and compelling evidence kindled further interest, and led us to arrange a session on 'Methodology in the Sociology of Science' at York in June 1974. By this time, so much material had been generated along such a vast spectrum of disciplines, that we felt it important to set out the domain as it appeared to us, and to put on record some of our studies, as instalments of 'work in progress'. This book is the result. In an attempt to bring together and clarify some of the important issues involved in the study of scientific disciplines, we have prepared a general editorial introduction. This introduction was drafted by Michael Mulkay, and was then revised in the light of comments from the other three editors.

In presenting this collection of essays, we make no grand promises. The problems involved in agreeing upon common formulations, and comparable categories, are formidable. Nonetheless, we believe our exercise has been constructive and we would like to share the sense of our meetings with others. In the time which has elapsed since these meetings were proposed, four of the papers in this volume have appeared, by agreement, in *Science Studies* (now *Social Studies of Science*) and *Social Science Information.* We are grateful to the editors and publishers for their permission to republish these essays in slightly modified form. Not all the essays presented at our meetings are included in this volume. Those which were not are listed in the PAREX Guide, available from the Maison des Sciences de l'Homme, 54 boulevard Raspail, 75270 Paris Cédex 06.

We are pleased to find that many of the objects which prompted us to meet, have also formed the *terminus a quo* of other groups in Europe. In July 1974, the Institute for Advanced Studies in Vienna sponsored a colloquium which has resulted in a volume entitled *Determinants and Controls of Scientific Disciplines* (Dordrecht: D. Reidel, 1976) edited by K. D. Knorr, H. Strasser and H. G. Zilian. In 1975, a special edition of the *Kölner Zeitschrift für Soziologie und Sozialpsychologie* was devoted to the sociology of science and included much work on the study of new disciplines. This issue is edited by Nico Stehr and is entitled, *Wissenschafts-soziologie – Studien und Materialien* (Opladen: Westdeutscher Verlag). In September 1975, a special meeting on the sociology of science, which included material on new disciplines, was held at York under the joint chairmanship of Nigel Gilbert and Michael Mulkay. A selection of papers from this conference will appear in a special issue of *Social Studies of Science* in August 1976.

The editors would like to thank the Maison des Sciences de l'Homme, the Social Science Research Council and the Universities of Sussex and York for providing us with financial support and secretarial organization for our meetings.

The Editors
January 1976

GÉRARD LEMAINE a fait ses études supérieures à la Sorbonne. Licencié en psychologie, diplômé de l'Institut de Psychologie de l'Université de Paris, de 1960 à 1965 il est chercheur au CNRS. Depuis 1965 il est sous-directeur d'études à l'Ecole des Hautes Etudes en Sciences Sociales (autrefois Ecole pratique des Hautes Etudes, 6ᵉ section). Il a fait des travaux sur la créativité, sur la différenciation et l'influence sociales, mais ses recherches portent de plus en plus sur le fonctionnement de la communauté scientifique. Il vient d'achever un travail sur les recherches psychologiques, neuro-physiologiques et biochimiques sur le sommeil.

ROY MACLEOD studied at Harvard and Cambridge, and is now reader and chairman of History and Social Studies of Science at the University of Sussex. He is, with Gérard Lemaine, a 'co-animateur' of PAREX and is engaged in comparative historical studies of scientific ideas and institutions in Western Europe.

M. J. MULKAY took his B.A. at LSE, his M.A. at Simon Fraser University (Vancouver) and his Ph.D. in sociology at Aberdeen. He is now a reader in sociology at the University of York, where he is studying scientific elites and the sociology of knowledge.

PETER WEINGART received his *Diplom* and his doctorate from the Free University of Berlin. He is now Professor of Sociology of Science and Science Policy at the University of Bielefeld and is involved in studies on the interaction between scientific development and the articulation of public and political opinion.

Problems in the Emergence
of New Disciplines

One of the characteristic features of the modern industrial societies in which we live is their inclusion of a relatively distinct community devoted to the continuous extension of systematic knowledge about the natural world.[1] Particularly since the nineteenth century this scientific research community has come to play a significant part in extending industrial and military technology. It has also come to exert a considerable influence on conceptions of the natural world dominant in the wider society. Moreover, the scientific community has grown even faster than industrial society at large. It has, therefore, taken up an increasing proportion of the resources of industrial societies and has absorbed a growing proportion of their members.[2] Yet despite the evident importance of science in economic, political and intellectual life, our knowledge of the ways in which science develops and of the factors which foster or impede its growth is still fragmentary and highly tentative.

One reason for this is, of course, that scientific development is a highly complex process. Consequently, there has been a tendency for those engaged in its empirical study to select for close attention one strand or a small number of strands from the complicated web of social and intellectual factors at work. Many historians, for example, have dealt primarily with the internal development of scientific knowledge within given fields of inquiry. Sociologists, in contrast, have tended to concentrate on the social processes associated with the activities of scientists; but at the same time they have largely ignored the intellectual content of science. These two broad approaches to the study of scientific development are not necessarily incompatible, even though in the past little attempt has been made to bring them together. It is our hope that these two main perspectives on scientific development, and their several specific variants, can be made to be supplementary and that new opportunities in the social history and the historical sociology of science will more clearly emerge. This book is intended as a move in that direction.

We have collected in this volume a number of recent case studies by historians and sociologists of the development of research fields in the natural sciences. These case studies are mostly concerned with the emergence and growth of particular new fields, although there is one study of the decline of an established area. By choosing studies of this kind we have tried to give the collection a certain coherence. At the same time, however, we have thereby omitted from direct consideration certain kinds of perfectly legitimate approaches to the study of scientific development. We have excluded, for instance, studies of the growth of the scientific community in particular countries and studies of the overall growth of science.[3] This latter type of study has, nevertheless, influenced the way in which we have defined our range of problems. For one of the central conclusions to be derived from an examination of the growth of science in general is that science, as both social and intellectual activity, has evolved by means of a cumulative proliferation of new areas of inquiry, by means of a continual branching out into fields of investigation previously unexplored and often totally unexpected. It is for this reason that we have chosen to concentrate here on the emergence of new research areas. In the rest of this introduction we shall attempt, firstly, to illustrate the full range of questions which can be formulated in relation to this broad problem.[4] We shall then briefly discuss some of the case studies presented in part 1, drawing attention to those questions which were taken as central in particular studies. The basic assumption behind this exercise is that we shall come closer to a systematic and generalised understanding of scientific development only if we have answers to a wide-ranging and comparable set of questions for a considerable variety of scientific fields and for a variety of cultural and national contexts.

In one way or another, all new areas of scientific investigation grow out of prior research or out of the extension of an established body of scientific and/or technical knowledge. Accordingly, it is always possible to trace the intellectual origins of any given field and to show that its emergence at a particular time was at least partly due to previous scientific-cum-technical developments. For example, the emergence of genetics at the turn of the last century can accurately be seen as the end-product of a long line of scientific thought, which can be followed back to the time of Linnaeus and beyond.[5] If we concentrate on this aspect of scientific development, such questions as the following must be asked.

What were the distinctive scientific problems which provided the focus for the new research area? How did these problems come to be formulated? Were they the logical outcome of a major theoretical advance? Or were they the result of attempts to resolve anomalies generated in the course of previous research?[6] Were they unexpectedly derived from the accumulation of empirical data? Or was empirical information sought to solve explicit theoretical issues? Did research techniques play any part in changing the direction of scientific inquiry?

These are all important questions which must be answered if we are to understand why a particular field arose and prospered when it did. In the case of genetics, these questions (or some similar but perhaps more refined set of questions) could be used to provide a framework within which to trace the gradual emergence of the new field throughout the second half of the last century. Thus Darwin's theory of evolution drew particular attention to the nature of the principles of variation of inheritance. This problem eventually became the focus for the new discipline. However, Darwin's work raised more difficulties than solutions in relation to this specific topic. Mendel's laws of inheritance, arising largely out of a long tradition of work into plant hybridization, constituted what later came to be regarded as a major step toward resolving these difficulties; a step which had been foreshadowed in Darwin's own work.[7] But Mendel's research was ignored by a whole generation of scientists largely because, it seems, its central assumptions about particulate inheritance were inconsistent with theoretical conceptions dominant at the time. Leading scientists such as Nägeli were simply unable to perceive the significance of Mendel's results.[8] At the same time, however, research was proceeding on the fertilization process and on the role of the chromosomes, by Hertwig, Strasburger, Weismann and others. This work led to a view of inheritance as arising from the recombination of separate units of hereditary material, that is, as dependent on what are now called 'genes'; and to the rediscovery of Mendel's results by Correns and De Vries. It also led to the widespread use of statistical techniques. From this point on, genetics existed as a distinct area of inquiry in something like its modern form, with a corpus of established knowledge and technique, and with the beginnings of a cumulative research programme deriving from this body of knowledge.[9]

This sketch of the origins of genetics is necessarily brief and superficial. It is intended to do no more than illustrate how we can in principle provide a valuable account of the emergence of a new field by concentrating solely upon a sequence of intellectual developments. But the statements proposed above in relation to genetics can easily lead to quite different kinds of question. At the most general level, we can ask: what were the social processes occurring within the research community which were associated with these scientific developments? More specifically we can raise such issues as: was Mendel's work ignored initially because he failed to communicate with those scientists who would have been more receptive to his work? Did the social organization of the research community affect the dissemination and reception of Mendel's results? What was the intellectual background of those scientists who laid the foundation for modern genetics? What was their position in the research community? Did scientists with a different position and background respond differently to the new scientific developments? These are some of the more obvious questions which come to mind as soon as we begin to regard as problematic the social processes directly associated with specific intellectual advances. We do not intend to try to answer these questions here in detail. Nevertheless, we can illustrate the kinds of answers which might be formulated on the basis of available evidence.

In the first place, we know that Mendel's contact with the wider research community was mediated through the eminent scientist Nägeli.[10] This situation, in which relatively unknown men depend on a particular eminent colleague, is not unusual in science. There is, in fact, considerable evidence to show that in many fields there exists a stratum of leading scientists, each of whom guides the work of a number of less prominent researchers.[11] Thus Mendel's relationship with Nägeli was by no means unique. It was rather a typical product of the social organization of science. Moreover, it had important consequences for the way in which Mendel's work was received. For it seems likely that the *leaders* in Mendel's field were most committed to the dominant conception of inheritance and, therefore, least receptive to his new ideas.[12] Further support for this view is revealed when we examine the characteristics of those men who eventually succeeded in creating the new field. Firstly, they were rather young. Secondly, either they tended to have come from fields only tangentially related to the study of inheritance or they were recognized as iconoclasts even without their support of Mendelian ideas.[13] In short, these were men who occupied relatively lowly positions within the research community and who were least committed to established notions of inheritance. There is, then, at least a *prima facie* case for arguing that the emergence of genetics as a distinct field of inquiry was dependent on a combination of intellectual and social factors within the scientific community. Mendel's work, and that of his successors, was a response to scientific problems. But the scientific implications of their results were not pursued until there existed a strong group of scientists who, owing to their academic background and their position in the research community, were willing to abandon established conceptions.

There exists now a preliminary body of literature which enables us to view the intellectual development of research areas in science as systematically related to the internal social processes of the research community. In some, and perhaps many, cases the growth of a new area starts with the perception, by scientists already at work in one or more existing areas, of unsolved problems, unexpected observations or unusual technical developments, the pursuit of which lies outside their current field. Thus the exploration of a new area is often set in motion by a process of scientific migration.[14] In the case of genetics, scientists initially came from nine or more different fields.[15] Scientific migration is not a random process, for the scientists moving into a new field tend to come from other areas with specifiable characteristics. In particular, they come from research areas which have experienced a pronounced decline in the significance of current results; from areas where there are few or no avenues of research easily available; from areas whose members have special competence in or knowledge of techniques which appear to have wider application; and from areas which have been disrupted, often by events originating outside the research community, and whose members have consequently no firm commitment to an established field.[16] They tend to move into areas which appear to offer special opportunities for productive research, for the utilization of their particular skills and, consequently, for career advancement.

During the earliest stage of a research area's development, workers at different places take up the same or closely related problems, often unaware of similar work proceeding elsewhere. The lack of communication and the concern with relatively crude exploration of fairly obvious problems leads to multiple discovery, anticipation of results and open competition.[17] An early lead in the competition for results tends to be taken by those with best access to such resources as suitable techniques, graduate students, research funds and publication outlets. It seems likely that a crucial factor in this early phase is sponsorship by scientists of high repute who, by guiding their protégés into new and promising areas, confer legitimacy on the areas of their choice and contribute to the rapid exploration of these areas.[18] The initial results tend to be scattered among various disciplinary journals, general purpose journals and the journals of learned societies.[19] As a result of these first publications, the communication network is extended and strengthened, as some of those previously working independently on similar problems become aware of their common interests and establish informal contact. Where informal communication is not established, growth appears to be seriously impeded.[20]

During the early stages of exploration, research problems tend to be loosely defined and results are often open to widely differing interpretations. This was true of 'genetics' during the 1880s and 1890s. At this stage, in cases where there is a firmly established definition of the field already in existence, any radically new conception is likely to meet with considerable resistance and initially to be strongly supported only by those who are in some way marginal to the area. Gradually, however, as a result of continual debate informally and through the journals, agreement over scientific issues tends to increase. Growing consensus is accompanied by associated changes in intellectual and social processes within the network. For example, publications appear increasingly in more specialized journals. Similarly, the proportion of references to papers by authors not centrally engaged in the field declines markedly.[21] At the same time, a small number of fairly early contributions come to be recognised as paradigmatic and to be cited regularly. As these important contributions become known to workers in other areas and to potential graduate students, the rate of recruitment into what is coming to be regarded as a 'new and interesting field' increases rapidly. As a result, in many cases, the number of researchers active in the area and the amount of published material grows rapidly.

As the network increases in size, research teams and clusters of collaborators form who recruit new entrants to the field and train them from the perspective of the increasingly firm scientific consensus.[22] Both research groups and individual scientists take up specialist lines of inquiry, which are chosen so as to minimise overlap and, consequently, the likelihood of competition.[23] This process ensures that a relatively wide range of issues is explored.[24] Research teams and groupings of collaborators tend to be led by highly productive scientists who exert an important influence on the direction of intellectual development, not only because they are responsible for many of the basic advances, but also because they play a major part in the informal dissemination of information within the network.

Research areas tend to develop in response to major innovations which appear early in the growth sequence, such as that of Mendel in the case of genetics. Subsequent work tends to consist primarily of elaborations upon these central contributions. Consequently, a major proportion of what participants see as innovative work is completed before the field has begun to acquire a significant proportion of its eventual membership.[25] This means that the perceived interest of the field falls sharply after the very earliest period and that, consequently, opportunities decline for making what will be recognised as a notable scientific contribution. As this becomes evident to participants and, more slowly, to potential entrants, the rate of growth decreases.

In some areas, the decline of interesting and/or solveable problems may be followed by a rejection of the existing consensus, and by its replacement with a new and fertile research framework.[26] But this is probably unusual. The central feature of the *typical* sequence seems more likely to be that the pursuit of the problems with which the network was originally concerned either generates a number of new problems and unexpected observations or produces results which are seen to have implications for work in other areas. Thus growth usually turns imperceptibly into decline as recruitment falls away and established members of the network move elsewhere into problem areas in process of formation (see de Certaine's essay in part 1). However, research areas which have become well established take a long time to die out altogether. There is always *some* work that can be done. In many fields, therefore, a few scientists are likely to remain, carrying on the research tradition long after the focus of interest has shifted elsewhere.[27] In some fields, however, although the initial problems are quickly solved, the first period of exploration produces a rapid efflorescence of loosely related avenues of investigation. In such instances the sequence of preliminary exploration, exponential growth and levelling off, can be clearly observed at the level of the specialty or discipline.[28]

This account of the processes of scientific development emphasises the way in which science grows through the branching of new lines of research. It is, therefore, particularly consistent with, and receives support from those quantitative studies in which the cumulative increase in numbers of research papers, separate journals, scientific abstracts, specialist societies, and so on has been described.[29] Indeed the literature summarised above begins to give us an idea of the ways in which social and intellectual processes combine within the scientific community to produce its distinctive pattern of growth and internal differentiation.

Yet this account, focusing exclusively on development inside the research community, is clearly incomplete. For there are several kinds of external influence upon scientific development. It sometimes happens, for instance, that ideas, observations or techniques evolved in the course of practical activities are transmitted to those concerned with the systematic extension of scientific knowledge and that this information changes the direction of their research. As we indicated above, the practical knowledge of plant and animal breeders was increasingly incorporated into the work of biologists, and particularly those concerned with inheritance, throughout the nineteenth century. A similar transmission of technical knowledge, acquired in the course of the development of the steam engine, had a major impact on the scientific study of heat and energy, and on the emergence of the field of thermodynamics.[30] Such 'technical' information can pass into the research community in at least three ways. It can be transmitted by the movement of scientists, technologists or informed laymen from one social context to another. It can also be transmitted through personal contact between scientists and relevant non-scientists. And it can be transmitted by means of formal media of communication, such as professional journals.

The limited evidence available on this issue indicates that the last of these three communication channels is, in general terms, the least important.[31] However, in any specific case, we must be prepared for the possibility that, in one way or another, the direction of scientific advance has been influenced by an input of technical information from outside. We must try, therefore, to answer such questions as: to what extent was scientific development affected by the introduction of technical information generated outside the research community? Who was responsible for the transmission of this information? Did those responsible occupy a special position either in the research community or in the lay community? Were all researchers equally receptive to this information? What social and intellectual factors were associated with a favourable response? Was the transfer or acceptance of information due in any way to a particular set of institutional arrangements? These questions are all fairly obvious, once we have recognised that technical information does flow across the boundary of the research community in both directions. Nevertheless, they are not always posed explicitly in studies of the emergence of new fields and we are sometimes left uncertain whether no technical information from outside was involved or whether the issue was never investigated.

The most interesting of the questions formulated immediately above, for the purpose of our present discussion, is that concerning institutional arrangements. For this question draws attention to another set of external influences upon scientific development, namely the immediate institutional contexts in which scientific research is undertaken. There are a number of studies which show that the institutional context of research can affect both the rate of scientific growth and also its direction.[32] It seems likely that genetics, for example, was able to develop particularly quickly in the US during the first decade of this century, at least partly because the American university system was expanding at that time and also because American agricultural colleges and experimental stations provided a reasonably receptive environment for the new genetics and, in some cases at least, a context in which research could be undertaken.[33] A somewhat different example of how changes in a national academic system can affect the emergence and growth of new areas can be found in the case of the medical sciences in Germany during the second half of the last century.[34] Between 1850 and 1870 physiology emerged there as a distinct discipline. The number of university chairs expanded quickly in this field and the number of discoveries increased dramatically. But the German university system itself did not expand. Consequently, by the 1870s all the possible chairs in physiology had been established and occupied by relatively young men. From this date, therefore, the attractiveness of a career in physiology declined markedly and there was an immediate shift of interest within the medical sciences away from physiology toward such fields as pathology, pharmacology and experimental psychology, where opportunities for professional advancement were less restricted.[35] As a result of these processes, the rate of innovation in German physiology fell sharply and remained low for a generation; whereas in the other medical sciences new departures were set in motion.

In the light of these examples, it seems necessary in any comprehensive account of the emergence and/or growth of new scientific fields to consider the part played by the academic context and by associated institutions. Accordingly, questions such as the following should be raised. Did research into the new area originate and spread within the university system or within some other social context? Were any changes occurring in this social context which were especially favourable or unfavourable to the exploration of the new field? Did entry into the new field confer any special social or economic advantages? Clearly, answers to questions of this kind will in some cases contribute to our understanding of the emergence of new fields. But, once again, the answers that we are likely to get will lead us toward a new set of questions. They will lead us, in particular, to consider the economic and political processes at work in the wider society.

We suggested above, with special reference to genetics, that a new academic area would become more easily established if its inception coincided with the expansion of the university system. But systems of higher education do not expand in a social vacuum. Rather they tend to respond to changes in the national economic situation and to changes in political policy and political context. The ways in which the economy and the political process impinge on scientific development are varied, often highly complex, and in general not well understood. We shall offer just a few illustrative examples. In the case of genetics, the availability of agricultural colleges and experimental stations interested in research on inheritance was merely one by-product of a broad Federal government policy designed to help American agriculture.[36] Situations like this, in which government support for an area of public interest fosters the growth of a clearly relevant scientific field, are probably fairly common.[37] In contrast, the expansion of the German university system during the last century, and the accompanying emergence of many new fields of inquiry, appears to have been an indirect consequence of the dynamics of the German political structure. Because the German cultural area exceeded the limits of any single German state, no central national university existed. Instead there was a large number of separate universities, all of which were in competition for academic reputation. Thus, it has been argued, the university system was decentralized and competitive because the political system was decentralized and competitive. Accordingly, as the German universities sought to outdo each other, they became more receptive to supporting new areas, in which none of their competitors could have established a commanding lead.[38]

These are examples of historical connections between political structure and policy, on the one hand, and scientific development, on the other hand. There are, in addition, instances where economic factors have been particularly important. The expansion and reform of science education in Britain during the later part of the last century is a good illustration of how changes in the economy can influence the institutional context in which science evolves. For the reorganization of British science teaching at this time, which brought with it a radical alteration in the nature of scientific research and recruitment of scientific personnel, was a direct response to the apparent economic decline of the United Kingdom in comparison with scientifically more advanced societies, and in particular, in comparison with Germany.[39]

The impact of economic factors on the development of scientific disciplines has not always been mediated through changes in the institutional context of research. The work of Pasteur, for example, on the fermentation of beer and on silkworms, in the course of which he began to develop his germ theory of disease and to lay the foundation for the discipline of bacteriology, was a direct response to the 'needs' of French industry.[40] But Pasteur's scientific ideas were by no means produced solely by his study of the technical problems facing the manufacturers of French beer and silk. Rather Pasteur's analysis of these practical problems was guided by conceptions he had already begun to develop in the course of prior, and more exclusively scientific, researches.[41] If this example is at all typical, it seems likely that the direct connections between the economy and scientific development will involve a two-way process and will depend greatly on the flow of technical information.

The connections between scientific development and economic and other practical problems are perhaps most obvious in the biological and medical sciences. Thus many of the discoveries and, even more, the changes of outlook that have transformed biology during this century have been associated with attempts to satisfy the needs of practice; for example, in fields such as entomology, ecology, immunology, and so on.[42] But links of this kind between broad social developments and the evolution of scientific knowledge are not necessarily confined either to the biological sphere or to the twentieth century. It has been argued, for instance, that the emergence of modern physics in the seventeenth century was not unrelated to the rise of the bourgeois class and military and economic demands; and that the focal scientific problems of classical physics, such as problems of floating bodies and projection of bodies through resistant media, were direct responses to technical issues which had become important as a result of broad socio-economic changes.[43]

In the light of the earlier discussion, it seems to us unsatisfactory to claim that broad changes in the structure of society have determined the course of scientific development in any simple, direct or uniform fashion. It appears necessary, nevertheless, to formulate a series of questions relating to the influence upon science of economic and political factors. For example: did scientists respond directly to specific technical problems in the economic sphere? Were there changes in the economy which affected governmental or industrial support for particular types of scientific research? Was the inception or the growth of the field influenced in any direct or indirect way by special features of the political context? These general questions must, of course, be made much more specific in the study of particular fields. The value of such general formulations is that they help us to ensure that we do not ignore factors which may be of crucial importance in specific cases.

In various ways, then, the internal development of scientific research has been influenced by the wider political and economic context.[44] In many cases this influence has been relatively indirect, largely because those responsible for economic and political policy have in the past tended to assume that direct intervention by laymen would only disrupt pure research and that an autonomous scientific community would not fail to set in motion a more or less continuous supply of practically useful and beneficial knowledge. Consequently, although the support given to research by both government and industry has been on a selective basis, academic scientists have been left relatively free in Western countries to determine the detailed distribution of funds in accordance with scientific criteria. In recent decades, however, the cost of much scientific research has increased dramatically. As a result, governments, which provide most of the funds for pure research, have come to require a more tangible return for their support. Increasingly, therefore, attempts have been made to assess the benefits of research in relation to economic growth, welfare, armaments and national prestige.[45] Furthermore, governments have become increasingly committed to a 'policy for science' which reflects social, economic and political, as well as scientific, priorities.[46] Thus, science has come to be seen as competing with other areas of governmental policy for scarce resources. Accordingly the view has formed that, despite the internal logic of scientific development and the undeniable element of unpredictability in scientific advance, an explicit policy must be formulated to control the direction in which science evolves in such a way that 'the maximum social benefit' is extracted from scientific knowledge.[47]

In addition to this change of view in official circles, there has been an evident decline of general support for science. One sign of this is the recent fall in recruitment into science, which has been noted in Western Europe, Britain and the USA.[48] Another sign is the growing momentum of an increasingly critical perspective on science. From this new perspective, science comes to be seen as inseparable from such unwelcome developments as pollution and the hydrogen bomb; and the activity, even of the academic research scientist, is more and more regarded, not as a morally neutral search for truth, but as embodying a narrow, and in some respects equivocal, moral position. These views are by no means confined to laymen. Many of the leaders of the scientific community appear to have become aware of the difficulty of the moral problems facing them. In addition, there are signs of more widely based movements of opinion within the scientific community. For instance, certain national societies for social responsibility in science have considered requiring their members to make an ethical statement of principle concerning their intentions in research. Similarly, a number of schools of 'critical science' have developed recently whose aims – to investigate and understand the consequences of modern science and technology and to ensure that any abuses are abolished or controlled – are both political and scientific.[49]

We do not know at present whether this climate of opinion with respect to science will be lasting; nor do we understand in detail how it is likely to influence intellectual advance in science. If it does last, if critical debate about the place of science in modern society continues and if explicit policies embodying attempts at rational control of science become permanent features of modern government, it seems likely that non-scientific considerations will come to play an increasingly important part in determining the direction of scientific development and that academic scientists will have to become significantly more receptive than in the past to the requirements of lay audiences. Those engaged in the study of science must, therefore, be ready to investigate the nature of the possible links between scientific development and views of science current in various sectors of society at large.[50] In the case of many past developments, the availability of research personnel and the existence of a general support for science were not problematic. In the future, however, this is unlikely to be so. There is every indication that the supply of new researchers will continue to diminish and that there will be an increasing concern among laymen, politicians and scientists to regulate scientific development in accordance with social and moral standards as well as purely scientific criteria.[51] As a result, especially in the case of scientific fields which have emerged in the last decade or so, we must be ready to pose such questions as: was this field particularly attractive to new entrants to science and, if so, why? Was it seen as being especially significant in relation to specific social values? Was there any negotiation involved between scientific leaders and those able to provide funds and facilities? Was there any organised or diffuse movement among scientists (or among laymen) in its favour?

So far in this introduction we have drawn attention to a series of what can be called, for the sake of convenience, 'problematic spheres' in relation to the emergence of new areas in science. These may be summarized as follows:
— internal intellectual processes
— internal social processes
— external intellectual factors

— immediate institutional context
— specific economic and political factors
— diffuse social influences.
The order in which these items are listed does not represent their degree of significance. How these factors interact in particular cases remains empirically open. What we have tried to show above is simply that every sphere can, at least in some instances, influence appreciably the course of scientific development. More specifically, we have illustrated how these spheres may be seen as bearing on the *rate* of scientific development, on the *direction* of scientific development, and on the intellectual *content* of scientific development.

These important notions of rate, direction and content, which have been implicit in the preceding discussion, need a little clarification at this juncture. By 'rate of scientific development' we are referring to the speed with which scientific information accrues within a particular field or within a number of related fields. It can be measured, in a manner which is crude but adequate for many purposes, by counting the number of researchers active in the area or the number of research reports published in the area over a period of time.[52]

Although rate of development is, in most cases, closely linked to direction of development, the two notions must be kept analytically distinct. 'Direction of scientific development' refers to the exploration of one area of intellectual endeavour rather than other areas. To use an example given above, certain facets of the German political and educational systems appear to have influenced the direction of scientific development during the last century by encouraging scientists to search for and to open up new fields of medical research. Of course, these changes in direction entailed changes in the rate of development of the various medical sciences involved, with older fields slowing down as the new fields began to grow. However, changes in the rate of growth need not always involve alterations in direction. For example, new government policies may make available more funds and more research personnel for a relatively mature field of inquiry which is seen as having important practical implications. In such a situation, the rate of development may accelerate within this field without there being either a change in the direction taken by scientific research or even a fall in the rate of development of other areas.

There can be no doubt that both the rate and the direction of scientific development are influenced by social as well as by intellectual factors. It is by no means so clear that the content of science – and by this we mean scientific principles, explanatory propositions, and empirical findings –

has been or can be *directly* influenced by social factors. Certainly it has been argued, by both philosophers and sociologists of science, that although the speed of scientific advance and the direction it has taken may be affected by social processes, the actual content of scientific thought is an outcome solely of the internal logic of scientific ideas and scientific research methods.[53]

It is clearly important to bring to bear on this point the empirical findings provided by case studies. In our view, none of those contained either in this volume or elsewhere, demonstrate unequivocally the effect of social influences on the content of scientific thought. In the case of radio astronomy and in that of radar meteor astronomy (see the essays by Mulkay and Edge, and by Gilbert), for example, it is certain that the technical advances made in the course of war-time research on radar, as well as the social groupings then formed, were crucially important in setting in motion the growth of these new research areas immediately after the Second World War. However, there is no way in which we can discover from the evidence at present available whether the propositions in relation to meteors or radio emission from celestial phenomena which are now generally agreed, would have been any different if their origins had been totally independent of external influences. Similarly, in the case of tropical medicine (see Michael Worboys' essay), it can reasonably be argued that political factors merely hastened the application of bio-medical perspectives to diseases such as elephantiasis, leprosy and malaria; and that the way in which these diseases were interpreted by the practitioners of tropical medicine was determined entirely by 'scientific' considerations.

The case of agricultural chemistry (see the first essay in this volume) comes close to demonstrating the impact of external economic and demographic factors on scientific content. In this case it is argued that, due to the pressing need to increase agricultural yields and within the context of developments in chemistry, practical goals were translated into a specific scientific development, namely Liebig's theory of the cycle of plant growth, which allowed the production of artificial manure. But the influence of these external factors on the content of a particular scientific development must not be mistaken to refer to a simple uni-directional and *direct* process. Rather, the case of agricultural chemistry demonstrates the extremely complex nature of this process, in which previous scientific knowledge, economic problems, and political and institutional factors may all interact. We only know for certain that by this process external influences are 'translated' into scientific knowledge which remains subject to the internal logic of science.

The last essay in this volume, on the 'Resistance and Receptivity of Science to External Direction', deals with one attempt to conceptualize this process. Perhaps the only situation in which a conclusive inference could be made in relation to this issue would be one in which there were two available scientific perspectives which dealt with the same range of phenomena and which were judged by participants to be of equal scientific merit. In such circumstances, it might be possible to show that support for one perspective rather than another was a consequence of religious, political, economic, or other social influences, and not solely a consequence of scientific judgments. It is, however, unlikely that such a clear-cut situation could ever be observed. For example, even if scientists' adoption of one perspective rather than another was 'really' due to political factors, those involved would probably tend to justify their choice on scientific grounds, thereby making it difficult, if not impossible, for the investigator to show that the political sphere exerted a determining influence on the content of scientific ideas.

There is, then, considerable difficulty in showing that social factors, whether internal or external, actually mould the *content* of scientific ideas.[54] It is not surprising, therefore, that in the studies below little attempt is made to establish such a strong relationship. Rather the main concern is to describe how social factors have influenced the incidence, dissemination and acceptance of new scientific ideas and, thereby, the rate and direction of scientific development. These studies also try to show how scientific innovations have exerted a reciprocal influence on accompanying social developments. These reciprocal relationships can be clearly seen in the case of radio astronomy. This specialty would not have emerged when it did, nor would it have grown up so quickly, if radar techniques developed during the war had not been available or if university research groups had not been formed by scientists who had been employed in war-time radar research establishments. At the same time, however, research into radio emission from celestial objects would not have been pursued with such energy if the scientific results had not appeared significant in the light of current conceptions. The appearance and rapid development of radio astronomy in Britain and Australia immediately following the Second World War was clearly due to a conjunction of social, scientific and technical factors. That all these factors were involved in the emergence of the new specialty can be seen from the fact that, where this conjunc]ion did not occur, the growth of radio astronomy was much more hesitant and largely dependent upon prior scientific and social developments in these two countries.

A dynamic relationship between intellectual and social processes can also be observed in the case of physical chemistry (see the essay by R. G. A. Dolby). In this instance, the growth of the area was facilitated by the existence of peripheral regions in the scientific community within which the new perspective could emerge and prosper; and by the formation of a 'school' around the figure of Ostwald, which played an important part in sponsoring the new ideas of physical chemistry and in attracting and training new recruits. Once again, however, these social factors combined with intellectual developments. Ostwald and his school were able to make such a major intellectual impact at least partly because they were able to systematise a considerable body of previously scattered scientific work, and also because they based their claim for scientific legitimacy on powerful new theories which in due course proved to be fruitful in various areas of chemical inquiry.

As we have already noted, the relationship between intellectual and social processes is further illuminated if we look at the role of the institutional setting of science. Institutions are social processes which have achieved a considerable degree of permanence and perceived legitimacy. Science is institutionalized in universities in the form of teaching and research activities. The organizational structure of the university system acquires its own weight and dynamics, for instance, by social separation between disciplines on intellectual grounds, by the formalization of recruitment and resource allocation procedures, by its dependence on state authorities or private boards, and so on. As a result, although the structure of the academic world can become a barrier to scientific innovation, it is sometimes possible for scientists to use the social dynamics of the university system to gain support and acceptance for new intellectual departures. Thus the proponents of physical chemistry were able to take advantage of the diversity of the German university system to obtain a secure base and to set in motion the cumulative growth of their field, despite the intellectually and institutionally dominant position at that time of organic chemistry. In some instances, the impact of the immediate institutional context may be selective, favouring one specialty or discipline rather than another. To show this clearly, however, we need to demonstrate that the institutional context operates differentially upon scientifically equivalent fields. At other times, it seems that changes in the institutional context affect a wide range of areas in a more or less uniform fashion. Thus the expansion of the American university system at the turn of the century helps to explain the rapid establishment in that country not only of physical chemistry, but also of many other fields.

In the case of agricultural chemistry we have an instance where scientists deliberately used institutional mechanisms in order to overcome opposition from established disciplines and to facilitate the diffusion of their own scientific convictions. Agricultural chemistry was a discipline whose development was strategically planned in response to requests from outside the scientific community for a chemical science which would bring about a definite improvement in agricultural productivity. Liebig, the major figure involved, was convinced that when a new theory replaced an old one it tended to stand in direct opposition to it. Consequently, he believed that it was important to promote the growth of the new perspective through the training of students. Within his own laboratory he adopted an explicit policy of directing students into research in agricultural chemistry. This alone could not have been successful, however, if Liebig had not also taken steps to ensure that career opportunities were available for his students.[55] In reports on the situation of chemistry in Prussia and Austria he attacked the incompetence of existing teachers in order to gain influence over future appointments in the interests of his own students. In addition, he was in command of the leading international journal for organic chemistry, in which he gave his field and his students a prominent place. Finally, Liebig was not only influential in establishing professorial chairs for agricultural chemistry in several universities, but he was also able to restrict the development of the agricultural academies, whose members tended to oppose his views.

Although in the case of agricultural chemistry the strategic use of institutional mechanisms was particularly pronounced, the development of many scientific specialties shows a similar pattern.[56] The nature of the institutional context and the use of that context made by innovators are often crucial factors in the establishment and diffusion of novel ideas in science. However, the operation of institutional mechanisms alone can explain in full neither the success of innovations nor the removal of resistance to these ideas. Liebig, for example, was not recognised as successful until he had demonstrated the agricultural superiority of his artificial manure and, by implication, the validity of his theory.

In the chapters which follow, the emphasis placed upon intellectual, institutional and other factors unavoidably varies, according to the nature of the case under study and the perspectives of particular authors. Consequently, although the connections between the development of scientific knowledge and various problematic spheres are examined in part 1, no single study gives a full and detailed discussion in relation to every sphere. The studies presented cannot be used, therefore, as an empirical base for the formulation of reliable generalizations about the social production of scientific knowledge. Their value lies rather in the way in which they document the existence of certain relationships between the problematic spheres and the way in which they illustrate the importance of specific factors within some of these spheres. Thus our attempt to delineate here a set of problematic spheres provides no more than a 'first ordering scheme', designed to facilitate and to systematise further analysis. It leaves virtually untouched the highly complex task of specifying in a consistent, precise and general form, the links between the various factors involved and the exact manner in which they affect the rate, direction and content of intellectual development in science. For the moment, we must remain content with the guiding assumption that each of the spheres identified above has a degree of autonomy, an internal dynamic, as well as being related to and in many cases directly affected by the other spheres.

At various points in the discussion above we have referred to issues of a methodological kind. On several occasions, we have mentioned the difficulty of drawing conclusive inferences by means of systematic comparison between various cases of scientific innovation. Some, and perhaps most, of the methodological problems which arise in the course of research into scientific development are common to many areas of historical and sociological inquiry. Accordingly, they present no *special* difficulties and we can draw on a large body of methodological literature as we try to resolve them. Others, however, grow out of certain rather distinctive features of this field of research, and particularly out of our concern with scientific knowledge and scientific knowledge-claims. Thus, in the study of the emergence of new areas of scientific investigation, we are necessarily faced with the difficult task of understanding esoteric, technical cultures. We need to decide, therefore, just how detailed and how technical our accounts of these cultures need to be. We also need to learn how the cognitive content of science can be acquired and analysed most effectively.

Little attention has so far been paid to these special methodological problems by those engaged in studying the social dimensions of science; or indeed to methodological questions of any kind. The range of methodological issues requiring attention is considerable, extending from problems of conceptual elaboration and identification of variables, similar to those raised in this introduction, to the refinement of specific techniques of observation and inference. Given the preliminary nature of current research in this field and the general absence of explicit methodological discussion, it would be inappropriate for us to attempt here any systematic review of methodological issues. Nevertheless, because we are convinced that, as the body of empirical material grows, questions concerning research strategy, approaches to theory building, techniques of inference, and comparative analysis will increasingly force themselves upon our attention, we have included in part 2, following the case studies, a series of essays in which methodological issues are the main concern.

NOTES

1. How the boundaries of the 'natural' world are defined varies over time and from one society and one social group to another. Consequently, the scope of scientific study can be seen to vary. Thus in Britain there is a tendency to regard the natural world and the physical world as equivalent and, as a result, to make a definite distinction between the physical and the social sciences. In other societies, this distinction is frequently absent or, at least, much less clear cut.

2. D. J. de Solla Price, *Little Science, Big Science* (New York: Columbia University Press, 1963).

3. See respectively, R. Taton, 'Emergence and Development of Some National Scientific Communities in the Nineteenth Century', *International Social Science Journal* 22:1 (1970) 94–110; and de Solla Price, *Little Science, Big Science*; L. J. Anthony/H. East/M. J. Slater, 'The Growth of the Literature of Physics', *Reports on Progress in Physics* 32 (1969) 709–767.

4. We do not mean by this that we shall try to formulate every possible question. We mean only that we will try to give examples of as wide a range as possible of relevant questions. For the sake of clarity we will formulate these illustrative questions explicitly, even though they may sometimes appear obvious in the light of previous discussion.

5. In order to preserve continuity in the discussion which follows, we shall use wherever possible the development of genetics, a field not covered in our case studies, as an example. Our references to genetics are meant to be no more than illustrative.

6. See T. S. Kuhn, *The Structure of Scientific Revolutions* (University of Chicago Press, 1962, second edition 1970).

7. C. Zirkle, 'The Knowledge of Human Heredity Before 1900' pp. 35–57 in: L. C. Dunn (ed.), *Genetics in the Twentieth Century* (New York: Macmillan, 1951).

8. B.;Glass, 'The Long Neglect of a Scientific Discovery: Mendel's Laws of Inheritance' pp. 148–160 in: G. Boas *et al.* (eds.), *Studies in Intellectual History* (Baltimore: Johns Hopkins University Press, 1953).

9. Dunn (ed.), *Genetics in the Twentieth Century*.

10. B. Glass, 'The Establishment of Modern Genetical Theory as an Example of the Interaction of Different Models, Techniques and Inferences' pp. 521–541 in: M. Clagett (ed.), *Critical Problems in the History of Science* (Madison: University of Wisconsin Press, 1959).

11. D. J. de Solla Price/D. Beaver, 'Collaboration in an Invisible College', *American Psychologist* 21 (1966) 1011–1018; D. Crane, *Invisible Colleges* (University of Chicago Press, 1972).

12. E. B. Gasking, 'Why was Mendel's Work Ignored?', *Journal of the History of Ideas*

20 (1959) 60–84.

13. A. H. Sturtevant, 'The Early Mendelians', *Proceedings of the American Philosophical Society* 109:4 (1965) 199-204.

14. G. Holton, 'Models for Understanding the Growth and Excellence of Scientific Research' pp. 94-129 in: S. R. Graubard / G. Holton (eds.), *Excellence and Leadership in a Democracy* (New York: Columbia University Press, 1962).

15. Sturtevant, 'The Early Mendelians', 204.

16. For these three areas, see respectively N. C. Mullins, 'The Development of a Scientific Specialty: The Phage Group and the Origins of Molecular Biology', *Minerva* 10 (1972) 51-82; D. L. Krantz, 'Research Activity in "Normal" and "Anomalous" Areas', *Journal of the History of the Behavioral Sciences* 1 (1965) 39-42; D. Fleming / B. Bailyn (eds.), *The Intellectual Migration: Europe and America, 1930-1960* (Cambridge, Mass: Harvard University Press, 1969).

17. F. Reif / A. Strauss, 'The Impact of Rapid Discovery upon the Scientist's Career', *Social Problems* 12:5 (1965) 297-311.

18. As we have noted above, eminent scientists often oppose the introduction of major changes of perspective within their own areas of research. For several reasons, however, this is not inconsistent with their sponsoring major contributions in new areas. For example, these new fields are frequently scientifically undeveloped, so that often there are no bodies of established conceptions which are likely to be undermined by the new advances. Moreover, in many cases where a well established scientific framework is threatened by new departures, the eminent scientists who sponsor innovative work have made no significant contribution themselves to this framework and consequently are not particularly committed to its maintenance. In addition, research which eventually brings about major scientific reformulations is frequently seen at its inception as being no more than an interesting, but by no means fundamental, elaboration of the current perspective.

19. C. S. Gillmor / C. J. Terman, 'Communication Modes of Geophysics: The Case of Ionospheric Physics', *Eos* 54: 10 (1973) 900-908.

20. J. E. McGrath / I. Altman, *Small Group Research: A Synthesis and Critique of the Field* (New York: Holt, Rinehart and Winston, 1966). The evidence presented in this source is from the social rather than the natural sciences.

21. Crane, *Invisible Colleges*, 68.

22. B. C. Griffith / N. C. Mullins, 'Coherent Social Groups in Scientific Change', *Science* 177 (1972) 961.

23. J. Gaston, *Originality and Competition in Science* (Chicago and London: University of Chicago Press, 1973).

24. W. O. Hagstrom, *The Scientific Community* (New York: Basic Books, 1965).

25. Holton, 'Models for Understanding', 124; Crane, *Invisible Colleges,* 70.

26. Kuhn, *The Structure of Scientific Revolutions,* 6 *et passim.*

27. C. S. Fisher, 'The Last Invariant Theorists', *Archives of European Sociology* 8 (1961) 216-244.

28. Mullins, 'The Phage Group', 74-9.

29. H. W. Menard, *Science: Growth and Change* (Cambridge, Mass: Harvard University Press, 1971); de Solla Price, *Little Science, Big Science,* 9-10; Anthony / East / Slater, 'The Literature of Physics', 711-18.

30. J. D. Bernal, *Science in History* (Harmondsworth: Penguin Books, third edition 1965).

31. W. H. Gruber / D. G. Marquis (eds.), *Factors in the Transfer of Technology* (Cambridge, Mass: MIT Press, 1969); J. Langrish *et al., Wealth from Knowledge* (London: Macmillan, 1972).

32. J. B. Morrell, 'The Chemist Breeders: the Research Schools of Liebig and Thomas Thomson', *Ambix* 19 (1972) 1-46; G. L. Geison, 'Social and Institutional Factors in the Stagnancy of English Physiology, 1840-1870', *Bulletin of the History of Medicine*

46:1 (1972) 30-58.

33. C. Rosenberg, 'Factors in the Development of Genetics in the United States', *Journal of Medical History* 22 (1967) 27-46.
34. A. Zloczower, 'Career Opportunities and the Growth of Scientific Discovery in Nineteenth Century Germany, with Special Reference to Physiology' (unpublished thesis: The Eliezer Kaplan School of Economics and Social Sciences, Hebrew University of Jerusalem, n.d.).
35. See for example J. Ben-David/R. Collins, 'Social Factors in the Origins of a New Science: The Case of Psychology', *American Sociological Review* 31 (1966) 451-465.
36. Rosenberg, 'Factors in the Development of Genetics', 41-2.
37. For instance, research on cancer, space research and moon research. For the latter, see I. I. Mitroff, *The Subjective Side of Science* (The Hague: Elsevier, 1974).
38. J. Ben-David/A. Zloczower, 'Universities and Academic Systems in Modern Societies,' *European Journal of Sociology* 3 (1962) 45-85.
39. D. S. L. Cardwell, *The Organization of Science in England* (London: Heinemann, 1972); R. MacLeod, 'The Resources of Science in Victorian England: The Endowment of Science Movement, 1868-1900' pp. 111-166 in: P. Mathias (ed.), *Science and Society, 1600-1900* (Cambridge University Press, 1972).
40. There are parallels here with the development of agricultural chemistry. See part 1 below.
41. J. D. Bernal, *Science and Industry in the Nineteenth Century* (London: Routledge and Kegan Paul, 1953); M. J. Mulkay, *The Social Process of Innovation* (London: Macmillan, 1972).
42. Bernal, *Science in History*, III. 867-876.
43. B. Hessen, 'The Social and Economic Roots of Newton's *Principia*' pp. 151-212 in: N. Bukharin *et al.*, *Science at the Crossroads*, Papers presented to the International Congress of the History of Science and Technology, June 29 to July 3, 1931 (London: Kniga, 1931; reprinted Frank Cass, 1971); see also Shigeru Nakayama *et al.*, *Science and Society in Modern Japan* (Tokyo: Tokyo University Press, and Cambridge, Mass: MIT Press, 1974).
44. We are concerned here with research undertaken to improve the validity and range of academic knowledge. There has, of course, been an enormous expansion in the employment of scientists for practical ends by industry and government.
45. I. C. Byatt/C. V. Cohen, *An Attempt to Quantify the Economic Benefits of Scientific Research* (London: HMSO Science Policy Studies No. 4, 1969).
46. H. Brooks, *Science, Growth and Society* (Paris: OECD. 1971); S. Blume, *Towards a Political Sociology of Science* (London: Collier Macmillan, 1974).
47. C. Freeman *et al.*, 'The Goals of R and D in the 1970s', *Science Studies* 1:3/4 (1971) 357-406.
48. H. Rose/S. Rose, *Science and Society* (Harmondsworth: Penguin Books, 1969).
49. J. R. Ravetz, *Scientific Knowledge and its Social Problems* (Oxford: Clarendon Press, 1971).
50. Y. Ezrahi, 'The Political Resources of American Science', *Science Studies* 1:2 (1971) 117-133.
51. de Solla Price, *Little Science, Big Science*, 30-32.
52. Our 'rate of scientific development' is much the same as what Ben-David has called 'scientific productivity'. See J. Ben-David, 'Scientific Productivity and Academic Organization in Nineteenth-Century Medicine', *American Sociological Review* 25 (1960) 828-843.
53. E.g., K. Mannheim, *Ideology and Utopia* (London: Routledge and Kegan Paul, 1926). See also the discussion in R. K. Merton, *Social Theory and Social Structure* (New York: Free Press, 1957) and in W. Stark, *The Sociology of Knowledge* (London: Routledge and Kegan Paul, 1958).

54.   One of the very few attempts is that of Hessen, mentioned above.
55.   Morrell, 'The Chemist Breeders', 18-19.
56.   Hagstrom, *The Scientific Community,* 208-209.

1
Studies of Scientific Development

WOLFGANG KROHN / WOLF SCHÄFER

The Origins and Structure
of Agricultural Chemistry

INTRODUCTION

It is the purpose of the present case study to point out some interconnections between social needs, cognitive patterns and institutional strategies which are relevant to a sociological theory of scientific development. Studying agricultural chemistry, we have tried to trace the interactions between an actual problem (in this case, a population explosion), the perception of this problem (by, in this case, T. R. Malthus), the recognition of limitations in the problem-solving capacity of science (from the work of H. Davy and A. D. Thaer), the beginning of experimental techniques and of model building (in the formulation of a paradigm) and the institutionalization achieved by what we shall call a 'cognitive variant'.

The structure of these interactions in agricultural chemistry makes it an example of a type of dynamic in science we have elsewhere described as 'finalized science'.[1] This type of scientific enterprise falls between those which are concerned with analysis of the 'construction of reality' and operating independently of social demands, and those which are primarily concerned with the application of knowledge to specific technical problems, where the pertinent theoretical formulations are already applicable. In the case of agricultural chemistry, we find social goals giving impulse to the emergence and cognitive formation of fundamental theories.

This external influence on science can assume various forms. First, it can appear in the weak form of a stimulus to resource allocation and institutional guarantees (as can be found, for instance, in the case of research on magnetism with reference to measuring longitude and latitude at sea).[2] Such historical influences are independent of the cognitive structure; to argue the opposite would be a genetic fallacy – a confusion of genesis and structure. Second, external factors can influence the contents of theories. As a rule this applies in particular to the semantics of a theory: the habits of thought of the social superstructure preform the patterns in which empirical knowledge is expressed, as is often claimed for the Darwinian theory of evolution so far as it overlaps with economic liberalism. Such patterns may considerably influence the heuristics of research. In principle, however, they are exchangeable, as are different interpretations of an identical calculus. Finally, external factors can influence the constitution of the subject matter of the respective research field. This is the case where the concepts delineating the subject matter of a research field involve social norms which cannot be held to be properties of a natural reality.

This third type of external influence is exemplified by agricultural chemistry. In this study, agricultural chemistry is defined as the field which has as its object determining the chemical interrelations between the atmosphere, the soil, plants, animals and men *via* the mechanisms of respiration, nutrition, absorption and putrefaction, and the subjection of these to control. The object of agricultural chemistry is to acquire knowledge of the chemical conditions of the primary natural reproduction of culture, which had been seriously threatened by the exploding population. Therefore agricultural chemistry played a key role in the social development of the nineteenth century. Moreover in this field, one can trace several social norms which assume theory-building functions, and which are transformed into the 'paradigm'. However, it is not the social norms alone which enable agricultural chemistry to emerge as a specialty. In the 'prehistory' of agricultural chemistry, current knowledge of chemistry and rational agriculture could offer only relatively restricted and *ad hoc* prescriptions despite the fact that the practical problems involved were clearly acute. Scientific disciplines are only to a certain degree receptive to social problems, depending on the cognitive state and the stage of institutionalization of the disciplines themselves.[3]

The following six points characterize the development of agricultural chemistry and the structure of our paper:

1. There come into existence defined needs, external to science, which stimulate the rise of agricultural chemistry and influence its content.
2. Agricultural chemistry – since Wallerius an academic subject and part of the research programme of rational agriculture – could not

be advanced successfully, either by means of the phlogiston theory or by means of early agricultural science.[4]

3. Agricultural chemistry was not a necessary step in the development of chemistry. In fact, it constitutes a special development, beginning about 1840.

4. On the other hand, agricultural chemistry was not feasible without the existence of relatively mature fields of mineral and organic chemistry, offering a number of fundamental laws and methods of investigation (or what may be described as the paradigmatic stability among 'mother disciplines').

5. Agricultural chemistry was not only the application of fundamental disciplines, but also a development of theories, which led to special heuristics, research methods, and explanatory models.

6. Agricultural chemistry was institutionalized strategically. Its establishment was based not only on its theoretical and experimental success, but also on research planning by the men of science involved.

THE DEMOGRAPHIC CONTEXT OF AGRICULTURAL CHEMISTRY

It was not in order to find an answer to the 'internal' question of plant nutrition but, rather, to solve 'external' problems of human nutrition that chemistry was applied to agriculture and physiology. The coincidence of the population explosion and the industrial revolution in the eighteenth and nineteenth centuries gave rise to a new relationship between man and the material world, and agricultural chemistry took part in establishing this relationship.

A new relationship with the material world can be brought about in two ways: either by exploiting new powers, as was the case with the industrial revolution, or by reforming an already existing attitude toward nature, as in the case of agricultural chemistry. When new forces of nature are exploited we speak of *technological progress* (exemplified in Watt's steam engine) and when a conventional attitude toward the material world is reorganized, we speak of *progressive technology* (for example, the development of Liebig's artificial manure). It was the latter kind of progress which was expected of agricultural practice from the beginning of the industrial revolution. But agricultural practice 'prior to 1840' (this is Liebig's own periodization, coinciding with the year of the first edition of his *Agricultural Chemistry*) had not taken up the challenge of traditional

agriculture. On the contrary, 'after 1840' the 'practical man' of agriculture had to be made to comprehend that the practice of intensifying
agriculture and stock-breeding common during the eighteenth century
was based on methods which exhausted the fertility of the soil; the practical man, 'the sworn enemy of all "theory", had theorized that his soil's
fertility was inexhaustible and . . . had acted completely according to the
theory that the sources . . . to reproduce harvests in his fields . . . were
inexhaustible!'[5]

The basis of this optimism was questioned for the first time in the
closing years of the eighteenth century. T. R. Malthus in his *Essay on the
Principle of Population* tried to calculate the catastrophic disparity between revolutionary population explosion and conservative food production. The proposition of his 'Principle of Population' is well known; he
assumed 'that population, when unchecked, goes on doubling itself every
twenty-five years, or increases in a geometrical ratio', whereas 'the means
of subsistence, under circumstances the most favourable to human
industry, could not possibly be made to increase faster than in an
arithmetical ratio.'[6] Although we have learned since that the naturalistic
determinism implied in this concept is false, for the decline of the birth
rate towards the end of the nineteenth century contradicts the assumption
of historically-sociologically invariant generative behaviour, we cannot
underestimate the essay's power of perception, nor its historical impact.
Malthus had recognized the limitations of traditional agriculture in
regard to demographic factors, and had produced a vision of a *secular
subsistence crisis:*

> When acre has been added to acre till all the fertile land is occupied, the
> yearly increase of food must depend upon the melioration of land
> already in possession. This is a fund, which, from the nature of all soils,
> instead of increasing, must be gradually diminishing. But population
> . . . would go on with unexhausted vigour; and the increase of one
> period would furnish the power of a greater increase the next, and this
> without any limit.[7]

The new situation, the widening gap between population growth and
increase in food production, had become evident between 1750 and
1800; in the same fifty years, the world's population had grown by more
than 150 million (from 728 to 906 million) people.

This first wave of the population explosion, together with the 'practical
man's' intensified exploitation of the soil, should have led to the conventional 'problem-solution' of a sudden rise in mortality, rather than to a
lasting increase of agricultural production. Further population growth

combined with the impact of Malthus' theories had become an external stimulus for the development of agricultural chemistry (statistics show a population increase in Europe of more than 75 million people between 1800 and 1850 — from 187 to 266 million; while the population of England and Wales grew during the first phase of the industrial revolution, between 1780 and 1840, by 100% to 16 million).[8] Liebig, contrary to Malthus, did not believe in 'preventive checks to population' but searched for an alternative to 'present husbandry' and asked whether chemistry could achieve the conditions necessary for obtaining 'big and ever increasing harvests lasting eternally'.[9] By this, the fatalistic vision of Malthus came down to earth and the dilemma became both real and manageable at the same time. As Liebig wrote:

A combination of coincidences has caused a population increase in all European countries which does not correspond to the production capability of these countries and is therefore unnatural, and to such an extent that if present cultivation remains the same it can be sustained only under two conditions: 1. if, by a divine miracle, the fields regain their yield capacity which folly and ignorance have taken from them; 2. if beds of Guano manure are discovered which are, for example, as large as the English coal fields. No reasonable person will say that the realization of these conditions is either probable or possible. In a few years, the Guano reserves will be depleted, and then no scientific nor, so to speak, theoretical disputes will be necessary to prove the law of nature which demands from man that he cares for the preservation of living conditions . . . For their self-preservation, nations will be compelled to slaughter and destroy each other in cruel wars in order to obtain balance, and if, God forbid, there are two years such as the starvation years of 1816 and 1817 then those who live through them will see hundreds of thousands perish in the streets. Add a war thereto and mothers, as during the Thirty Years' War, will drag home the bodies of the slain enemy in order to still with their flesh the hunger of their children; as in Silesia in 1847, the corpses of animals having died of diseases will be excavated in order to prolong the agony with the carcass. These are not vague and dark predictions, images of a sick phantasy; for science does not prophesy, it calculates; not *if*, but *when*, is undecided.[10]

Today — 'after 1840' — we are able to comprehend the antinomy between the industrial and demographic revolution and the intensification of traditional farming. For the latter, whatever it may have appeared to be, was no agrarian revolution but the completion of the neolithic exploitation of nature. If indeed the *past* 'future of European countries . . . was suspended on the tip of a needle', then we are indebted to agricultural chemistry for part of *our* future.[11] For agricultural chemistry, provoked by the secular problem of feeding the population, clarified the 'Chemical Process of the Nutrition of Vegetables' (the title of the first volume of the classic seventh edition of *Agricultural Chemistry*, which appeared in 1862), and thus analyzed 'modern agriculture as a system of exhaustion'.[12] The agricultural chemical re-interpretation of 'modern' agriculture as exploitation of the soil enabled a progressive agriculture to emerge, characterised by the application of artificial fertilizer, and the significance of which for natural history was a new form of integrating nature — as unexploiting 'as a tidal movement within a cycle'.[13]

THE PRE-HISTORY OF AGRICULTURAL CHEMISTRY

Agricultural chemistry, like any other special development in chemistry, was based on foundations set forth by *inorganic chemistry*. These may be summarized shortly as follows: the definition of the chemical element and the chemical compound; the fundamental laws of Lavoisier (conservation of weight), Proust (constant proportions), Dalton (multiple proportions), Gay-Lussac and Humboldt (simple volume proportions); as well as of the atomic theory (Dalton) and of a theory of compounds (Berzelius).

However, it was the success of *organic chemistry* which made it possible to speak of the maturity of chemistry for special theoretical developments. For whereas the theoretical and experimental focus of inorganic chemistry was the analytical isolation (i.e. the discovery) of chemical elements and the description of their physical and chemical qualities, organic chemistry signified the breakthrough in describing complex processes of composition and decomposition. Owing to the low number of elements involved in organic processes, the analysis of their characteristics became less important than the characteristics of the compounds and of elementary compound groups. Chemical processes gained importance in relation to new techniques of analysis. The development of elementary chemical analysis allowed the quick determination of relative proportions in weight of high molecular organic compounds, together with knowledge of atomic weights drawn from inorganic chemistry. This determination was relatively independent of the individual skills of the person carrying out the experiment. Combining new compound theories (such as the radical theory of Dumas and Liebig; and the nucleus theory of Gerhardt and

Laurent) with new experimental techniques paved the way for a series of analyses to which the varieties of plants, parts of plants (in different stages of growth), soils and atmospheres could be subjected. Without this knowledge one could perhaps assume chemical cycles in the reproduction of life but one could make no assumptions about their chemical reconstruction and partial technical construction. The necessity for series of experiments, requiring routinization of processes and simplified apparatus, was constantly stressed by Liebig, sometimes even at the expense of reducing accuracy in measurement.[14]

According to Liebig's view, chemistry necessarily had to reach a state of maturity, which by 1840 had been attained:

Chemistry had become among the sciences so independent in its structure that it could participate in the development of other areas; and in that the efforts of the chemists were turned to studying the living conditions of plants and animals, they touched upon agriculture . . . Chemistry began to study according to its strict methods all the parts of plants as precisely as possible; it examined what was in leaves, stems, roots, and in fruit; it pursued the processes of the animals' nutrition and what was to become of the nutrition in their body; it analyzed arable lands in different regions of the world.[15]

The significance of these developments in organic chemistry for agricultural chemistry may be indicated by a comparison between Liebig and Humphrey Davy. In the first decade of the nineteenth century, Davy delivered his 'Elements of Agricultural Chemistry in a Course of Lectures for the Board of Agriculture'.[16] He defined agricultural chemistry as a simple addition of phenomenologically adopted agricultural elements; it was a 'department of knowledge, which has not yet received a regular and systematic form'; it was 'a science as yet in its infancy' so that there was a strong difference between expectations and output.[17] This kind of 'paradigmless' agricultural chemistry could perhaps be made useful in certain ways; it could not, however, provide a theory of agriculture which could disprove alternative theories.

A third factor shaping the pre-history of agricultural chemistry, was the development of *plant and animal physiology*. During the eighteenth century, many physiological chemists and chemical physiologists studied problems essential to agricultural science — including Priestley (on the generation of oxygen by the leaves of green plants exposed to sunlight), Ingen-Housz (on carbon dioxide emission of plants by night), and Senebier (on photosynthesis).[18] Physiology and chemistry had not been clearly separated either methodologically or by subject matter. This separation did take place, however, after the foundation of organic chemistry, when physiology no longer remained bound to the morphological and functional analysis of organs but extended to analysis of the substances building up and maintaining these organs. Since then physiology has assumed an important heuristic function in the constitution of a comprehensive agricultural science; for with respect to man's physiological needs, plants and animals together with their own physiology are included in the function cycle of chemical metamorphoses.

These influences of chemistry and physiology were gradually superimposed upon theories of practical agriculture, which took their lead from the older 'oeconomia ruralis et domestica'. This development in the mid-eighteenth century led to pragmatic experimental economy, and finally to the 'rational agriculture' of the Thaer school, in the first half of the nineteenth century. A. D. Thaer in his *Introduction to the Knowledge of English Agriculture and its New Practical and Theoretical Advancements* gave an account of the technological progress achieved in this field during the eighteenth century, including melioration and cultivation; the general use of enclosures; improvement in the three-field system; the introduction of crop rotation; the cultivation of new vegetables; the improvement of stock breeding; and improvements in the plough and similar tools.[19] The agriculturalists conducted various experiments to get higher returns by adjusting agricultural devices to the special conditions of a given farm. Higher earnings could result from *technical* improvements or from bigger profits depending on rationalization and a suitable sale, the decisive factor being the *economic* aspect of management. From these experiments evolved two chief theories, the *humus theory,* which regarded humus as the main means of nutrition for plants, and the economic *theory of location.*[20] The gradual isolation of all relevant variables helped to provide the disciplinary background of agricultural chemistry. But the scientific deficiencies of the pragmatic approach were grave. The economistic mode of thinking neglected the ecological problems of exhaustion. The humus theory (dominated by the phlogiston theory and by vitalism) lagged behind the chemical knowledge of the time, and experimental findings could not be generalized beyond the realm of local conditions.

THE PARADIGM OF AGRICULTURAL CHEMISTRY:
THE PROCESS OF SEGMENTATION

In order to explain the central position Liebig held in agricultural chemistry, attention has usually focused upon his institutionalization strategies and polemics.[21] These interpretations frequently regard any kind of strategic behaviour within the scientific community or vis-à-vis society as illegitimate. Furthermore, they are too simple, disregarding the contribution made by the reconstruction of existing knowledge. In the case of Liebig this reconstruction is the formation of a comprehensive, in principle reliable, and applicable paradigm. It claimed competence to elucidate agricultural processes, to construct these processes according to human needs and to integrate economic and technical knowledge. This paradigm was the source of his influence. Liebig himself in later editions of his *Agricultural Chemistry* expressed this metaphorically:

> In my agricultural chemistry I have simply tried to put a light into a dark room. All the furniture was there, even tools and objects of comfort and fun; all these things, however, were not clearly visible to the society using this room for their welfare and to their advantage. Groping haphazardly one person found a chair, another one a table, the third one a bed in which he made himself as comfortable as possible; yet most were blind to the harmony of the furnishings and their interrelationship. After each object had received some, though weak, light, many began to complain that the light had not made any significant change in the room; one person had known and used this, the other person something else, together they felt and touched what was given. Chemistry, this light of knowledge, can never without harm be removed *from this room.* This goal has been totally achieved.[22]

The particular history of the genesis of Liebig's book from 1840 sheds light on the systematic process by which agricultural chemistry developed by segmentation from the mainstream of chemical science.[23]

During Liebig's visit to England in 1837, the chemical section of the British Association for the Advancement of Science in Liverpool conferred upon him 'the honourable task of preparing a Report upon the state of Organic Chemistry'.[24] How is it to be explained that having accepted this request Liebig then wrote a work about agricultural chemistry? Organic chemistry was initially defined as the science of the chemical processes of organic substances in nature or as the science of the chemical conditions of life.[25] Hence if Liebig in his report intended to apply 'the principles of natural philosophy to the development and nourishment of plants', this intention holds strictly to the programme of organic chemistry.[26] However, the development of organic chemistry from 1820 to 1840 had taken an entirely different direction. Since urea was synthesized in 1828 by Liebig and Wöhler, most chemists were convinced that all organic compounds could be synthesized. Thus organic chemistry abandoned its original goal, and developed into what we today term the chemistry of carbon compounds, the properties of which are not conditioned by organisms but by the structure of carbon. Against the background of this factual development of organic chemistry, adherence to the goal of a chemistry of vital processes led to a special development — theoretically as well as empirically.

REPRODUCTION CYCLES

The fundamental concept of agricultural chemistry is that of the *reproduction cycles of organic processes.* As Liebig wrote:

> Our present research in natural history proceeds from the conviction that laws of interaction exist not only among two or three but rather among all phenomena which in the realm of minerals, plants and animals condition life on the surface of the earth. Thus none of them is separate but at all times joined to one or several others, all of them linked together without beginning and without end. The sequence of these phenomena, their origins and their departures can be compared to the tidal movement within a cycle.[27]

It can be supposed that Liebig did not derive the idea of cyclical organization only from agronomy and biology (where it is suggested phenomenally by the ontogenetic scheme and by the seasonal cycle) but also from the political economy of Adam Smith and John Stuart Mill, to whom he frequently refers.[28] Liebig criticised the agronomists for failing to make the distinction between efficient practices which reduce natural working capital and those which raise returns and interests. For the cycle to be maintained in equilibrium the capital turn-over must exclude diminishing returns. Otherwise extended reproduction would lead sooner or later to a breakdown:

> Agricultural production does not differ fundamentally from the regular industrial enterprise. Factory-owner and manufacturer know well that their investment and working capital must not continuously diminish if their business is not to come to an end. In the same way, a judicious agricultural enterprise requires the farmer who wants higher yields to increase the number of active components in his soil which are conducive to production.[29]

Presumably the concept of 'cycle' as an analogy to capital circulation is of consequence precisely because it makes the transition from natural cycles to cycles based on cultural norms more easily conceivable. Treating the difference between capital turn-over (= natural cycle) and capital returns (= agricultural earnings) by analogy requires 'agriculture to dispose of a reliable yardstick to measure the value of its experiences' regarding investments.[30] Does an increase in year X represent returns or is it concealed loss of capital? Only science can give prognostic answers. For example, does loosening the soil by mechanical means bring higher returns or does it increase its exhaustion?

The notion of the cycle has various connotations — e.g., the revolution of the stars in astronomy; the circulation of the blood in medicine; the circulation of money in economics; the notion of feedback cycles in technology; supply-demand mechanisms in capitalistic economics.[31] Two independent factors can be found underlying this variety: firstly, the assumption of a starting position, which will be re-established by a chain of metamorphoses; secondly, the notion of an equilibrium which is maintained by means of control mechanisms. In the tradition of political economy these aspects were initially separated from each other. The physiocrats, and Quesnay in particular, concentrated on the production-consumption cycle and thus on the reproduction of expended substances. The English school, and Smith in particular, had as its focus the mechanisms required to maintain a labile equilibrium. With Marx, the two aspects became combined.

Though Liebig's concept of cycles bears a strong resemblance to its equivalent in political economy, the concept's specific meaning grew out of chemical considerations: what explains the fact that although the nutrition of plants and animals constantly consumes certain resources of the atmosphere and of the soil, these resources remain constant over time? There are three possible solutions. Either these resources are infinite, or they are spontaneously generated, or they are regularly reproduced. The first and second solutions can be falsified by chemistry. If the quantity of oxygen consumed by animals were calculable and the atmospheric mass known, the exhaustion of the oxygen constituent in the atmosphere could be estimated. According to Liebig:

> In 800,000 years the atmosphere would no longer contain any trace of oxygen. It would, however, have become entirely unsuitable for respiration and combustion processes much earlier for already a reduction of its oxygen content to 8 per cent . . . would have produced a lethal effect on animals.[32]

The second solution is ruled out by a successful basic hypothesis of the chemical paradigm: chemical elements cannot be transformed into each other. Therefore, the concept of the cycle is the only possible scheme whereby the chemical conditions of life processes can be conceptualized. Nature *must* follow cycles if what is empirically observed is to be made intelligible.

Theoretically the concept of the cycle presupposes the concept of an 'ought-value', namely a norm which determines that the cycle has come to its completion: the initial conditions in respect of which all later events are interpreted and analyzed. Yet if the initial conditions are marked out as the 'ought', to be achieved by future events, the degree of deviation — that is, the actual value — and possible corrections must be detectible. Thus Liebig defines circulation 'on the surface of the earth' as 'continuous change, constant disturbance and recovery of the balance'.[33]

Liebig's conception of circulation contained both factors of reproduction and self-control. It was, however, impossible for Liebig to offer a teleological explanation for these processes. Thus, the principle of circulation made new demands on causal analysis in chemistry. In the complex interplay of the processes of composition and decomposition in the atmosphere, in the soil and in plant physiology (including physically determined osmoses and diffusions), a guiding thread had to be found to enable scientists to follow all these chemical transformations.

A preliminary form of the concept of cycle was the concept of metamorphosis developed in organic chemistry. This relied on a concept of balance. In economics, the keeping of a balance sheet presupposes that inputs and outputs of a qualitatively different nature can be traced as transformation of a given value. This was precisely the problem in chemistry and physiology. Which element and which product (the plant as product of the soil and the air; the animal as product of the fodder and the air) has what equivalent among the production factors? The discovery of these modifications of matter (called metamorphoses by chemists and physiologists at the time) was among the pioneering activities of the physiologists of the eighteenth century.

From a methodological point of view, the principle of cycles of reproduction involves two experimental essentials. In the first place, experimentation in agricultural chemistry demands the observance of 'in vivo' conditions. Such experiments must intend to identify *all* and *only* the necessary conditions of physiological processes.[34] In his *Organische Chemie* Liebig accused the plant physiologists of conducting experiments which were 'valueless for the decision of any question' (p. 42) because they had no theory of procedures to control their experiments:

They conduct experiments, without being acquainted with the circumstances necessary for the continuance of life— with the qualities and proper nutriment of the plant on which they operate — or with the nature and chemical constitution of its organs. These experiments are considered by them as convincing proofs, whilst they are fit only to awaken pity. (p. 41)

Similarly, Liebig reproached the animal physiologists, to whose field the 'in vivo' postulate also applied. His criticism referred particularly to a question of practical consequence, i.e. whether carbohydrates could be converted into fats or not:

> Without being acquainted with the conditions or even asking whether such conditions exist they first of all exclude everything which would make it possible to answer the question. The animals are put into a state of artificially induced disease, deprived of all nourishment; with the greatest care they exclude all those matters which play a part in blood formation and in the sustenance of vital functions acting on fat formation. They then believe that these miserable and cruel experiments have furnished proof that sugar, a nitrogenous substance, cannot be converted into fat, another nitrogenous substance.[35]

To answer a question by experiment requires knowledge of the conditions under which the question is answerable. Liebig introduced this theory-dependent relation of theory and experiment into agricultural chemistry by means of the concept of 'chemical metamorphosis'.

The second methodological aspect in experiments relates to the time horizon in which agricultural experiments are framed. When experimenting in agriculture, 'it takes a year or even longer before one has all the results . . .'.[36] Besides the fact that experiments can find and explain innumerable details of physiological processes, a final answer to the question of whether the chemical experiment has made transparent one of the segments of the actual cycle will be known only after at least one period has passed; and indeed, because of a minimal accumulation of marginal changes, it is often known only after several periods.[37]

THE CONSTRUCTIVE VARIATION OF CYCLES

The principle of reproduction cycles and its implications, however important, form only one part of the paradigm of agricultural chemistry. So far nothing has been said about the 'culture' of agricultural chemistry. This principle refers to the 'conditions necessary for the life of all vegetables . . .'.[83] But agricultural chemistry is not merely the science of natural cycles and their stability, but also the science of their variation in keeping with human needs and purposes. In what manner these purposes affect the content of the paradigm, will be briefly outlined.

While the immanent finality of nature, in a manner of speaking, is rooted in the enduring stability of natural reproduction, the farmer's immanent interest is:

> to cut as many shoes as possible out of the inexhaustible stock of leather in the soil and the best teacher will be the man who has made the most of such intensive cultivation of the soil . . .[39]

Nonetheless, once it has become evident that over-exploitation of the soil has catastrophic consequences, the farmer's interest and that of society no longer coincide. Society's interest must be in 'achieving big and ever increasing harvests for ever and ever'.[40] To solve this problem is, according to Liebig, the purpose of agricultural chemistry. Its object then is no longer confined to the discovery of the laws of reproduction governing vegetable life, but to construct natural reproduction cycles which will benefit man. The purposes that have to be achieved in such constructions with the means of nature are not purposes of nature. Thus, agricultural chemistry becomes a social science operating with the methods of natural science. At first sight this seems to be the usual connection between science and technology: once discovered, natural laws enable technical constructions within nature. But in agricultural chemistry the social purpose is not the *result* of scientific knowledge but the *condition* of scientific inquiry. Agricultural chemistry does not provide insights into *why* agriculture functions but rather constitutes a design of *how it must* function.

The inter-relation between goals and theory construction in agricultural chemistry becomes evident as soon as one apprehends that knowledge of agricultural chemistry is directed toward goals which are not natural goals. The general notion of 'achieving big and ever increasing harvests for ever and ever' finds specification in a whole set of norms (or 'oughts'), when the concept of 'increase' is operationalized. 'Increase' as signifying an additional yield is a concept which is not derived from nature:

> In a free and uncultivated state the development of every part of a plant depends on the amount and nature of the food afforded to it by the spot in which it grows. A plant is developed in the most sterile and unfruitful soil as well as in the most luxuriant and fertile, the only difference which can be observed being in its height and size, in the number of its twigs, branches, leaves, blossom and fruit.[41]

It makes no sense to say that a dwarf-pine is less perfect than a pine grown in the forest only because their individual organs differ; a dwarf-pine 'increased' in its height and size would not be capable of existence. In this sense, if we take agricultural chemistry to be a science of the continuous removal of cultural utilities from nature, it is a science which treats laws of social nature. These laws make reference to norms which are superimposed upon natural qualities: in part on the qualities of plants, in part on those of the soil, in part on those of the reproduction cycle.

With respect to plants, such norms are, according to Liebig: to obtain an abnormal development of certain parts of plants; and to obtain an abnormal development of certain vegetable substances. Or, to put it more concretely, fine pliable straw, giving strength and solidity, or more corn from the same plant, or a maximum of nitrogen in the seeds, and so on.[42] The norms for the soils are in particular: different degrees of fertility (depending on the sum of nutrients which can be absorbed), and the duration of fertility (depending on the sum of nutrients present in the soil).[43] Norms which relate to the reproduction cycles are derived from the selection of the crops and their succession.[44]

Now it is obvious that by whatever method one tries to order these norms systematically, they will still not be coincident with a scale of natural states of things. In this respect agricultural chemistry differs from classical medicine, which is concerned not with diverse forms of health but with eliminating disease. Deviations from an 'ought' state of affairs which is thought to be naturally given, can, in principle, be ordered on a scale. However, when such deviations are defined as the goals of various maximization strategies (something which in medicine would be interpreted as a theory of alternative forms of possible good health and the means of improving health) it will be the goal-orientations themselves which determine, or more precisely, which have a determining influence on the descriptive pattern and the methods of the theory.

The teleological structure of 'finalized' theory in agricultural chemistry signifies that the construction of suitable soils, manures and plants (and ultimately of a suitable ecological system) is not just an application of scientific results, but the goal of obtaining knowledge. This is because the concept of suitability is a theoretical concept which cannot be derived from the state of things as found in nature but itself structures possible states nature can adopt. Agricultural chemistry is explicitly a cultural conceptualization of nature. This statement should not lead to misunderstanding: it is not intended to say that the actual results of agricultural chemistry (causal explanations and laws) are not objective natural laws.

They are laws of nature in the sense of being theoretically derivable from general laws formulated by chemistry, physics and physiology, and in the sense that the resulting experimental and technical practice entails objective experimental rules and procedures. Therefore, if we speak of finality in this connection this does not refer to the form of these laws but to the possibility of their being conceptualized.

Thus the hard core of agricultural chemistry is not the concept of reproduction cycles but its social goal-orientation, achieving a continuous increase of crops with perpetual continuance. The goal so defined has a complex structure which seems at first sight inconsistent: if on the one side there is posited the connection between all processes of animal, plant, soil and atmospheric chemistry as constituted by a system of circulation, and if on the other side it is stipulated that an increasing mass of substances will be removed from circulation, how can stability of circulation be ensured? Liebig's paradigm cleared the way to change the various cycles, according to social goals, without disturbing the natural equilibrium given. The removal of any substance from a system of circulation necessarily implies the integration of that same substance into other chemical-physical processes. In these processes, each 'disappearance' of a substance has to be linked to a reorganization of cycles. This reorganization must, however, safeguard the reproduction of the initial conditions of the original cyclical process. Only then are 'ever increasing yields' no longer an idle dream but a realizable goal.

THE 'PROGRESSIVE PROBLEMSHIFT' IN AGRICULTURAL CHEMISTRY

For the institutionalization of agricultural chemistry it was decisive that the paradigm formulated by Liebig possessed an important theoretical impact and was empirically generative. This can be demonstrated by six points.

1. The concept of the cycle — that is to say the first part of the paradigm — led Liebig to the discovery of fundamental chemical processes such as the nitrogen cycle, the hydrogen cycle and the interdependent oxygen-carbon cycle. This made possible the explanation of the constant composition of the media (atmosphere and soil) and it led to inferences about the decrease of carbon in the air prior to the emergence of the animal world and the equivalence of the mass thus lost to natural carbon deposits.

The heuristic relevance of the category of the cycle can scarcely be overestimated. The concept affects animal physiology, links animal and plant physiology and can be used practically in the process of 'recycling'. The concept connects interdependence with causality and structures a systematic concept for the reproduction of physical-chemical-biological processes of the earth.

2. The concept of metamorphosis gained from organic chemistry performed a key function in agricultural chemistry. Berzelius, referring to it, wrote:

> In our study of organic bodies our attention was primarily centered on the particular product . . . while we almost neglected the by-products. Gradually we began to notice some, finally all of them. Actually, it was Liebig and Wöhler who were the first to take up these studies . . . and who shed light on an entirely new field in the study of organic chemistry . . . that of the chemical metamorphosis of *organic oxides.* The excellent work they did on the transformation of uric acid came just at the moment when it could best serve us as a guide in these complex questions . . . The time has come now to pay the closest attention to these metamorphoses.[45]

In agricultural chemistry the concept of chemical metamorphosis guided the analyses of the processes of fermentation, decay and putrefaction as well as of nutrition and respiration. Here knowledge of all the products formed in such transformations was fundamental for an understanding of the chemical unity underlying the reproduction of animal and plant life. The same held true for knowledge of the effects of substances artificially introduced into nature.[46] The chemistry of organic decomposition exhibited a systematic connection with agricultural chemistry and thereby acquired a consistent pattern itself.

3. The experiments performed by rational agriculturists became susceptible to scientific interpretation only within the frame of agricultural chemistry:

> What Thaer found good and proper in his fields at Moeglin came to be held as good and proper for all German soils and what Lawes discovered on the small strip of land at Rothamstead came to be held as axioms applying to all English soils.[47]

Liebig did not intend to advocate inductionism. On the contrary, he realized that there must be a theoretical standard explaining the range of techniques, for only on this basis could 'trial' become 'experiment':

> If the agriculturist, having no proper scientific principle to guide him,

carries out experiments . . . then there will be small chance of success. Thousands of agriculturists carry out similar experiments in various ways, the result of which in the end will be an agglomeration of practical experiences, comprising a method of culture, whereby the goal sought will be obtained for a certain area. However, the next door neighbour will fail using this method. Imagine the amount of capital and effort lost in *these* experiments! How totally different, how much safer, the path followed by science; once on it, science does not subject us to the danger of failure and bestows upon us all guarantees for success.[48]

In agricultural chemistry a series of new experimental devices were generated, permitting laboratory experiments with artificial nutrient fluids, analysis of physical transformations and serial research on comparative physiology.[49]

4.   It took some twenty years before artificial manure was obtained; but the early failures were not owing to theoretical errors as much as to insufficient knowledge. Apart from this, agricultural chemistry proved successful in predicting the effects of manure of different kinds upon plants. In the history of artificial manure, the difficulties encountered were of two kinds.[50] Firstly, the almost exclusively theoretical derivation of the chemical composition of manure proved incompatible with some of the empirical conditions. Liebig had expected rain-water to wash off the manure if it consisted of water-soluble substances and had not allowed for the fact that the physical properties of the soil prevented the manure from being absorbed by the plant. It took him some sixteen years to recognize why this occurred. Secondly, Liebig had underestimated the influence of nitrogen. He believed that plants could provide for themselves sufficiently with the nitrogen they absorbed from atmospheric ammonia.[51] It was only with considerable hesitation that Liebig conceded this point, because to recognize that manures needed to contain nitrogen clouded the clear differences between the traditional humus theory and Liebig's own theory of minerals. This did not seem desirable from either a strategic or an institutional point of view.

5.   The construction of artificial manure was based on two fundamental insights which, under the label of the 'law of the minimum', came to form a kind of technical natural law: a) the growth of plants is determined not by the organic but by the mineral substances of the soil (known as the 'mineral theory of plant nutrition'); and b) the substances contained in

the nutrient salts are not inter-substitutable.

The theory that the growth of a plant depends on the mineral substance which is exhausted first had been discussed by Sprengel.[52] Liebig did not think highly of Sprengel's contribution. Sprengel could present clear reasons for the importance of mineral substances to the growth of plants by the analysis of ashes.[53] However, he did not distinguish between the actual constituents of plants and the required quantities of each constituent (or their possible substitutes) which, according to theory, were indispensable. Plants absorb all soluble salts from the soil. As Liebig wrote:

> Because of this capacity no conclusion can be deduced for the necessity of the presence of certain salts in plants or of their presence being merely accidental. All inorganic constituents present in the ashes could not be considered necessary without further investigation.[54]

This distinction between *actual* constituents present in plants and *necessary* ones makes the 'law of the minimum' non-trivial; it cannot be established by analytic observation only, but on the basis of theory and experiment for particular plant species. As an experimental law, it had strategic and technical significance: it rendered possible the discovery of absent substances and thereby their addition or substitution.

6.   As Liebig's theory could not be invalidated by various faulty suppositions — furthermore could falsify these very suppositions — its stability as a *theory* became established. The initial failure to construct artificial manure, which prevented academic acceptance of agricultural chemistry, did not undermine Liebig's theory. Faulty suppositions (for instance, the view that plant cells did not need to respire oxygen or Liebig's views about the irrelevance of microorganic processes) did not destroy the structure of agricultural chemistry. Rather, once corrected, they served to extend and develop it.

The 'progressive problemshift' which occurred in the paradigm of agricultural chemistry indicated that agricultural chemistry had become more than just the successful application of accumulated chemical knowledge. Nonetheless, there exists an important difference between a discipline of this type and, say, classical mechanics or inorganic chemistry. Agricultural chemistry had nothing as fundamental to offer as, for example, axioms of mechanics or the chemical laws of simple and multiple proportions. Yet it is one of the characteristics (although not a necessary one) of a 'finalized theory' that its foundation does not rest on the relevance of its propositions within the construction of the 'natural' reality, but is structured by the urgency of social problems. To win acceptance, the theories which can take these purposes into account and find the respective problem-solutions need no longer evince the same fascination as do fundamental theories. On the other hand, they must possess paradigmatic stability for evaluative standards of progress to emerge and to define the next layer of problems to be considered. If such paradigmatic autonomy does not exist, the respective field will, as a rule, become the assembly-point of findings from a great variety of research fields. In this sense, even if there had not been Liebig's paradigm, there would have developed an agricultural science eclectically assimilating the results of physiology, botany, physics, and so on. But such a science would have lacked the characteristics of a progressive problemshift based upon paradigmatic structures. Finalized disciplines take their rise in this middle-ground between an interdisciplinary eclecticism, which is performed *only* by social needs, and a scientific interest generated solely by theory-guided problem constellations.

THE INSTITUTIONALIZATION OF AGRICULTURAL CHEMISTRY

So far our analysis has focused on the historical development of the cognitive structure of agricultural chemistry. The question now to be asked is whether that structure is associated with any determinate type of institutionalization. This seems likely, for if a discipline is based strategically on goals external to science it may be expected that its institutionalization will be strategically pursued.

For Liebig, the decision to shift the focus of his concern from organic chemistry to agricultural chemistry was not motivated by scientific reasons alone. His 'insuperable disgust and aversion against chemistry's activities at the present time' was based on the belief that chemistry was *asocial* and that 'useful applications cannot be obtained therefrom, neither for medicine, nor for physiology, nor for industry'.[55] He wished to prove 'that if physiologists and agronomists do not use the culture of chemistry, no permanent and valuable progress can be expected in physiology or in agriculture'.[56]

Liebig's view was that chemistry must turn to agriculture to prevent catastrophes of huge dimensions. Such a motivation rules out any 'ivory-tower' mentality of the 'pure' scholar. In order to institutionalize his concepts Liebig extensively used tactical and strategic methods. His behaviour was frequently characterized (and criticized) as over-ambitious. There is no need to deny these allegations since a science which comes into being for external reasons, and which operates on the basis of external goals, requires the active introduction of its findings and methodology into society. In his writings Liebig frequently touched on the problems of the establishment of new doctrines. His explicit opposition to the humus theorists and physiologists was grounded not only upon his mineral theory but also upon his understanding of the principles underlying effective opposition:

> Glancing at the history of science reveals that if a new doctrine takes the place of a prevalent one, the new doctrine will not be a further development but the very opposite of the old one.
>
> For a long time I believed that in agriculture it would suffice to teach the truth, in order to disseminate it, as is common in science, and to disregard errors; finally, however, I have realized that this was wrong and that the altars of the lie have to be shattered, if truth is to be based on a firm foundation.[57]

Liebig acted accordingly.

In the years following 1840, Liebig was so convinced of his theory that almost nothing shook his belief in the effectiveness of artificial manure, the formulas of which were mainly derived theoretically. Together with the manufacturer of his manure, he waged a publicity campaign in the English press which they hoped would promote the rapid diffusion of the manure. Widespread introduction of the new manure would have considerably increased the demand for agricultural chemists in rural areas, in industry, and at universities. However, the manure's inefficacy soon became obvious. As far as the institutionalization of agricultural chemistry was concerned the manure programme proved a complete failure. As one historian has commented, 'Liebig's teachings seemed so much discredited that the *Journal of the English Agricultural Society* refused to publish Liebig's answer to reports by Lawes and Gilbert.'[58] It took Liebig fifteen years to explain the failure of the manure. His battle against the 'practical men' of rational agriculture over acceptance of his claims took equally long. This underscores the significance of institutional success for a 'finalized' science. Within chemistry, the success of the reproduction cycle theory might have been sufficient for acceptance.

For Liebig, the training of students was of paramount importance for the institutionalization of his theory. As he was one of the first to found a laboratory in which students received regular training in the art of experimentation, he could easily promote agricultural chemistry as a special field of training. Liebig's purpose was to tackle the complex problems of agricultural chemistry by an effective division of labour and organization of research. But behind this organization of a system of division of labour there was yet another problem to which no solution had been found until Liebig's time: the standardization of experimental conditions and the practicability of speedy simultaneous analyses. Liebig's purpose in his activities as designer of experimental apparatus was to simplify the apparatus even at the cost of precision.

The regular training of students presupposed the existence of job opportunities. In several reports Liebig attacked his contemporary academic colleagues for their incompetence, hoping to push his students into their chairs.[59] Reflecting on his success in Austria, he wrote: 'For many years no candidate who had not received training in Giessen or had not completed his studies there could get a teaching post.'[60] In Hessen, Saxony and Bavaria these efforts proved successful; later, they were successful in Prussia, too. For this policy of 'public relations' Liebig did not need to found a special journal. He held a dominant position in the *Annalen der Chemie und der Pharmacie* (the leading German chemistry journal and, at the same time, the leading international journal of organic chemistry), and thus he could give agricultural chemistry the backing of organic chemistry which was developing with extraordinary success. To this end Liebig in 1840 modified the traditional classification of the *Annalen* (in which investigations in agricultural chemistry would have appeared only under the item 'Mixed Notes') and had all relevant publications, including his own works and polemics with other scholars, appear in the *Annalen*. In addition, Liebig ensured that agricultural chemistry was given a prominent place in many of the handbooks and textbooks published.

In Munich in the last period of his life (1859-1873) the institutionalization of agricultural chemistry was completed: in 1862 the first professorial chair for agricultural chemistry was established in Halle, followed by Leipzig in 1869, Giessen in 1871, Göttingen in 1872, Munich in 1874, Königsberg and Kiel in 1876, Breslau and Berlin in 1880. Accordingly, the academies of agriculture which had been the castles of the oppositional rational agriculture were dissolved: Regenwalde in 1859, Möglin in 1862, Waldau in 1868, Tharandt in 1869, Hofgeismar in 1871, Eldena in 1877, and Proskau in 1880. Others were taken by Liebig's students.

CONCLUSION

The theory of agriculture to which Liebig first gave a relatively complete formulation marks the beginning of a new type of theory-building in the natural sciences. We have called this type 'finalized science', a term chosen to indicate that human needs and interests explicitly take part in forming the subject field of a science. As teleological causes they are the cognitive impetus of theory-building. Thus the science of agriculture is a theory about the most rational organizing of nature to satisfy human needs and at the same time a science about the rationality of human needs vis-à-vis nature.

Obviously such a science differs from the classical disciplines of physics, chemistry and biology. In the latter the order of nature — the structure of reality conceived as independent of human interests — constitutes the subject of research, although of course applicable results follow from research and the patterns of scientific thought are not isolated from the prevailing cultural environment. Newton's classical mechanics, Einstein's theories of relativity or Watson's double helix are in this sense knowledge that is valid, independent of human needs and interests. On the other hand, no clear distinction can be made between agricultural chemistry and applied or engineering sciences or medicine. In these fields specific segments of nature are conceptualized under the perspective of satisfying human needs.

However, our concern is not to distinguish agricultural chemistry (as finalized science) from applied sciences, but rather to give the concept of applied science a precise meaning. The term 'applied science' is misleading in suggesting that it is nothing but the *application* of a given science, and not a contribution to science itself, resulting in the notion of the superiority of 'pure' over 'applied' science. In certain instances an applied science or technology may not require theoretical work but only need to establish certain strategies to gain new knowledge. As a rule, however, the production of applicable science will of necessity entail a process of theory-construction evolving independently from the mother disciplines. Such additional theoretical work is necessary not only because the respective application is a specialization, the refinements of which have no major significance for the mother disciplines; but also because these refinements cover *a limine* different types of objectivity: on the one hand, inquiry into nature unrelated to any specified purpose; on the other, nature constructed purposefully in terms of specific goals.

Historically agricultural chemistry is one of the first examples of successful goal-oriented theory. Goal-oriented sciences have since modern times been theoretical in the sense that they have formulated models and analogues for the phenomena observed. The eighteenth century offers many examples of the closer relationship between science and technology in textiles, agriculture and transport. But it was only in the latter half of the nineteenth century that Liebig and — a little later — the pioneers of mechanical engineering (Franz Reuleaux) and refrigeration and heating (Carl von Linde) for example, formulated theories which were deductive, comprehensive and heuristic and thus fulfilled the function of a paradigm.

Traditional philosophy of science has tended to neglect this type of applied sciences. Their theoretical status and their relationship to pure sciences have not been adequately clarified. Presumably, two causes may be held responsible for this neglect. First, object areas and problems limited to the study of disease, machines, manure and the like do not possess the dignity natural philosophy was ready to accord to universal properties of nature (e.g., forces, chemical compounds, and so forth). Secondly, inquiry into the artificial, the purposefully constructed, reality is held to possess less dignity than the 'natural state' of nature.

It is impossible to discuss on the mere basis of a case study the importance of the role of pure science in the progress of applied and technological sciences. We intended our case to show in what manner applied sciences are theory-developing research strategies. Finalized sciences, on the one side, presuppose mature disciplines in which entire areas of reality have been subject to scientification (e.g., fields of physics, chemistry). On the other hand, they presuppose advanced technologies, which furnish new processes, but encounter limitations, which cannot be overcome by mere empiricism. Special developments occur when specific technical or social goals are introduced into a basic science already matured. The philosophy of science reveals but one aspect of modern science – its reductionist programme. Another important aspect of modern science has been discussed here in terms of our concept of finalized science: that is, the construction of reality according to scientific methods and theories, directed by the changing goals of man in his natural environment.

Wolfgang Krohn / Wolf Schäfer, Max-Planck-Institut zur Erforschung der Lebensbedingungen der wissenschaftlich-technischen Welt, 813 Starnberg, Riemerschmidstrasse 7, Postfach 1529, FRG.

WOLFGANG KROHN received his doctorate from the University of Hamburg. He is currently a member of the Max-Planck Institute at Starnberg and works on a project concerned with the institutional and cognitive conditions of scientific development. As a lecturer at the University of Munich, he is concerned with the sociological and philosophical origins of modern science.

WOLF SCHÄFER received his M.A. in social history from the University of Munich. He is currently doing research at the Max-Planck Institute at Starnberg on the social history of science and technology.

NOTES

1. G. Böhme / W. van den Daele / W. Krohn, 'Die Finalisierung der Wissenschaft', *Zeitschrift für Soziologie* 2 (1973) 128–144. A revised English version entitled 'Finalization in Science' is to be published in *Social Science Information* 15:2 (1976).
2. Cf. Heinz Balmer, *Beitrage zur Geschichte der Erkenntnis des Erdmagnetismus* (Zürich: Sauerländer and Co., 1956) 141f.
3. Cf. W. van den Daele/P. Weingart in part 2 of this volume.
4. Cf. J. G. Wallerius, *Chymische Grundsätze des Ackerbaus* (Berlin: A. Weber, 1764); A. D. Thaer, *Grundsätze der rationellen Landwirtschaft,* 4 vols (Berlin: Realschulbuchhandlung, 1809–1812).
5. J. Liebig, *Die Chemie in ihrer Anwendung auf Agricultur und Physiologie,* 2 vols (Braunschweig: Vieweg, 1862) intro., 9. As there exists no authorized translation of the first volume, we were obliged to translate the quotations ourselves.
6. T. R. Malthus, *An Essay on the Principle of Population* (Seventh edition, 1872, reprinted New York: Kelley, 1971) 4 and 6.
7. *Ibid.,* 4.
8. W. Köllmann, *Bevölkerung und Raum in neuerer und neuester Zeit* (Würzburg: Ploetz, 1965) 1, 6.
9. Liebig, *Die Chemie* , I, intro., 12.
10. *Ibid.,* intro., 125f.
11. *Ibid.,* intro., 155.
12. J. Liebig, *The Natural Laws of Husbandry* (London: Walton and Maberly, 1863) xiv.
13. Liebig, *Die Chemie,* I, intro., 87.
14. J. Volhard, *Justus von Liebig,* 2 vols (Leipzig: J. A. Barth, 1909) I, 231, 239.
15. Liebig, *Die Chemie,* intro., 9f.
16. H. Davy, *Collected Works* (London: Smith, Elder and Co., 1840) vol. VII.
17. *Ibid.,* 177, 117.
18. Cf. C. A. Browne, *A Source Book of Agricultural Chemistry* (Waltham, Mass: Chronica Botanica Company, 1944) ch. 5.
19. A. D. Thaer, *Einleitung zur Kenntnis der Englischen Landwirtschaft,* 3 vols (Hannover, 1798–1804).
20. J. H. Thünen, *Der isolierte Staat in Beziehung auf Landwirtschaft und Nationalökonomie* (Hamburg, 1826).
21. Browne, *A Source Book,* 264, 279.
22. Volhard, *Justus von Liebig,* II, 32.
23. J. Liebig, *Die organische Chemie in ihrer Anwendung auf Agricultur und Physiologie* (Braunschweig: Vieweg, 1840).
24. J. Liebig, *Chemistry in its Application to Agriculture and Physiology* (London: Taylor and Walton, 1842) 4.
25. J. R. Partington, *A History of Chemistry* (London: Macmillan, 1972) vol. 4, 233.
26. Liebig, *Die organische Chemie,* dedication to Humboldt.
27. Liebig, *Die organische Chemie,* I, intro., 87.
28. *Ibid.,* 134ff.
29. *Ibid.,* 147ff.
30. J. Liebig, *Chemische Briefe* (Leipzig/Heidelberg: Winter, 1878) x.
31. O. Mayr, 'Adam Smith and the Concept of the Feedback System', *Technology and Culture* 12 (1971) 1-22.

32. Liebig, *Die Chemie*, ι. 18 (note).
33. J. Liebig, *Chemische Briefe* (Heidelberg: Winter, 1844) 178.
34. Liebig, *Die organische Chemie*, 36ff.
35. J. Liebig, *Bemerkungen über das Verhältnis der Thierchemie zur Thier-Physiologie* (Heidelberg: Winter, 1844) 40.
36. Liebig, *Die Chemie*, ι. xiv.
37. *Ibid.*, ι. 290.
38. *Ibid.*, ι, 137.
39. *Ibid.*, ι. intro., 5.
40. *Ibid.*, ι. intro., 12.
41. *Ibid.*, ι. 157.
42. *Ibid.*, ι. 159.
43. *Ibid.*, ι. 252f.
44. *Ibid.*, ι. 257.
45. J. J. Berzelius, 'Über einige Fragen des Tages in der organischen Chemie', *Annalen der Pharmacie* 31 (1839) 20f.
46. Liebig, *Die organische Chemie*, 199ff.
47. Liebig, *Die Chemie*, ι. xiii.
48. *Ibid.*, ι. 180.
49. See, respectively, J. Liebig, 'Die Wechselwirtschaft', *Annalen der Chemie und Pharmacie* 46 (1843) 73, and O. Kellner / H. Immendorf, 'Beziehungen der Chemie zum Ackerbau', *Die Kultur der Gegenwart*, 3. Teil, 3. Abteilung, 2. Band (Leipzig/Berlin: Teubner, 1913) 415, 464.
50. Cf. L. Schmitt / H. Ertel, *100 Jahre erfolgreiche Düngerwirtschaft* (Frankfurt: J. D. Sauerländer, 1958).
51. Liebig, *Die organische Chemie*, 84.
52. C. Sprengel, *Die Bodenkunde oder die Lehre vom Boden* (Leipzig, 1837).
53. Browne, *A Source Book*, 233.
54. J. Liebig, *Die organische Chemie in ihren Beziehungen zu den Herren Dr. Gruber und Sprengel* (Heidelberg: Winter, 1841) 36.
55. J. Carriere, *Berzelius und Liebig. Ihre Briefe von 1831-1845* (Munich/Leipzig: J. F. Lehmann, 1893) 210-11, letter to Berzelius dated 26 April 1840.
56. *Ibid.*, 215, letter to Berzelius dated 3 September 1840.
57. Liebig, *Die Chemie*, ι. intro., 13, and ι. xv.
58. Volhard, *Justus von Liebig*, ιι. 37.
59. J. Liebig, *Über das Studium der Naturwissenschaften und über den Zustand der Chemie in Preussen* (Braunschweig: Vieweg, 1840); J. Liebig, 'Der Zustand der Chemie in Österreich', *Annalen der Pharmacie* 25 (1838) 339-347; J. Liebig, *Herr Dr. Emil Wolff in Hohenheim und die Agricultur-Chemie* (Braunschweig: Vieweg, 1855).
60. Volhard, *Justus von Liebig*, ι. 369.

P. COSTABEL

Du Centenaire d'une Discipline Nouvelle: la Thermodynamique

L'histoire de la science a-t-elle une contribution positive à apporter au présent débat, même si l'on admet que cette histoire recouvre aujourd'hui des activités multiples qui ne concernent pas seulement des phénomènes antédiluviens et des temps révolus? On peut poser la question sans aucune pointe d'ironie. L'étude de la naissance de disciplines nouvelles, telle qu'elle a été proposée ici, correspond à l'état actuel du phénomène scientifique et il n'y a aucun doute que cet état semble défier toute référence au passé.

Dans la mesure même où le terme de discipline évoque cependant une réalité familière de l'enseignement organisé, il ne paraît pas indécent de se demander si le développement de la science au XIXe siècle — époque de forte structuration universitaire — n'a pas quelqu'exemple à fournir pour une réflexion utile.

Si la thermodynamique vient aussitôt à l'esprit, dans cette perspective, c'est à coup sûr parce que son nom est composé, et il semble bien que ce qui s'est manifesté ainsi dans le vocabulaire, il y a un siècle, n'est pas sans rapport avec le développement des études d'interconnexions qui prolifèrent aujourd'hui.

Reste, pour l'historien, à faire la preuve qu'il ne se donne pas bonne conscience à peu de frais.

L'apparition de termes composés dans la classification des sciences suit de près les efforts des Encyclopédistes du XVIIIe siècle pour présenter, avec cette classification, non seulement une révision radicale des conceptions anciennes, mais encore une ébauche d'organigramme ouvert sur l'évolution à venir.[1] Il faut ici se limiter à cette indication fugitive. Au début du XIXe sie cle, la physique mathématique est le premier exemple caractéristique de création de vocable nouveau pour signifier un type d'activité autonome, distinct de ce qu'évoque chacun des mots entrant dans sa composition. Tandis que l'adjectif 'physico-mathématique' était en usage depuis deux siècles pour désigner un certain type de considérations ou de 'problèmes',[2] c'est seulement avec l'essor de la science française sous le premier Empire que l'adjectif mathématique vient définir une branche de la physique. On le constate aussi bien dans les documents concernant la science en train de se faire, comme les rapports académiques de Delambre,que dans les titres de traités didactiques, comme celui de Biot.[3] Le phénomène correspond à un dépassement de la distinction, voire de l'opposition, entre théorie et expérience: le primat de l'expérimentation dans les sciences de la nature est reconnu comme conjoint à la nécessité d''assujettir au calcul' les démarches du physicien, c'est-à-dire de demander à la mathématique de prendre le relais de la vieille 'philosophie naturelle' pour diriger et suggérer. D'où un type particulier de spéculations qui tient à la fois de la mathématique pure et de l'expérimentation, et qui conduit rapidement à une transmission dans l'enseignement, le lieu privilégié étant en France l'Ecole polytechnique. Bien entendu, ce schéma très simplifié doit être aussitôt assorti du complément qui lui donne son véritable sens: l'universalité de la notion de force étant l'essentiel de la 'philosophie naturelle' de Newton, c'est la mécanique qui est le modèle fondamental, au moment même où elle accède d'ailleurs à un statut rationnel qui paraît exempt de toute contestation.

Ce que la physique mathématique signifie au début du XIXe siècle touche directement notre propos. Les promoteurs de cette activité, comme en témoignent leurs bibliographies, n'ont pas opéré de spécialisations étroites dans leurs recherches. Qu'il s'agisse d'optique, d'électricité ou de chaleur, on les retrouve tous participant à un effort d'ensemble dans lequel la mécanique rationnelle est le modèle de référence, et où l'espoir de conserver cette unité d'inspiration est manifestement le moteur principal.[4] Ce n'est pas par hasard que l'expression de théorie mécanique de la chaleur est utilisée encore cinquante ans plus tard, même à l'époque où l'on commence à parler de thermodynamique et jusque sous la plume d'un créateur en la matière comme Clausius.[5]

Le nom que je viens d'évoquer est pourtant celui d'un maître et d'un vulgarisateur; c'est le nom du personnage auquel on peut effectivement rattacher la naissance de cette discipline nouvelle dont je veux parler. Il m'est apparu utile de marquer dès l'abord comment, d'un point de vue global, s'est reproduite pour elle, avec une évolution beaucoup plus rapide, la situation de la physique mathématique elle-même.

Il faut, d'ailleurs, apporter des précisions supplémentaires. Aujour-d'hui encore la plupart de ceux qui veulent bien admettre que le terme de thermodynamique est juste centenaire s'imaginent volontiers que son apparition marque la nouveauté de relations entre chaleur et mouve-ment, et c'est là un cas typique de formulation ambiguë. L'idée de telles relations remonte à la plus haute antiquité et on la rencontre constam-ment au XVIIe siècle, associée aux recherches sur la nature de la lumière. La découverte des lumières froides fut à cette époque un obstacle et Pascal qui connaissait la phosphorescence de la pierre de Bologne,[6] *Spongia solis,* se riait de ceux qui voulaient assimiler agitation corpus-culaire et chaleur.[7] Le thème ne fut pas pour autant éliminé, tant s'en faut, mais il eut à s'adapter à l'évolution des divers aspects de la notion de mouvement, ainsi qu'à des observations venues en plus grand nombre de la sphère technique: échauffement dans les machines en raison des frotte-ments, dégagement de chaleur dans les chocs. D'autre part, au début du XIXe siècle, la machine à vapeur mit en évidence la possibilité de créer du mouvement en consommant du feu, et comme deux siècles auparavant dans le cas des lunettes, le produit de l'ingéniosité technicienne appelait de manière pressante la réflexion théorique tout en l'orientant sur des voies nouvelles.[8]

Il est donc à la fois vrai et faux que l'idée des relations entre chaleur et mouvement se fasse seulement jour après les premiers efforts de la physique mathématique. Il est vrai, surtout, que les relations en question ont été, durant toute la première moitié du XIXe siècle, illustrées tout autrement que par le passé, tout autrement qu'à travers la spéculation pure. Rien d'étonnant dès lors à ce que, vers 1850, au moment même où la réflexion théorique commence à aboutir, un adjectif spécial soit utilisé pour désigner les phénomènes étudiés: à la forme plus précise et plus concrète prise par ces phénomènes correspond dans le langage la néces-sité de les nommer correctement.[9]

Quant au passage de l'adjectif au substantif, il s'est réalisé en moins de vingt ans. Témoin cette publication du ministère de l'Instruction publique en 1867, intitulée 'Rapport sur les progrès de la Thermodynamique en France' et rédigée par M. Bertin, maître de conférences à l'Ecole nor-male.[10] Encore que ce document officiel ne fasse dans son contenu qu'un usage très limité du nouveau vocable et garde la préférence aux expres-sions antérieures, il ne contredit pas son titre; il manifeste l'existence d'une discipline nouvelle. De telle sorte que l'analogie entre la physique mathématique et la thermodynamique s'inscrit dans un processus doué d'accélération. Et cela suffit, à mon avis, à faire pressentir l'intérêt de l'exemple.

Le rapport Bertin, auquel je viens de faire allusion, peut nous servir de guide pour un examen plus détaillé. En possession d'une information historique très remarquable, l'auteur sait que l'idée fondamentale de ce qu'il appelle la science moderne, c'est-à-dire les transformations de l'énergie à travers des équivalences, n'est pas entièrement nouvelle. Il cite le physicien français Fresnel qui, dès 1822, et à propos de certains phénomènes lumineux, déclarait que 'la quantité de forces vives qui disparaît comme lumière est reproduite en chaleur'.[11] Mais il insiste sur le fait que seule une longue épreuve pouvait permettre à l'idée de se perfectionner et de se transformer jusqu'à la structure nécessaire à la constitution d'une science.

Bien entendu, il distingue les travaux préparatoires qui ont eu un rôle décisif entre 1842 et 1849, c'est-à-dire ceux de Mayer, Colding et Joule, et l'élaboration 'claire et méthodique de procédés d'investigation et de raisonnement' qui fut de 1849 à 1851 l'oeuvre de Clausius, Rankine et William Thomson.[12] Bertin, cependant, ne tombe pas dans le travers qui conduisait en 1928 Charles Fabry, alors professeur à la Sorbonne, à écrire dans ses *Eléments de thermodynamique* la note suivante: 'Du point de vue historique, il est curieux de constater qu'alors que les notions de travail et de quantité de chaleur étaient déjà clairement établies, on ne réussit pas à découvrir cette relation si simple [équivalence du travail dépensé et de la chaleur dégagée]. Il semble qu'on se soit bouché les yeux pour ne pas la voir.' Le point de vue historique de Fabry était surtout celui de l'ignorance, une ignorance allant jusqu'à considérer comme 'clairement établi' ce qui ne l'était pas encore entre 1820 et 1840. Ayant moi-même appris la thermodynamique sous M. Fabry, j'ai bien quelque raison de regretter que l'enseignement que je reçus comme étudiant ait été si peu éclairé quant aux conditions cognitives réelles dans la trame de l'histoire. Si Fabry avait lu Bertin — ce qu'après tout il pouvait faire — il n'aurait pas cru les choses si simples et nous aurait mieux fait comprendre les difficultés de la pensée scientifique aux prises avec la création.

D'ailleurs, tout en insistant sur le fait que la découverte de l'équivalence précise entre travail et chaleur a déclenché la constitution de la thermodynamique, Bertin signale fort heureusement comment le terrain était préparé à un autre point de vue. Bien qu'il attribue à Sadi Carnot, dans son célèbre petit ouvrage de 1824, *Réflexions sur la puissance motrice du feu,* une conception du 'fluide calorique' qui n'est pas exacte, Bertin mentionne les acquisitions dues à ce jeune savant français: le fait qu'il est nécessaire, pour produire du travail en consommant de la chaleur, de disposer d'une source chaude et d'une source froide, et d'opérer sur une chute de température; la possibilité de raisonner sur cycles d'opérations. Bertin ajoute: 'Clapeyron a éclairci ce que le mémoire de Carnot avait d'obscur et a montré comment on devait traduire analytiquement et représenter géométriquement ce mode de raisonnement si neuf et si fécond. Ces deux géomètres ont créé en quelque sorte la logique de la science. Lorsque les véritables principes ont été découverts il n'y a eu qu'à les introduire dans les formes de cette logique, et il est à croire que, sans les anciens travaux de Carnot et de Clapeyron, les progrès de la théorie nouvelle n'auraient pas été à beaucoup près aussi rapides.'

Ces notations sont tout à fait justes.[13] Vous savez tous plus ou moins que ce que l'on appelle le second principe de la thermodynamique, celui qui vise la dégradation de l'énergie, est en germe dans l'ouvrage de Sadi Carnot, et il vous est peut-être déjà arrivé d'entendre cette question naïve: comment se fait-il que l'élaboration avancée du second principe ait précédé la découverte du premier principe? Les numéros d'ordre sont le fruit de l'exposé didactique, ils apparaissent avec la discipline constituée. Ce serait donc vous faire injure que de prendre au sérieux une question que j'ai dite naïve pour m'en tenir à une expression modérée. Mais il m'a semblé que cette question n'était pas, en fait, inapte à nous faire mieux saisir ce qui est ici le plus important. Comme le dit Bertin, les principes ont mis quelques décennies à parvenir à une formulation satisfaisante et les notions de base à se préciser, et ceci sans l'ordre que l'on reconnaît a posteriori; mais la rapidité avec laquelle la constitution de la discipline se cristallise s'explique essentiellement grâce à l'invention d'une logique qui est la forme, le moule, prêt à recevoir et à modeler une matière adéquate.

Si l'histoire impose à cet égard le nom de Sadi Carnot, c'est qu'une pareille affaire exige l'activité de pointe d'un esprit clair, d'un esprit qui se pose à un moment donné des questions que personne d'autre ne pose.[14] En l'occurrence les questions suivantes: y a-t-il, pour les machines à feu, un rendement maximal qu'il est vain de chercher à dépasser en augmentant, par exemple, les pressions de vapeur? Est-il raisonnable d'admettre comme on le fait que les chaleurs spécifiques d'un fluide gazeux ont un rapport constant? Les réponses fondamentales de Carnot, à savoir qu'il y a un rendement maximal et que la constance est à placer dans la différence des chaleurs spécifiques, sont effectivement le fruit d'une logique toute leibnizienne: le mouvement perpétuel est impossible et il n'y a pas de création ex nihilo. Que cette logique ait surpris les contemporains et qu'il ait fallu dix ans pour qu'elle soit prise au sérieux avec Clapeyron, en

1834, c'est un beau sujet de méditation sur lequel on est loin, aujourd'hui encore, de pouvoir conclure.[15] Le fait que l'ouvrage de Carnot n'a été édité, à compte d'auteur, qu'à 600 exemplaires, le contexte technique et social dans lequel il est apparu, et bien d'autres raisons sont à considérer. Le colloque qui doit se tenir en juin prochain pour la célébration du 150e anniversaire des *Réflexions sur la puissance motrice du feu* permettra peut-être d'avancer vers une compréhension satisfaisante.[16] Quels que soient les résultats de cet effort, il restera vrai que les idées de Carnot doivent à la traduction analytique de Clapeyron d'avoir pu atteindre les créateurs de la thermodynamique. Et de ce fait le passage de Bertin que nous avons cité plus haut appelle un complément d'importance.

Quiconque ouvre l'opuscule de Sadi Carnot ne peut manquer d'être frappé par le peu de place accordée par l'auteur à l'usage de l'analyse mathématique. Au point que l'on pourrait douter de la formation de cet auteur dans la célèbre Ecole polytechnique.[17] Si Bertin a raison de situer Clapeyron dans la ligne de pensée logique qui prend son origine chez Sadi Carnot, il faut cependant mettre davantage qu'il ne le fait, l'accent sur le rôle de la mathématisation introduite par Clapeyron. La logique de Carnot n'a pris force et consistance, n'a eu de puissance de communication, que lorsqu'elle a été conjointe à un langage opérationnel.

Je ne crois pas utile de m'étendre plus longtemps. A considérer les trente années qui, de 1820 à 1850, recouvrent la préparation de cette discipline nouvelle qu'est la thermodynamique, la moisson de données est riche, tout particulièrement en ce qui concerne les 'conditions cognitives.' Si l'historien que je suis privilégie ces conditions par rapport à toutes les autres susceptibles d'être invoquées et qui mettraient en ligne de compte les considérations sociales ou la politique de la science et de la technique, ce n'est pas parce que j'ignore ces autres conditions.[18] Mais c'est encore une fois parce que rien ne permet de remplacer l'action d'un esprit comme celui de Sadi Carnot pour poser des questions que personne ne pose, et pour faire rendre au contexte historique large et complexe ce qu'il contient de favorable au dépassement des paradigmes reçus. Et pour ce dépassement, le primat à reconnaître à la pensée logique ne peut être disjoint de l'expression dans un langage approprié.

Il me semble que les quelques mots qui me restent à dire pour vous conduire jusqu'au centenaire proprement dit que j'ai évoqué en commençant, ne peuvent être que la confirmation de cette première constatation. Ne nous attardons pas sur le fait que les physiciens français ont sous le second Empire poursuivi une très importante tâche expérimentale et ont progressivement pris conscience de leur retard par rapport aux savants étrangers sur le plan théorique. Ne nous attardons pas à détailler comment des oeuvres méritoires de traduction et d'information, telles que celles de Verdet ou de François Moigno (1804-1884), ont permis à la physique française de récupérer ce qu'elle n'aurait pas dû perdre, la tradition de ces pionniers. Mais disons plutôt ceci: au moment où se réalise en France, de 1872 à 1878, la réédition des *Réflexions* de Carnot et au moment où les retrouvailles donnent lieu à la satisfaction rétrospective, Boltzmann en Allemagne formule son interprétation statistique de l'entropie — bouleversement de la conception du second principe de la thermodynamique et véritable fondement nouveau, fondement que la science moderne reconnaît encore comme tel.[19]

Or, quel est le motif des recherches dont la théorie de Boltzmann marque l'aboutissement? C'est la redoutable nécessité de comprendre l'irréversibilité que la dégradation de l'énergie impose à l'attention du physicien. La logique de Carnot comportait à cet égard une lacune. Je crois que c'est dans la mesure même où cette lacune était évidente que le relais a été pris si vite par un autre esprit privilégié, pour compléter et donner à l'élaboration rationnelle sa forme achevée.

Il y aurait lieu, sans aucun doute, de dire combien un Boltzmann a été servi par l'organisation de l'université allemande, par l'élan donné outre-Rhin à la recherche aussi bien expérimentale que théorique.[20] Les contacts que Boltzmann a eus avec les maîtres de Berlin, l'étude approfondie qu'il fit à Vienne de l'oeuvre de Maxwell, l'obligation dans laquelle il se trouva, de par ses fonctions universitaires, d'enseigner la science en marche, tout cela compte de manière considérable dans l'avancement de ses travaux.[21] Et l'on pourrait établir une comparaison utile avec la situation en France. Mais en définitive, comme précédemment, on ne trouverait dans ces considérations que la meilleure connaissance de ce qui fut dans telle société et à telle époque plus favorable qu'ailleurs.

Le paradoxe de la réversibilité, qu'il s'agissait de conjurer pour faire le pont entre la mécanique classique et la science des phénomènes de la chaleur, et dont la solution a vraiment fondé une discipline nouvelle, était en définitive affaire de pensée scientifique et cela seulement.

L'accélération de l'histoire qui est celle de notre science contemporaine me paraît tenir aussi, en majeure partie, au perfectionnement des structures logiques et des langages opérationnels qui accompagne de près désormais toute démarche scientifique.[22] Ma conclusion, au terme d'un regard sur le passé vieux d'un siècle, c'est que la prolifération des disciplines, le développement prodigieux des découvertes, résultent avant tout des progrès de la méthodologie multipliant les possibilités des esprits moyens de participer à l'effort créateur, sans pour autant éliminer les génies.[23]

P. Costabel, Centre de Recherches Alexandre Koyré, Ecole des Hautes Etudes en Sciences Sociales, 12 rue Colbert, 75002 Paris.

P. COSTABEL, ancien élève de l'Ecole Normale Supérieure (promotion Sciences 1932), agrégé de mathématiques (1935), a été secrétaire du Comité national français d'histoire et de philosophie des sciences de 1956 à 1971. Entré dans les cadres de l'Ecole des Hautes Etudes en 1957, il y est directeur d'études depuis 1963 et consacre ses séminaires à l'histoire des sciences exactes du XVIIe au XIXe siècles.

NOTES

1. Cf. *Système figuré des connaissances humaines* grand in fol. plano contenu dans le prospectus de lancement de l'*Encyclopédie* rédigé par Diderot et diffusé en octobre 1750, reproduit à la fin du Discours préliminaire tome I de la publication (1751). *Essai d'une distribution généalogique des sciences, etc.* par Ch. F. G. Roth (Weimar 1769), placé en tête du tome I de la Table générale de l'*Encyclopédie* (1780).
2. Cf. notamment Mersenne, *Cogitata physico mathematica* (Paris 1644).
3. Jean-Baptiste Joseph Delambre (1749-1822) *Rapport historique sur les progrès des sciences mathématiques depuis 1789 et sur leur état actuel* (Paris 1810) 284-308; Jean-Baptiste Biot (1774-1862) *Traité de physique expérimentale et mathématique* (Paris 1816).
4. Siméon-Denis Poisson (1781-1840) est l'auteur le plus significatif à cet égard: cf. Programme de la *Mécanique physique* donné en tête d'un Mémoire à l'Académie (14 avril 1828). Voir aussi les premiers volumes d'un *Traité de physique mathématique: Nouvelle théorie de l'action capillaire* (Paris 1831) et *Théorie mathématique de la chaleur* (Paris 1835).
5. Rudolph Clausius (1822-1888) *Die mechanische Wärmetheorie . . .* 1e édition 1864 (rassemblement de travaux commencés en 1850); *Théorie mécanique de la chaleur*, traduits de l'allemand par F. Folie (Paris 1868-69).
6. Cf. la controverse Galilée-Lagalla-Liceti *Opere Gal.* Ediz. Naz. XVIII pp. 233-234 — Pascal, *Pensées* 91 Brunschwig-660 Lafuma.
7. Cf. Pascal, *Pensées* 368 Br.-686 Laf.
8. L'invention empirique de la lunette se situe en Hollande au début du XVIIe siècle, et le premier ouvrage à donner une théorie satisfaisante des instruments d'optique est la *Dioptrique* de Huygens 1692, publié en 1704. Mais si un siècle a été nécessaire pour que la science assume ainsi l'invention, le travail théorique correspondant, inauguré par Kepler en 1611, n'a cessé d'être commandé par les problèmes posés aux artisans techniciens et les améliorations successives réalisées par eux. Pour la machine à vapeur, on note de même à partir de James Watt (1736-1819) que l'idée d'utiliser la *détente* de la vapeur en augmentant la pression de la vapeur saturante dirige pendant une trentaine d'années — et toujours en avance sur la réflexion théorique — l'ingéniosité technicienne. Pour le détail de cette très importante considération, voir l'édition critique des *Réflexions sur la puissance motrice du feu* de Sadi Carnot que Mr Robert Fox doit publier aux éditions Vrin à Paris fin 1976.

9. L'adjectif 'thermodynamique' pour désigner les phénomènes qui font l'objet de la théorie mécanique de la chaleur est employé par Clausius dans ses premiers mémoires.

10. 'Publication faite sous les auspices du ministère de l'Instruction publique, à l'Imprimerie impériale.'

11. Augustin Fresnel (1788-1827) *Supplément à la chimie de Thomson* [Thomas] (Paris 1822) 40.

12. Julius Robert von Mayer (1814-1878); Ludwig A. Colding (1815-1888); James Irescott Joule (1818-1889); William J. M. Rankine (1820-1872); William Thomson (Lord Kelvin) (1824-1907).

13. Elles sont d'ailleurs pratiquement empruntées à Verdet (Marcel Emile) (1824-1866) qui a joué dans l'information du milieu français, en ce qui concerne les travaux de W. Thomson et de Clausius, un rôle de premier plan — et qui a fait passer dans son enseignement à la Sorbonne aux alentours de 1860-65 des exposés très utiles relatifs au progrès de la théorie.

14. Sadi Carnot (1796-1832). Les Actes du colloque cité ci-dessous paraîtront aux éditions du CNRS en juin 1976.

15. Emile Clapeyron (1799-1864). Cf. *Journal de l'Ecole Polytechnique* (1834).

16. Ce colloque a eu lieu à l'Ecole polytechnique au mois de juin 1974.

17. Pour la filiation que Sadi Carnot manifeste, du point de vue de l'attitude fondamentale de l'esprit, par rapport à son père Lazare et à son oeuvre concernant la théorie des machines, voir *Lazare Carnot Savant* par Charles E. Gillispie et A. P. Youschkevitch (Princeton 1971), traduction française en cours de publication.

18. En France le développement des chemins de fer, auquel le gouvernement de Louis-Philippe a donné un rôle politique considérable, a certainement conditionné un grand nombre d'expériences nouvelles et l'on ne peut pas ignorer que le résultat de ces expériences est présent dans les divers travaux théoriques entre 1835 et 1840. En même temps d'ailleurs le Génie maritime fournit des illustrations parallèles (cf. l'oeuvre de Reech à Lorient).

19. Ludwig Boltzmann (1844-1906). Cf. 'Ueber die Beziehung zwischen dem zweiten Hauptzatze der mechanischen Wärmetheorie . . .' *Weiner Berichte* 76 (1877).

20. Cf. *Histoire Générale des Sciences*, sous la direction de R. Taton, (Paris: PUF. 1961) III. 620-629.

21. Cf. René Dugas, *La Théorie physique au sens de Boltzmann et ses prolongements modernes* (Neuchâtel/Paris 1959). L'ouvrage permet de conjuguer la connaissance des problèmes scientifiques mis en cause, le style de vie d'un universitaire contesté et obligé à de fréquents changements de poste, tandis que la physique bénéficiait dans l'ensemble des universités allemandes d'un élan remarquable.

22. Au début du XIXe siècle, la notion confuse de 'quantité de chaleur totale' contenue dans un corps et la tendance à la dominer par une traduction dans le langage des fonctions analytiques ont été responsables de beaucoup de fausses manoeuvres, ce qui explique en grande partie l'attitude de Sadi Carnot. L'attention portée aux 'préalables' marque le progrès fondamental de la pensée scientifique.

23. C'est ainsi que se réalise un voeu de Leibniz (cf. Pierre Costabel, 'Deux inédits de la correspondance de Leibniz', *Revue d'histoire des sciences* 2:4 (1949) 316 et 326) et que l'insertion plus profonde de la science dans le corps social détermine en retour des possibilités d'influence plus grandes, sur la science, d'actions ou de dirigisme externes.

R. G. A. DOLBY

The Case of Physical Chemistry

In the late nineteenth century, physical chemistry went through a crucial phase in its development, a phase associated with its emergence as a self-conscious scientific specialty.[1] The central episode was the rise to dominance of a research school around Wilhelm Ostwald. The sense of common identity felt by the members of Ostwald's group — through their association with the professor and with one another in the teaching research laboratory, through their adoption and defence of important productive new theories, through the founding of a new journal and a new textbook tradition — has been widely considered to be crucial in the rise of the new discipline. The school systematised previously scattered scientific work, and provided impetus to directions of research which were to be of major importance in the development of science. The school dominated the application of thermodynamics to chemistry, but built in particular on J. H. van't Hoff's theory of solutions and S. A. Arrhenius's theory of the permanent dissociation of electrolytes in solution. The influence of the group was recognised by both its supporters and by those who opposed it, though the desirability of its influence was quite differently assessed. Many of the novel ideas it disseminated became part of the scientific consensus, although not until the claims had been subjected to a process of criticism and resultant modification. The scale of influence of the school is illustrated by the fact that sixty-three of Ostwald's students were later to become professors.[2]

Histories, obituaries and textbooks written by those in contact with physical chemistry in the decades immediately after the events just described tended to say that there was a very sharp transformation of physical chemistry in the 1880s, or even in the year 1887 (when the theories of van't Hoff and Arrhenius were first linked, when Ostwald became professor of physical chemistry at Leipzig and founded the *Zeitschrift für physikalische Chemie*). In such retrospects, which have tended to dominate later historical accounts, the significance of earlier work in physical chemistry which did not contribute key ideas was minimized.[3] The acknowledged influences were represented as isolated and scattered fragments drawn together by van't Hoff, Arrhenius, and Ostwald and his school. However, when one attempts to build up quantitative measures of the growth of physical chemistry, no sharp change in the 1880s appears. This is clearly illustrated by the top curve of the graph in the figure, which provides an approximate measure of the historically significant innovatory activity in physical chemistry.[4] There is a fairly uniform rise throughout the nineteenth century. Measures of the total numbers of scientific papers published and abstracted in physical chemistry in the second half of the nineteenth century give a similar impression of steady growth, but as the classificatory headings in the relevant fields were changing during the period it is hard to give a precise numerical indication of the continuity of growth.

The contrast between historical retrospects and quantitative measures can be understood when a distinction is made between the focal and peripheral topics of a science, how these change with time, and how historical accounts tend to assess their relative importance. A focal topic is one which receives a great deal of attention, so that it attracts many research papers and, eventually, textbook summaries. The focal topics of the new physical chemistry in the 1890s were the theories of solutions and electrolysis, and the applications of thermodynamics to chemistry. A peripheral topic is one at the fringes of scientific interest in a field, perhaps attracting the attention of a few isolated individuals. Work on photochemistry, although attracting attention for brief periods in the nineteenth century, never generated a growing tradition of innovative research and was therefore a peripheral topic for most of the century. The lack of growth of interest in photochemistry is illustrated by the lowest line of the graph in the figure.

The *subject* of physical chemistry was recognised throughout the nineteenth century; indeed, the label 'physical chemistry' to identify the application of physical theory and technique to chemical phenomena dates from the eighteenth century.[5] There was a focus of interest in French chemistry in the late eighteenth and early nineteenth centuries on physical phenomena and conceptions. As this was central to chemistry as then conceived, however, it did not form the basis of an additional *discipline* of physical chemistry. By the second half of the nineteenth century,

Rate of Citation of Primary Material in the Physical Chemistry Chapters of J. R. Partington,
A History of Chemistry (London: Macmillan, 1964) volume IV

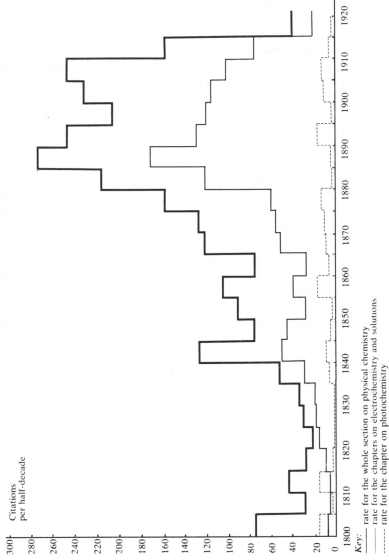

300 ⌐ Citations
per half-decade
280
260
240
220
200
180
160
140
120
100
80
60
40
20
0
1800   1810   1820   1830   1840   1850   1860   1870   1880   1890   1900   1910   1920

Key: ──── rate for the whole section on physical chemistry
──── rate for the chapters on electrochemistry and solutions
------- rate for the chapter on photochemistry

the focal topics of chemistry had moved far from physics. Work continued to be done in physical chemistry, but the subject area was not fashionable. For example, C. L. Berthollet's neglected conceptions of affinity and mass action attracted the attention only of scattered individuals. There was a steady but low level of interest in the physical properties of chemical substances. This had some practical and theoretical significance for organic and inorganic chemistry, but was a peripheral theme in the general chemistry of the third quarter of the century. The major area of research in physical chemistry in the decade before the late 1880s was thermochemistry. In some regions outside Germany this topic was becoming fashionable. However, the theoretical basis of the work was inadequate, as it was incompatible with the second law of thermodynamics. It was strongly attacked in the early 1880s by men with better knowledge of thermodynamics, who went on to become important in the new physical chemistry.

In contrast to the gradual rise in overall activity in the general subject area of physical chemistry, the work that was to be focal to the new physical chemistry of the 1880s had emerged relatively rapidly. The important applications of thermodynamics to chemistry began with the work of the American mathematical physicist, J. W. Gibbs, in the mid-1870s. It was some time, however, before the theoretical topics attracted much attention. Not until after mathematically qualified chemists had been trained (especially by the Ostwald school) was the associated experimental work taken up on a significant scale. Studies of electrochemistry and of solutions, which were so important to the new physical chemistry, had been peripheral activities in the three decades before the 1880s. It is therefore easy to see why later historical accounts of physical chemistry saw the 1880s as a pivotal decade. Much of the earlier work in physical chemistry was irrelevant to the issues which became focal then, and thus tended to be given less significance. The rate of discovery in electrochemistry and the theory of solutions rose sharply in the 1880s, as the middle line of the graph in the figure illustrates. It was the limited amount of immediate ancestry for the new specialty's first focus of interest which made its emergence seem so much more sudden than the growth of the general subject area of physical chemistry would suggest.

The distinction between focal and peripheral topics is of special value in exploring the manner in which new scientific specialties can be formed. T. S. Kuhn's account of paradigm-sharing communities, for example, used retrospective understanding to locate the focal scientific topics (and the people who work on them) in communities which do not have clearly located boundaries.[6] His account does not give clear theoretical guidance, however, on questions concerning the changing relationship between communities which do not share focal topics. Changing community structure may often be represented by the appearance of new focal issues at the periphery of older communities, or by the fusion or separation of focal issues in established sciences. There are, of course, many ways in which new specialties can emerge. They may arise as the response to an external social pressure, as a result of which new lines of research into important practical problems become institutionalised on a large scale. They may arise by redrawing community boundaries after revolutionary change in an older, differently defined field. Or they may appear when a totally new and unexpected branch of phenomena comes to be exploited systematically.

Let us, however, consider a mechanism suitable for examining the emergence of new disciplines in subject areas which have long been known, but which have previously seemed unproductive and unfashionable.

1. New ideas or techniques appear at the periphery of established fields.
2. In some cases, the scientists developing the idea, or others learning of it, form localised groups which exploit it and expand it into a distinctive scientific approach. If successful, increasing numbers of scientists become interested and in university-based subjects, many students are trained.
3. If the organisation of science makes it possible, the interests and skills of such a group may be diffused over a wider geographical area without losing their distinctive character by dilution with the prevailing patterns of science. (This is only possible if there is no significant assimilation of the new topic by those concerned with the focal topics of the established sciences.)
4. In some cases, the new approach achieves full institutional status as a separate science.

These four stages can readily be distinguished for physical chemistry. However, as each stage occurred most readily in a different geographical region, careful national comparisons are needed to understand the full process. The science in different geographical regions is not always in complete harmony. In particular, the topics which attract greatest attention in one region may be of peripheral interest in another. By making national contrasts, we can sort out the effects of such differences on how new sciences appear. We must also take into account the institutional settings of science in different countries, which are invariably of great importance in determining the rate at which new approaches in science are able to grow.[7] Since the national institutionalisation of science tends to affect different sciences in a similar way, institutional factors can be separated from local variations of focal and peripheral topics by comparing the emergence of physical chemistry with other new sciences appearing at the same time. For example, the development of experimental psychology, which followed a path similar to physical chemistry at about the same time, provides a useful point of comparison.[8]

A brief sketch of the development of physical chemistry in several countries in the late nineteenth century indicates how national comparisons can highlight the main features in the emergence of the new discipline. Let us consider Germany, where a distinct specialty of physical chemistry first emerged. There, the internal development of chemistry away from inorganic and physical topics had been most extreme in the nineteenth century. German chemistry had grown very rapidly, following the pattern of laboratory use established by Liebig in which doctoral students were trained in chemistry by doing modest original research projects. Organic chemistry thrived because it proved especially amenable to this approach, as H.N. Stokes explained in 1897:

Most students of nature do not willingly enter upon entirely new fields of research. The pupils of the great masters of organic chemistry, Liebig, Dumas, Hofmann, Wurtz, Kolbe, Kekulé, and others, found enough to do in following in the footsteps of their teachers, and were not inclined to seek new pastures. The requirements of candidates for the doctorate, whereby the experimental material for the dissertation had to be accumulated in a comparatively short time, led to the assignment of topics with which the instructor was familiar, and which were fairly sure of giving positive results within a year or two, and as we all know, no branch of chemistry yields results so readily as the study of carbon compounds, with its highly developed synthetical methods. As the Chemiker-Zeitung has recently pointed out, even at the present day the full professorships in Germany are almost invariably held by organic chemists, while inorganic chemistry is left to subordinates. The weight of authority and influence being on the side of organic chemistry, the student who looks forward to a university career sees that his chances of promotion are better if he follows the organic rather than the inorganic direction. I need hardly add that the more mercenary hope of obtaining a new dyestuff or a new remedy, or of replacing nature in making an alkaloid, has also been a powerful incentive to many.[9]

Just because physical chemistry received so much less attention than organic chemistry, it was less likely that the relatively few Germans working in the area (almost all of whom were students or associates of R. W. Bunsen) would produce major and influential innovations. In fact, the key innovations of the 1880s came from Holland (van't Hoff), from Scandinavia (Arrhenius) and Latvia (Ostwald). The most dynamic of the three, Ostwald, accepted a chair in physical chemistry in Leipzig (the second chair in chemistry at that important university), where he was able to attract sufficient numbers of able students to establish a thriving school which exploited the new discoveries. Students, especially foreigners, coming to Germany to gain their doctoral degrees in the leading scientific nation of the time, first heard of Ostwald's work by accident, or on reading his influential *Lehrbuch der allgemeinen Chemie* (Leipzig, 1885-6), studied with him, and then went back home to spread his reputation and so attract more students. In his six years as professor at Riga, Ostwald said he had only one good student dedicated to research. In Germany a new research school could grow far faster than in any other European country. Only in Germany was there sufficient diversity in the university system to permit minority interests to flourish. Only there was the system of teaching students how to do experimental research established on a large scale. So while it was difficult for new developments to emerge in physical chemistry in Germany, once they were established, institutional factors accelerated their development. Furthermore, the sharp separation of physical chemistry from the focal area of organic chemistry meant that the new approach was not immediately absorbed into the mainstream of German chemical research.

In the 1890s, the new physical chemistry spread rapidly to America. This again owed much to general institutional factors. From the 1860s on, the American higher education system went through a period of reform and growth. One major feature was the growth of graduate schools modelled on German patterns of linking teaching closely to original research. In the natural sciences, subjects in which research techniques could be taught in the experimental laboratory were transmitted especially effectively from Germany to America. In the last decades of the nineteenth century, a flood of Americans went to Germany to prepare themselves for a career of university teaching. The German Ph.D. was a useful qualification, which indicated that they had acquired the German attitudes and skills of disciplined and industrious research. Of course, those who were chemists most often studied organic chemistry, the leading branch of German chemistry. But after 1887, a number were attracted to Leipzig to study the newly fashionable physical chemistry in Ostwald's laboratory. In a study of all the readily traced Americans who stayed in Ostwald's laboratory, fifteen returned to an academic career in America. (Seven others went into Government or industrial research.) Most of these set up laboratories in which further generations of American graduate students were taught the principles of research in physical chemistry.[10]

Many of the general institutional factors which were important in the development of the new physical chemistry were also reflected in the development of experimental psychology. Once a nucleus for the new research area had been established in Germany, the two disciplines followed similar paths. Like Ostwald, Wilhelm Wundt set up a teaching and research laboratory in Leipzig (in the first years after his appointment in 1875), and his conception of the new discipline spread through Germany and to America. Wundt had come from a different discipline (physiology) rather than a different country, but like Ostwald, he built up the nucleus of a new experimental discipline which his laboratory graduates could spread.

With the help of Wundt's textbooks and journals, experimental psychology quickly became the focal interest of the *subject* area of psychology. Psychology had previously been dominated by philosophical psychology, which now became more peripheral, and many established philosophical psychologists assimilated the new approach. Experimental psychology was not clearly demarcated from philosophical psychology in Germany, but as the Americans returned home from Wundt's laboratory, they tended to leave behind Wundt's philosophical system, and to found experimental laboratories in which the investigatory techniques were related to the preoccupations of their own culture. In America, psychology changed from a physiologically-oriented adjunct to philosophical psychology into an experimental discipline which studied biological or functional problems, exploiting practical applications with enthusiasm. Thus the separation of psychology from philosophy was far sharper in America than it was in Germany.

The development of both physical chemistry and experimental psychology appears simplest if one concentrates on Germany and America. Indeed, the historical writings of those Americans who found their intellectual origins in Germany support the pattern of a new discipline emerging relatively suddenly in Germany and then spreading outwards. But the story is not quite so clear if one looks back at developments in other countries. In France, for example, physical approaches within chemistry were not so peripheral, and the development of physical chemistry took a different course. Work was being done in physical chemistry by two important French schools in the second half of the nineteenth century. M. Berthelot had an extensive research programme in thermochemistry, and H. Saint Claire Deville exploited a technique for the sudden cooling of gases to study dissociation at high temperatures. However, neither of these schools was restricted to physical chemistry, and there were obstacles to the rapid growth of physical chemistry within them.[11] In general, the centralised bureaucratic organisation of French science seems to have made it slow to respond competitively to external developments, and German developments in physical chemistry and experimental psychology were not able to take effective root there. French work in the general area of physical chemistry did continue to develop during the last decades of the nineteenth century, but it did so by building upon indigenous developments in the subject area, which were mainly peripheral to the faster growing research interests of Germany and America. Similarly, French psychology did not follow the pattern established in Germany, but developed more gradually by building on the strong French interest in psychopathology which was encouraged by the fact that a career in French psychology required taking positions closely associated with medicine and psychiatry. The German-American bias in many histories of both physical chemistry and experimental psychology has tended to under-represent what French activity there has been, because much of it was on topics peripheral to the main developments in other countries.

In Britain, the university system was strongly influenced by Germany in the later nineteenth century, and although not growing as fast as that of America was able to take up new developments. In psychology, laboratories devoted solely to psychological experiments were slow to be established, but a science rather similar to that in America was eventually established. In the case of physical chemistry, graduates from the Ostwald school were initially able to establish themselves within chemistry departments, and then gradually to build up specialist facilities and organisations. However, there were initial difficulties for the new physical chemistry in Britain. In the early 1880s, there was a considerable British interest in the theory of solutions, a focal topic of the new physical chemistry. The prevailing British approach favoured qualitative chemical methods that aspired to explain the phenomena of solutions at all concentrations, while the Ostwald school employed quantitative physical methods successful only for extremely dilute solutions. As the ideas and the graduates of Ostwald's school penetrated Britain, there were several stages of intense debate, which sharpened the contrast between the old approach and the new.[12] Since the Ostwald approach eventually rose to dominance (it was the obvious choice for the new generation of mathematically competent physical chemists), the losing side in the debate tended to be forgotten. But the debate had many indirect effects on physical chemistry, not least by sharpening the contrast between the new discipline and the rest of chemistry.

We see, therefore, that the rise of physical chemistry is not quite as simple a story as orthodox historical accounts suggest. Moreover, we see that by comparing different countries and subjects, employing conceptual distinctions between focal and peripheral areas of research, we can make more critical use of historical evidence in assessing the relative role of social and cognitive factors in the emergence of new disciplines.

R. G. A. Dolby, Unit for the History, Philosophy and Social Relations of Science, Physics Laboratory, The University, Canterbury, Kent CT2 7NR.

R. G. A. DOLBY received his M.Sc. in chemistry from Victoria University of Wellington (NZ) and his M.A. in history and philosophy of science from Princeton University. He is senior lecturer in the Unit for History, Philosophy and Social Relations of Science at the University of Kent at Canterbury. His main interest is the investigation of the significance of social factors in scientific knowledge and scientific change, particularly as revealed by the development of scientific disciplines in the late nineteenth century.

NOTES

1. This paper is based on my longer study, 'Social Factors in the Origin of a New Science: The Case of Physical Chemistry', which is to be published in *Historical Studies in the Physical Sciences.*

2. This figure is given by F. Szabadvary, *History of Analytical Chemistry* (Oxford: Pergamon Press, 1966) 354. Not all sixty-three became professors of physical chemistry, however.

3. For example, A. Findlay and T. Williams, in *A Hundred Years of Chemistry* (London: Duckworth, 3rd edition, 1965), stress the crucial importance of the 1880s. See p.86. A.J. Ihde, in his *Development of Modern Chemistry* (New York: Harper and Row, 1964) 341, writes, 'According to legend, physical chemistry was established as a separate discipline in 1887, when Ostwald founded the *Zeitschrift für physikalische Chemie'.* He goes on to qualify the legend, however.

4. The graph is a count of the number of citations of primary material per half-decade in J.R. Partington, *A History of Chemistry* (London: Macmillan, 1964) vol. IV. Partington attempts an exhaustive study of historically significant work in chemistry and although he has some biases in his selection, they do not significantly affect the general trends for the nineteenth century revealed in the graph. (Note, however, that the tailing off after the 1890s is a consequence only of Partington's reduced interest in a full treatment of twentieth-century developments.)

5. *Ibid.,* IV, 569.
6. T.S. Kuhn, *The Structure of Scientific Revolutions* (University of Chicago Press, 1970) and 'Reflections on my Critics', pp. 231-278 in: I. Lakatos and A. Musgrave (eds.) *Criticism and the Growth of Knowledge* (Cambridge University Press, 1970).
7. The work of Joseph Ben-David has been of great value in highlighting the main themes in the institutional contrasts between nations in the nineteenth century, though not all his conclusions are fully acceptable. See, for example, J. Ben-David, *The Scientist's Role in Society* (Englewood Cliffs, NJ: Prentice-Hall, 1971) chapters 6-8.
8. Many of the ideas in J. Ben-David and R. Collins, 'Social Factors in the Origins of a New Science: The Case of Psychology', *American Sociological Review* 31 (1966) 451-65 have been most helpful, though their historical treatment is not entirely satisfactory. (See, for example, the comments by Dorothy Ross, 'On the Origins of Psychology', *American Sociological Review* 32 (6967) 46639, ane the reply by Ben-David and Collins, 69-472.)
9. H.N. Stokes, 'The Revival of Inorganic Chemistry', *Annual Report of the Smithsonian Institution for 1897-8* (Washington, DC) 295-6.
10. A more detailed discussion of the transmission of physical chemistry and experimental psychology to America is given in my unpublished paper, 'The Transmission of Two New Scientific Disciplines from Europe to North America in the Late Nineteenth Century'.
11. P. Duhem, in 'Une science nouvelle: La chimie physique', *Revue philomathique de Bordeaux et du Sud-Ouest* (1899) 205-219, 260-280, offered explanations of why French physical chemistry was eclipsed by the German.
12. See R.G.A. Dolby, 'Debates over the Theory of Solution. A Study of Dissent in Physical Chemistry in the English-Speaking World in the Late Nineteenth and Early Twentieth Centuries', *Historical Studies in the Physical Sciences* 7 (forthcoming).

MICHAEL WORBOYS

The Emergence of Tropical Medicine:
a Study in the Establishment of a Scientific Specialty

INTRODUCTION

Tropical meicine emerged as a scientific specialty around the turn of the century when it became a recognized field of teaching, research and professional practice.[1] As a distinct scientific specialty it emerged first in Britain, then in France, Italy, Belgium, Germany, Holland and, somewhat later, in the USA. This paper is concerned with its emergence in Britain in the period 1889 to 1901.[2] There are a number of factors that make tropical medicine an interesting case study. Firstly, it is obviously an 'applied' specialty, with close links to professional practice, whereas most studies of specialty emergence to date have discussed 'pure' or 'basic' scientific specialties.[3] Secondly, because of its association with European colonial imperialism, tropical medicine lucidly demonstrates the part played by 'external' social and economic factors in the establishment of scientific specialties. Finally, during the past 75 years tropical medicine has been the main scientific expression of Western medical and health policy for the Third World. Some understanding of the origins of such an important specialty should allow a clearer insight into the ways in which medical and health policies have taken form in the underdeveloped countries of the world.

This paper begins with a discussion of existing approaches to the study of scientific specialties and develops a framework to take cognizance of 'external' factors in the establishment of specialties. The nature of European medical theory and practice in the tropics in the nineteenth century is then considered in relation to the establishment of tropical medicine as a specialty, playing a significant role in late Victorian imperial development. Finally the paper discusses the nature of the specialty and its repercussions on medical and health policy in the British colonial empire.

THE EMERGENCE OF SCIENTIFIC SPECIALTIES

In recent years there has been criticism of purely intellectual histories of
science from many points of view.[4] The main criticism of such traditional
intellectual histories is not that they are untrue, but that they are incomplete and give an erroneous view of scientific development. With particular regard to the emergence of specialties, such histories rarely suggest the complexity of the whole process. Indeed, intellectual histories do
not even see the matter of specialty emergence as problematic. Viewed
retrospectively, specialties have emerged because they have proved to be
fruitful areas of scientific endeavour. However, as Kuhn points out, 'the
early developmental stages of most sciences have been characterized by
continual competition between a number of distinct views of nature'.[5] In
this sense, the study of specialties must be concerned with the viability,
validity and acceptability of scientific knowledge and modes of scientific
practice. In an 'immature' specialty there is little agreement or
comprehension of what are important problems, what are valid facts,
what are acceptable procedures or even whether the whole enterprise is
effective.[6] A decisive factor, therefore, in the emergence of a specialty is
the resolution of these questions, and it is once this has been achieved that
Ravetz terms a specialty 'mature'; that is, it has 'a certain underlying
stability which persists through all the rapid changes in results, problems
and even objects of inquiry'.[7] This notion of a 'mature specialty' is implicit
in the image of science articulated by Kuhn, who describes two types of
science: normal science, characterised by orthodoxy, consensus and
tradition, and revolutionary science characterised by incommensura-
bility, schisms and controversy.[8] Essentially the establishment of 'normal
science' and the associated notion of a 'shared paradigm' is analogous to
the emergence of a (mature) specialty.

> Men whose research is based on shared paradigms are commtted to the
> same rules and standards for scientific practice. That commitment and
> the apparent consensus it produces are prerequisites for normal sci-
> ence, i.e. for the genesis and continuation of a particular research tradi-
> tion.[9]

There are, however, important limitations to the generality of Kuhn's
explanation. Firstly, he is concerned with one, or possibly two, mechanisms of specialty emergence — that is, the process which occurs when an

established specialty undergoes an internal theoretical revolution through the appearance of anomalies, or when a preparadigm field coalesces to give a shared paradigm.[10] Secondly, Kuhn sees shared paradigms or specialties as essentially theory-based, but as Law suggests there are also subject-based specialties (e.g. entomology) and technique-based specialties (e.g. X-ray crystallography).[11] In these respects and others, Kuhn can still be seen in the tradition of intellectual history of science.

In their work on scientific specialties, sociologists of science have been working from the other extreme: that is, they have concentrated exclusively upon social factors and have largely ignored cognitive explanations.[12] An account typical in this tradition is that given by Hagstrom in his book *The Scientific Community,* in which the terms 'segmentation' and 'differentiation' are used to describe the process of specialty emergence.[13] Briefly, Hagstrom argues that new specialties emerge when competition for recognition and status within an established specialty becomes intense and subject to diminishing returns (in terms of recognition and status). In these circumstances, it is argued, scientists will tend to move out of that specialty and on to or to create one where recognition is more easily and readily won. Hagstrom's view stems from his central preoccupation with *social* control in science and it is only too clear that scientific ideas and cognitive change are not his concern.

An attempt to introduce the content of science into Hagstrom's general 'recognition-exchange' and 'social control' thesis has been made by Mulkay, who has suggested intellectual migration as a way in which new (Kuhnian) paradigms can be formed.[14] Scientists can either bring a new technique or methodology to an established specialty, or they can move to a previously unforeseen problem area. Mulkay develops these arguments in criticising Kuhn's exclusive concern with the internal generation of new paradigms; indeed he suggests that the term paradigm be dropped in favour of 'cognitive and technical norms'.[15] These ideas complement and extend Kuhn's view of science and can be developed to suggest ways in which wider social interests and change may influence the development of science: in defining significant problem areas and problems, in supporting professional practice, and in determining and legitimating certain forms of investigation rather than others. However, Mulkay does not develop the full potential of his argument, for he only goes on to discuss which members of the scientific community are likely to be 'innovative', without looking at innovation in science in relation to the wider society. Indeed, he admits that he has 'paid little attention to social factors

originating outside the research community' and is concerned 'solely with
"basic research"'.[16]

In extending Mulkay's approach it is instructive to consider it alongside
part of Hagstrom's account of specialty emergence; Hagstrom and
Mulkay base their work on very similar approaches. In a somewhat
unusual passage, Hagstrom observes that:

> Every established discipline possesses an ideology, a more or less ex-
> plicit justification of its privileges and the claims it makes upon the
> scientific world and the larger society. Corresponding to the ideologies
> of established disciplines are the utopias of newly emerging disciplines.
> . . [D]isciplinary utopias tend to be 'imperialistic', almost constricted in
> scope, oriented to very general audiences and explicit.[17]

It seems to me that what is being suggested is that during the emergence
of specialties scientists become involved in active 'scientism', that is,
they cultivate a particular image of their specialty to justify its existence.
Furthermore, Hagstrom suggests that this image becomes an everpre-
sent, if changing, feature of the social context of the speciality. This kind
of activity is well recognized in studies of the process of professionalization.[18] Indeed, there would seem to be many points of contact between the emergence of 'applied' specialties and professionalization which discussions of specialty emergence have yet to explore. For example, professionalization is concerned with the development
of socially-valued practice, is often linked to a practically oriented body
of knowledge and inevitably involves socialization into an appropriate
world-view. At a time when all scientific practice is undertaken on a full-
time, paid basis it is likely that there will be similar links with all types of
specialty, including the most basic research areas. This suggests that not
only must cognitive and sociological factors be considered, but that wider
social forces must be examined in discussions of the emergent specialty.

THE EARLY DEVELOPMENT OF MEDICINE FOR THE TROPICS

The term 'tropical medicine' appears to have been first used as recently as
1897. However, the history of the subject is much longer and goes back to
the earliest trading expeditions of Europeans. In the experience of Britain, there were three fragmented approaches to the study of tropical
diseases: through naval medicine, colonial medicine and the work of the
Indian Medical Service (IMS).

The earliest record of an English expedition being affected by a tropical disease dates from 1553, when the crew of a trading expedition to West Africa was decimated by an unknown fever. No surgeons accompanied such expeditions, as 'wounded' were not expected; in any case a surgeon could not have treated disease as such and a physician would have been a dubiously effective luxury. The first English book on tropical diseases was in fact the work not of a medical man but of an adventurer from the middle Americas, George Wateson. Published in 1598 under the bold title of *The Cures of the Diseased in Remote Regions Preventing the Mortality Incident in Forraine Attempts of the English Nation,* the book discussed scurvy, typhus, yellow fever, sunstroke and heatstroke.[19] For the next two hundred years, however, there was no systematic study of tropical diseases. Scurvy and surgery dominated what can be described as 'naval medicine', whilst tropical 'fevers' became accepted as a largely inevitable part of tropical ventures.

In the earliest attempts at European colonisation and exploitation of the tropics, very high mortality rates were considered unavoidable. This was the experience of Spain and Portugal in their American colonies and of Britain and France in the West Indies, in sub-tropical America, Asia and Africa. Theories of disease dominant in the eighteenth century were largely concerned with symptoms, rather than causes.[20] Among theories of causation, the 'miasmatic' theory of contagion was much in vogue; this supposed that fermentation, putrefaction and disease had much in common, and that diseases arose spontaneously from within the body or from 'unhealthy' environments. Accordingly, miasmatists stressed the unhealthiness of refuse, insanitary conditions, fogs and mists, high temperatures and particular geographical locations. The standard work on tropical diseases was J. Lind's miasmatist *Essay on Disease Incident of Europeans in Hot Climates.* First published in 1768 the book went to six editions, the last in 1808. To a convinced miasmatist, therefore, the tropics must have been totally oppressive. The earliest European settlements in the tropics tended to be in coastal areas or in river estuaries, where mists and fogs were common and where the settlements were notoriously insanitary.

A recent historian of naval medicine has remarked that medicine was vital to tropical imperialist activity:

. . . for the benefit of seamen, soldiers and emigrants in an age of warfare in the West Indies and of commercial expansion in the East. It was a subject of fundamental importance in British enterprise abroad. . . . [21]

The East India Company, which began a medical service in 1764, appointed from 1809 to 1819 a 'Lecturer in the Diseases of Hot Climates' to instruct their new officers prior to posting.[22] In West Africa, the unhealthiest British colony, conditions improved greatly during the first half of the nineteenth century for 'the combination of quinine therapy, better precautionary measures and the abolition of dangerous treatments was enough to make a real difference'.[23]

It was probably through the officers of the IMS, however, that Western medicine first came into contact with native populations on a large scale. Whatever else the IMS was famous for, it certainly had no record of achievement in the study, treatment or prevention of tropical diseases.[24] The only significant contribution made by an IMS officer to the study of tropical disease was Surgeon-Major Ronald Ross's famous work on the relation between malaria and the mosquito, work to which the hierarchy of the IMS were notoriously obstructive. In his autobiography Ross made what was intended to be a gentle criticism of the IMS and what reveals a damning indictment:

> The principal defects were that there was no proper or indeed scarcely any provision or encouragement for scientific investigation: no really adequate sanitary service: and no sufficient means for dealing with epidemics.[25]

It should be noted that the IMS was primarily a military service, serving the British soldier first, the Indian soldier second, and the native population in its 'spare' time. This ranking illustrates how imperial policy influenced the practice of medicine and medical science in a very direct way.

From these three fragmented and different approaches to tropical disease, it is not surprising that a consistent body of knowledge failed to emerge. The 'subject' was practised and 'studied' separately by individuals who were separated both geographically and professionally. Medical specialisation itself only became significant after 1850 and the number of doctors serving in the tropics was still comparatively small. Further, until the late nineteenth century, and even into this century so-called 'tropical' diseases such as malaria (ague), cholera, plague and yellow fever were prevalent in Europe and North America.[26] Ross once observed that he could have carried out his researches on malaria as well in the Thames estuary as in India.

'THE FATHER OF TROPICAL MEDICINE'

In 1865, Patrick Manson graduated in medicine from Aberdeen University. After a period of work in a lunatic asylum in Durham, he sought advancement, in the fashion of the age, through a career overseas.[27] In 1866, Manson was appointed to the Imperial Customs Service, was posted to Formosa and then Amoy, and worked inspecting ships and treating sick crewmen that passed through the ports. These duties were not very demanding in time or medical skill, so like most members of the Service he began to practise amongst the local Chinese community. In his work with the Chinese, Manson was confronted with diseases about which little was known and about which there was little he could do. He began, therefore, to make his own investigations on a number of these diseases, especially leprosy and elephantiasis. In 1875 Manson returned to Britain — as he wrote later, 'to drink at the fountain of science' and to learn all he could about tropical diseases.

In the ten years following Manson's graduation, a number of important medical developments had occurred. The germ theory of disease, first convincingly demonstrated by Pasteur in the 1860s, had begun to replace theories of disease associated with spontaneous generation and miasmata.[28] More generally there was a growing awareness of the value of medical research, illustrated in Britain by Lister's work on antiseptic surgery. This awareness was heightened by the 'successes' that microscopy was enjoying in natural history, zoology and, latterly, medicine where it was crucial to the development of Virchow's theory of cellular pathology.[29]

The scope of microscopic investigation undertaken in both natural history and medicine had shown the existence of a large number of parasitic worms and flukes in human tissues. From very remote times, 'worms' have been associated with ill-health and even with specific diseases, and from the early nineteenth century the idea of pathogenic parasites was accepted in medical science. In the 1840s and 1850s, investigations, primarily by Dutch zoologists, established two crucial concepts in parasitology: firstly, the theory of the alternation of generations, and secondly, the notion of the life cycle.[30] The alternation of generations means that the same species can exist in different morphological forms and habitats in different generations of its life. The associated notion of a life cycle describes how a parasite moves during its life in a cyclical manner between a primary host (or possibly, a secondary host) and a vector. These ideas were of crucial importance to an understanding of the etiology of parasitic diseases. They also provided the intellectual basis for the new specialty of parasitology, or more accurately helminthology, in that until the 1870s almost all known parasites were flukes or worms. The leading British 'parasitologist' was Spencer Cobbold, a medical graduate who chose a career in biology and eventually became Professor of Botany and Helminthology at King's College, London. During the 1870s Cobbold was making investigations into the life-cycle of a *Schistosome* worm found in Egypt, trying to show that an aquatic snail was the vector to its primary host — man.

Manson met Cobbold while on furlough from China, and on his return to Amoy became Cobbold's regular correspondent. Whilst in London, Manson studied journals and the reports of IMS Commissions looking for information on tropical diseases. In one IMS report, Manson found mention of a possible link between a nematode worm and elephantiasis, the worm having been observed in native blood samples. This was just the clue Manson had been seeking, so when he returned to Amoy he went armed with a microscope, the equipment necessary for the preparation of slides, and a research programme which entailed the examination of many samples of native blood. Having come to Britain 'to drink at the fountain of science', Manson returned to Amoy with little extra knowledge, but with the techniques and ideas to pursue research.

Manson was not back in Amoy long before he observed the elephantiasis worm (*Filaria sanguinis hominis*) and made two important discoveries. The first of these was that the *Filaria* only appeared in the blood at night (the phenomenon known as 'nocturnal periodicity'). The second was that as the patient's blood cooled on the slide the worms changed their form (an instance of alternation of generations). These two discoveries led Manson to postulate that the *Filaria* was associated in its life-cycle with a cold-blooded, nocturnal vector; furthermore, because of the infectious nature of the disease, it was probable that the vector was mobile. With these characteristics, the obvious candidate was a nocturnal flying insect and in particular the common mosquito (*Culex fatigans*).

Manson sent a paper describing the results of his work and his speculations on the 'insect-borne transmission of disease' to Cobbold in London, who subsequently read the paper to the Linnaen Society. According to reports the paper was heckled and greeted with incredulity; one Fellow asked, 'Did Patrick Manson expect them to believe that these minute *filaria* were provided with watches so as to know what time to retire to bed and what time to get up?'[31] Manson's subsequent investigations confirmed his hypotheses and earned him a reputation in parasitological research. His discoveries were, however, more of scientific value than of direct value in the treatment, control and prevention of elephantiasis.

In 1883 Manson left Amoy to set up private practice in Hong Kong. He stayed six years, helped to found the University of Hong Kong and saved enough money to retire to Britain to devote himself entirely to scientific work. He returned to Britain in 1889; in the following year the Chinese currency collapsed, Manson lost all his capital and was forced into medical practice in London. But he was still determined to pursue a scientific career and converted the attic of his home into a laboratory. London, now the centre of a large tropical Empire, proved to be rich in research materials. Through the missionary societies and the London Docks Manson gained access to patients suffering from the whole range of tropical diseases. This side of his work took precedence over his private practice when his maritime and tropical experience saw him appointed 'Visiting Physician' to the Seamen's Hospital Society in London. The Society ran the famous Dreadnought Hospital at Greenwich for European sailors and a small branch hospital at the Albert Dock for non-European sailors.[32]

By 1894 Manson was sufficiently well known to be invited to give a series of lectures on tropical diseases for intending missionaries. In the following year he began giving similar instruction to students at the Charing Cross and St George's Hospitals. The investigation and teaching of the etiology and treatment of tropical diseases was developing in an environment and culture totally different from the tropics. Work on etiology became exclusively scientific, based upon parasitological studies and the germ theory of disease. The clinical treatment of these diseases took precedence over prevention and epidemological studies on disease incidence and control. In the metropolitan situation, remote from the practical problems of the tropics, the study of tropical diseases became increasingly preoccupied with scientific problems rather than with the problems of poor health.

'CONSTRUCTIVE IMPERIALISM AND MEDICAL SCIENCE

In 1895, a quarter of a century of imperialism and colonial expansion culminated in the appointment of Joseph Chamberlain as Secretary of State for the Colonies, the first important political figure to occupy the post. Chamberlain instituted several programmes which radically altered the British Government's traditional policies in and for its tropical colonies.[33] He proposed that the Government should be active in promoting the 'exploitation' of these vast 'underdeveloped estates' — the policy he called 'constructive imperialism'.[34] The policy was based on two assumptions: firstly, the notion of 'exceptionalism', which held that in relation to the colonies exceptions could be made to the Government's traditional *laissez-faire* policies;[35] secondly, a belief that the tropics could provide markets for British manufacturers and held very rich and largely undiscovered natural resources which could supply Britain with all its raw material needs.[36] The partition of Africa and the need for strengthening imperial control in other colonies had already increased the demand for manpower, creating a recruitment crisis in the Colonial Service. The situation was most critical in West Africa, with not only the highest invalid rate, but also a notorious reputation as the 'White Man's Grave'.[37] Yet Chamberlain's ambitious policies of railway and harbour construction, of other public works and of the scientific exploitation of natural resources all called for more Britons to work in the tropical empire. Engineers, planters, managers, scientists, would all be needed to provide technological know-how and supervision for the schemes. The health of the British in the tropics became, therefore, an important matter of imperial interest and concern.

Up to this time, as discussed earlier, health in the tropics was poorly understood. Partly by virtue of the image of the 'noble, healthy savage' and partly because only the health of the white man had interested colonial doctors, the idea had grown up that susceptibility to tropical disease was a function of race and colour, the white man being particularly susceptible.[38] In 1898, Benjamin Kidd wrote a series of articles on *The Control of the Tropics,* in which he maintained that the white man would not be able to live and work in the tropics.[39] The idea of doing so, he argued in Social Darwinist terms, was against evolution and one of 'inate unnaturalness'. Kidd's arguments were in accord with the opinions of most experienced colonial theorists and ex-colonists. Sir Henry Johnston, the indomitable African empire builder, thought that 'there are many parts of the tropics where . . . [all] that can be hoped for . . . [is] the establishment of a sufficient number of whites to govern the blacks.'[40]

These ideas were vigorously opposed by the supporters and practitioners of the new knowledge of tropical diseases. Their opposition centred around the supposed universality of the germ theory of disease. All one had to do, they argued, was to discover the 'microbe' responsible for particular tropical diseases. This belief, founded on recent work in bacteriology and virology, had a tremendous effect on the practice of medicine everywhere. The 'new tropical medicine', therefore, embraces one application, in this case to the tropics, of a generalised European approach to medicine and disease. Manson summed up the opposition to the traditional view:

I now firmly believe in the possibility of tropical colonisation by the white races. Heat and moisture are not in themselves the direct causes of any important tropical disease. The direct causes of 99% of these diseases are germs . . . . To kill them is simply a matter of knowledge and the application of this knowledge.[41]

His faith was not only in the germ theory of disease, but in the power of science to combat the overall disease problem of the colonies.

By 1898 tropical diseases had become a subject of general public interest. The mosquito-malaria work of Manson's disciple Ronald Ross had found the columns of the daily as well as the medical press. Interest focussed on the 'imperial' potential of the discoveries and on the international scientific priority dispute that ensued. Ross was hailed as a worthy British successor to the Frenchman, Pasteur, and the German, Koch. In 1902, despite Italian protests, Ross was awarded the Nobel Prize for his work, the first Briton to receive the award for medicine. Manson himself gained a public reputation; indeed it was on the recommendation of Lord Lister that he was appointed physician and medical adviser to the Colonial Office in 1897. This position, previously equivalent to that of 'a firm's doctor', Manson transformed into an influential policy-advisory role, with direct access to the Secretary of State.

In October 1897, Manson opened his series of lectures at St George's Hospital with a plea for 'The Necessity of Special Education in Tropical Medicine'.[42] This appears to be the first use of the term 'tropical medicine', it represented a recognition of the possibility of a separate scientific specialty and provided the opportunity to articulate a 'disciplinary utopia'. Speaking to a medical audience, Manson remarked upon the ignorance of the British medical profession about tropical diseases. He pointed out that over a fifth of British medical graduates spent some period of their careers in warm climates, and that an increasing number of cases of tropical diseases faced home doctors, especially in the main city ports. Manson deplored the fact that no special instruction in tropical medicine was given in any medical school and that the novice 'tropical practitioner' had to teach himself about diseases such as malaria, beriberi, and filariasis. This lack of teaching, Manson concluded, was a 'very grave disease in our education system'. In a later public address Manson appealed more directly to imperialist economic and political objectives:

[Tropical medicine] strikes, and strikes effectively, at the root of the principal difficulty of most of [our tropical] Colonies — disease. It will cheapen government and make it more efficient. It will encourage and cheapen commercial enterprise. It will conciliate and foster the native.[43]

In the address at St George's Hospital, Manson did more than make a plea; he also proposed a plan to bring about the inclusion of tropical medicine in general medical education. He suggested that each medical school appoint a lecturer in the subject, thereby establishing tropical medicine on a par with specialties such as dermatology, ophthalmology and gynaecology. He thought that shipping centres such as London, Liverpool, Bristol and Glasgow would readily take such steps and that other medical schools would soon follow their example.[44]

In his role as Medical Adviser to the Colonial Office, Manson began to initiate changes in the training given to Colonial Medical Officers (CMOs). Until that time there was no special instruction given, apart perhaps from the odd visit to the IMS hospital at Netley. Some revision in training was also needed in view of the large expansion of the Colonial Medical Service planned as part of the groundwork for 'constructivm imperialism'. Manson took this dual opportunity to devise a scheme that offered both improved quantity and quality. Manson could not await the introduction of tropical medicine into the general medical curriculum, as the specialized needs of newly appointed CMOs were immediate and pressing. CMOs received no instruction in tropical medicine and yet were waiting, often at a moment's notice, to be posted to some far-flung corner of the Empire. They needed a short, intensive course on the essentials of tropical medicine. Manson suggested that the most suitable place for such instruction would be the Albert Dock Branch Hospital, where officers could see actual cases of a wide range of tropical diseases at first hand. The Albert Dock Branch had become Manson's main place of work for the Seamen's Hospital Society, following disputes with his colleagues at Greenwich in January 1896.[45] Publicly, these disputes concerned Manson's status as a visiting physician at the Dreadnought Hospital, but beneath this lay the rivalry of his colleagues about his growing reputation as Britain's leading expert on tropical diseases. This rivalry carried over into Manson's proposal to create a special teaching institution for CMOs and into the establishment of tropical medicine as a specialty.

In October 1898, the Colonial Office issued a memorandum stating their intention to found a School of Tropical Medicine at the Albert Dock Branch of the Seamen's Hospital Society.[46] The Office asked the Treasury for assistance and were given a government grant of £1,775, whilst a further £12,000 was raised at a charity luncheon presided over by Joseph Chamberlain.[47] The School was therefore assured, but it still met vehement opposition from several quarters. The disgruntled staff of the

Dreadnought Hospital felt their institution had been overlooked because of Manson's influence in the scheme and decried the very idea of a scientific institution built in the East End of London.[48] These petulant objections were followed by sterner opposition from the Royal College of Physicians and the higher echelons of military medicine. These were particularly annoyed that they had not been consulted; they felt that an expert advisory committee, representative of the medical profession, should have been created and that it was not wise for a politician to listen only to the advice of a single scientist.[49] A letter to *The Times,* signed by leading members of the IMS and the Royal College, objected that tropical medicine was already adequately taught at the Royal Navy Hospital at Haslar and at the Army and IMS Hospital School at Netley.[50] The writers argued that there was no need for a new institution; instead they proposed that intending CMOs should 'go through a four months' residential course at Netley and obtain the advantages which its hospital and school afford to candidates of the Army and IMS'. However, the questionable adequacy of Netley's training was common knowledge and its failings were soon made painfully clear in the debacle of the Boer War.[51]

There were also scientific objections to Manson's scheme. The President of the Royal College of Physicians argued that there was no 'scientific' difference between the etiology and pathology of tropical diseases and those diseases common in temperate climates.[52] While not crucial to the establishment of the School, this objection was important to the identity and cognitive status of tropical medicine as a specialty. It was also objected that the School would place too great an emphasis on 'dogmatic teaching' through lectures and would ignore observational and clinical work.[53] However, the proposed School was supported in correspondence to the press and medical journals. Colonial practitioners, home on leave, dismissed the scientific and educational objections as trivial when compared with the task facing them as colonial doctors.[54] Finally, with the backing of Chamberlain, the Colonial Office, various commercial interests and the SHS, Manson's scheme went ahead. In October 1899 the London School of Tropical Medicine opened with a class of 28 students, all of whom took the three-month course, and a small research staff.[55] The opening of the London School signified the establishment of tropical medicine as a specialty for teaching, professional practice and research.

TROPICAL MEDICINE: THE NATURE OF THE EMERGENT SPECIALTY

The first volume of the *Journal of Tropical Medicine,* 'devoted to the publication of papers on tropical disease and to discussion of subjects scientific and practical, affecting the interests of medical men in tropical and sub-tropical countries', was published in London in August 1898.[56] The *Journal* was published by Bale and Sons, and Daniellson, the leading colonial publishers, and was edited by two London doctors, James Cantlie and Professor W. F. Simpson. The early volumes of the *Journal* confirm that the concept of 'tropical medicine' was primarily a metropolitan one, the majority of contributions tending to be clinical studies and usually concerned with a specific disease or condition rather than with problems of general health. In fact, to the end of 1900 only two out of a total of nearly 200 articles were devoted to sanitation and public health, and one of these two dealt with conditions in the British Army in South Africa. The disease most commonly discussed was malaria, with nearly a third of all articles being devoted to its etiology, pathology and side effects. However, a wide range of diseases and conditions was discussed: from the mysteries of 'tropical heart' to the serious problems of cholera and tuberculosis. Initially, therefore, tropical medicine was a problem-based specialty in the widest sense, appearing to have no dominant theoretical perspective.

In his opening address to the London School in 1899 Manson attempted to articulate a 'theory' for tropical medicine.[57] He argued that the basis of tropical medicine ultimately lay in the germ theory of disease, but to this he added the notion of geographical distribution of diseases. He tried to distinguish two classes of disease, those that were cosmopolitan and those that were of limited geographical range. The former, according to Manson, were predominantly bacterial diseases, because their habitat was the 'cosmopolitan' one of the human body. They were transmitted from person to person, either directly (contagious) or indirectly (infectious), but in transmission the bacteria existed as dormant 'spores' unaffected by environmental conditions. None of this was particularly new, just a different approach to the dominant bacteriological medical approach. The diseases of limited geographical range were, argued Manson, primarily 'entozoal', or to use the modern term parasitic. He asserted that 'the great underlying principle of tropical disease. . . [was] the interdependence of man and beast in the matter of pathogenic germs'. The etiology of parasitic diseases was felt to be mainly dependent on the geographical distribution of vectors and secondary hosts. In short, what Manson was attempting to argue was that tropical diseases were parasitic diseases. However, he immediately had to admit that his theoretical construct was refuted by the experience of tropical practice, where bacterial, nutritional and physiological diseases were as common as parasitic diseases. It seems that Manson was not content to let the special problems of medical practice in the tropical colonies define what was to be 'tropical medicine', but rather sought a more 'scientific' or theoretical basis.

Two general points about the emergent specialty are particularly significant: firstly, its racialism and secondly, the emphasis upon 'science' and 'research'. The racialist element is seen primarily in the comparisons made between the susceptibility of natives and Europeans to various diseases.[58] Articles in the *Journal of Tropical Medicine* were suggestive: 'Do Adenoids Occur in Natives of the Tropical Countries?'; 'Are Asians who take to European Food and Drink Rendered Thereby More Liable to Diabetes?'; 'Trachoma and Race'. This racialism failed to distinguish between differences due to hereditary factors ('true' racialism) and those due to environmental factors. On the one hand it was assumed that the native was better acclimatized to the tropical environment and way of life, whilst on the other it was felt that there was some fundamental inherited biological difference. Certainly, the establishment of a unified tropical medicine, based on what is now called parasitology, would have tended to undermine the 'hereditary' racialism. However, at the time, differences, not similarities, were important. Hence, the fact that most so-called tropical diseases (such as cholera, malaria and sleeping sickness) struck both native and European alike was played down. Most of the articles in the early volumes of the *Journal of Tropical Medicine* were about native patients, with virtually no accounts or case histories of Europeans. The reasons were in part ideological and in part a true reflection of the difference in the incidence of the disease resulting from the better diet, living conditions and sanitary arrangements among Europeans.

The scientific emphasis of the new specialty, which came primarily from Manson and his group at the London School, is especially significant in understanding the subsequent development of tropical disease research and control. This can best be seen by reconsidering the differences that grew up between Manson and his former colleague, Ross. The accepted explanation of these differences is that in the 1890s Ross (then in India) and Manson (in London) became colleagues through correspondence, but that when Ross returned home there was a clash of personalities and the two men drifted apart.[59] Indeed, it would not be too much to say they became open enemies. This enmity was perhaps exacerbated by Manson's resentment of Ross's public acclaim and Nobel Prize, and by Ross's resentment of Manson's omnipotent status in British tropical medicine.[60] However, their differences were far more fundamental. The two men had radically different philosophies of health, which involved very different approaches to tropical medicine.

Manson, although trained as a doctor, developed during his career a preoccupation with the scientific aspects of tropical disease. His independent research work, his return to London to follow a research career and his hopes for the new specialty all testify to this emphasis. Manson's programme was essentially reductionist and stressed research rather than active control. It was somewhat different from the later reductionist programmes in tropical medicine which stressed the use of drugs and attacked the 'agents of disease', but it had very different goals from a public health programme. Manson stressed that greater knowledge of the pathology and etiology of tropical diseases would facilitate better control measures and increase the chances of effective protection, mainly for Europeans.

An alternative, 'holistic' medical paradigm saw general living conditions, diet and sanitation as the main determinants of health. This was a view Ross held strongly. As we have seen Ross regarded his IMS training as inadequate and inappropriate to the tasks of medical officers in the field. His dissatisfaction was first evident in 1889 when, whilst on leave in London, he became the first member of the IMS to take a diploma in public health; he did so voluntarily and at his own expense. Later, when in the throes of the final breakthrough in his malaria-mosquito work, he was posted to alternative work three times. Two of these postings he resented, but of the other, which involved sanitary work, he wrote:

> . . . unlike the two later interruptions, this first one was justified by the event, because it gave an almost unique experience in practical sanitation which was invaluable when we came after 1898 to apply the proved mosquito-malaria theory for the benefit of suffering humanity.[61]

Unlike Manson, therefore, Ross developed the practical implications of his scientific work, seeing malarial control as a matter of reducing the population of mosquitos by destroying or treating their breeding areas. In a way this approach was also reductionist, in that it attacked the agents of disease, or at least the vectors. However, in practice the approaches were very different. Once established as Professor at the Liverpool School of Tropical Medicine, Ross began to treat Britain as a base for expeditions and advisory work in the tropics.[62] Backed by Liverpool traders, he had by 1901 made a series of trips to West Africa. Typical was his visit to Freetown, the capital of Sierra Leone, where he advised on malarial control. The programme he suggested was to disrupt the life-cycle of mosquito and thereby prevent transmission of the disease. To this end he wanted systematic sanitary measures adopted: that is, garbage removed, ponds drained, puddles filled in, water containers covered, other breeding places treated with kerosene, undergrowth cleared and piped water provided.[63] Such a scheme, he argued, would not only reduce malaria, but would also improve the health of both Europeans and natives generally. In his attitude towards the native population, Ross differed greatly from the accepted British practice of Physical separation, seen in the separate British residences built away from the native settlements. In his later book, *Mosquito Brigades*, Ross quoted approvingly the views of Sir William McGregor, the Governor of Lagos, on the policy of separation:

> The policy followed in Lagos in this as in other matters is to take the natives along with the Europeans on the way leading to improvement. Here they cannot live apart or work apart, and they should not try to do so. Separation would mean that little, or at least less, would be done for the native, and the admitted source of infection would remain perennial.[64]

Ross's approach to tropical medicine was, therefore, holistic, practical, preventive and, for the times, progressive.

The different approaches and priorities of Manson and Ross had direct effects on policy. Manson was after all the medical adviser to the Colonial Office and head of the prestigious London School, whilst Ross was a consultant to various commercial interests and local colonial governors. Both accepted the 'theory of science for development' which postulated that disease was the main factor holding back tropical development.[65] The difference came over whether it was to be 'scientific research' for development, or 'public health' for development.

After the criticism of its handling of the establishment of the London School, the Colonial Office handled subsequent problems with regard to tropical medicine by the appointment of *ad hoc* committees of interest groups and scientists. In all about twenty committees were formed between 1895 and 1914.[66] A number of features of these committees are important. Firstly, they were essentially metropolitan agencies, meeting in London and staffed by British-based workers. Secondly, for the most part, the members were scientists, often pure zoologists and botanists with no medical or colonial experience. According to one Colonial Office official, 'co-operation was always readily forthcoming from the Royal Society, the universities, the Natural History Museum, Kew Gardens, and other centres of scientific work and knowledge. . .'[67] Finally, and as a consequence of the two former points, these committees tended to recommend research and information services, rather than practical projects or preventive policies. These committees reinforced the advice Manson was giving to the Colonial Office.

Kubicek excused the scientific and Eurocentric nature of these committees' work as 'understandable', 'given the complexity of local situations and the particular state of man's knowledge. . .'[68] However, such a view fails to acknowledge that at the same time Ross and his supporters were proposing an alternative policy. After his visits to West Africa around the turn of the century, Ross wrote to the Colonial Office suggesting a scheme whereby 'sanitary commissioners' be appointed to visit the colonies and report to London on the sanitary performance of local governments. In March 1901 a deputation from the Liverpool School and the Chambers of Commerce of Liverpool, London and Manchester visited the Colonial Office to press for the acceptance of Ross's scheme. Chamberlain, no doubt advised by Manson, refused to accept the proposals saying that they were impractical and likely to be much too expensive. He also made a remark which sought to put Ross in his place:

> These experts [i.e. the signatories to Ross's scheme] were not qualified, whatever their scientific acquirements might be. . . to undertake the full consideration of the financial aspect of the situation, and no corporation in this country would consent to put its finances in the hands of a sanitary commissioner, however eminent he might be.[69]

Clearly, as far as the Colonial Office was concerned, scientists should confine themselves to research and not become involved in practical policy. In his *Memoirs*, Ross comments perceptively on this episode:

> Chamberlain had done some good (and won much political capital) by suggesting the schools of tropical medicine; but in my opinion, his refusal of a proper sanitary organisation for the colonies largely cancelled then and since, the benefits which might have accrued.[70]

In 1930, Ross commented more scathingly on the differences between himself and Manson, and was in no doubt that tropical medicine had not developed as effectively as it could have done:

> I must say that I was rather disappointed with Manson's attitude towards the whole subject of practical . . . prevention. [He] never seemed very keen on it and was chiefly interested in the parasitological side of the subject while I was interested more in the practical side. . . . The British Empire has generally followed his example during the last thirty years.[71]

CONCLUSION

In an earlier section it was postulated that the emergence of a specialty could only be fully understood if the following factors were considered: the cognitive development of science, the socio-institutional aspects of science, and the influence of wider social conditions and social change. In conclusion, it is necessary to move towards an assessment of the import-ance of these various factors in the emergence of tropical medicine.

The cognitive background of tropical medicine lay in developments in nineteenth-century biology and natural history. The basis was not only heuristic, for it also led tropical medicine to become a 'scientific' specialty as such, rather than an instrument of general public health. It led the specialty to adopt a reductionist rather than a holistic programme and to become a metropolitan rather than a satellite activity. Without doubt tropical medicine sought to become a legitimate scientific specialty with its own social identity, norms and institutions. However, the social and institutional factors directly reflected wider social pressures, especially the demands of professional practice, and provided the context for meeting these social goals. The principal social factor was economic and political imperialism. British doctors were posted to the four corners of the world to service the imperial outposts that secured markets, trade and raw materials for the British economy. A School of Tropical Medicine was needed to increase the quantity and quality of these Colonial Medical Officers as an integral part of late nineteenth-century imperialism, the strengthening of political control and attempts at more systematic exploitation. In this context a *scientific specialty* of tropical medicine served the needs of imperial administration, economy and ideology. Administratively, Medical Officers trained in 'unified and universal' tropical medical science were seen as qualified to work in any part of the tropical Empire and could be used when and where required. Economi-cally, at least in the view of Manson and the Colonial Office, tropical medicine offered a cheap solution to the problem of disease in the tropical colonies. Its concentration on research and its attack on the agents of disease, in the short term provided an alternative to expensive public health measures. Finally, as a 'progressive' and 'exceptionalist' specialty, tropical medicine both reflected and supported the optimistic imperialist ideology of the late 1890s. Given these circumstances and the importance of good health to colonial imperialism, the emergence of the scientific specialty of tropical medicine was necessary and inevitable.

Michael Worboys, Department of History, Sheffield City Polytechnic, Pond Street, Sheffield S1 1WB.

MICHAEL WORBOYS took his first degree at Sussex, then M.A. in the Department of Liberal Studies in Science at Manchester University. He followed this with research on science and imperialism in the History and Social Studies of Science Subject Group at Sussex University. He is now lecturing at Sheffield City Polytechnic.

NOTES

1. The term scientific 'specialty' is used widely in the sociology of science and, in my view quite rightly, a detailed definition of the term has not been developed. See note 3 below.

2. The suggestion that international comparisons of the development of tropical medicine would be instructive was made strongly in the discussion on a shorter version of this paper given at the PAREX meeting in December 1973. I have not pursued this line of enquiry because my reading of colonial science suggests that the emergence of tropical medicine in Britain was foremost and typical. I would however like to thank various colleagues at Sussex University for comments on earlier drafts of this paper, and especially Roy MacLeod for his detailed criticism and suggested revisions. This research was supported by a grant from the SRC.

3. A review of the studies of scientific specialties is given in D. O. Edge/M. J. Mulkay, 'Fallstudien zu wissenschaftlichen Spezialgebieten' pp. 197-229 in: Nico Stehr (ed.), *Wissenschaftssoziologie*, Kölner Zeitschrift für Soziologie und Sozialpsychologie supplementary vol. 18 (Opladen: Westdeutscher Verlag, 1975).

4. For reviews of these developments see T. S. Kuhn, 'The History of Science', *International Encyclopedia of the Social Sciences* 14 (1968) 74-83; A. Thackray, 'Science: Has the Present Past a Future?' in: R. Steuwer (ed.), *Minnesota Studies in the Philosophy of Science* V (Minneapolis: University of Minnesota Press, 1970); J. Agassi, 'Towards an Historiography of Science', *History and Theory* 2 (1963).

5. T. S. Kuhn, *The Structure of Scientific Revolutions* (University of Chicago Press, 2nd edition, 1970) 2.

6. J. R. Ravetz, *Scientific Knowledge and its Social Problems* (Oxford: Clarendon Press, 1971; Penguin Books, 1972) 364-402. Ravetz's book contains by far the most detailed and valuable account of the 'craft' of science. It is in this context that he introduces the notions of 'immature' and 'mature' specialties.

7. *Ibid.,* 159. In my reading, Ravetz's use of the terms 'immature' and 'mature' is ambiguous. He seems to regard 'immature' specialties as both ineffectual and exciting, and 'mature' specialties as both effective and dull. Perhaps Ravetz cannot admit that science 'can have its cake and eat it'!

8. Kuhn, *The Structure of Scientific Revolutions,* 23-24, 92-110. Also see D. Shapere, 'The Structure of Scientific Revolutions', *Philosophical Review* 73 (1964) 383-394; I Lakatos and A. Musgrave (eds), *Criticism and the Growth of Knowledge* (Cambridge University Press, 1970). A good introduction to the debate on Kuhn's work is given in B. Easlea, *Liberation and the Aims of Science* (London: Chatto and Windus, 1973) 1-26.

9. Kuhn, *The Structure of Scientific Revolutions,* 11. Kuhn does make a distinction between what he regards as 'pure' science and 'applied' science; however, he does not develop the point beyond the following observation. 'In the sciences (though not in fields like medicine, technology, and law, of which the principle *raison d'être* is an

external need), the formation of specialized journals, the foundation of specialists' societies, and the claim for a special place in the curriculum have usually been associated with a group's first reception of a single paradigm' (19). Whether applied subjects like medicine have a different type of paradigm to the sciences' is not made clear. Furthermore, how an 'external need' is transformed into a cognitive and technical programme is not discussed.

10. This point is the main thrust of Mulkay's critique and development of Kuhn's work. See M. Mulkay, *The Social Process of Innovation* (London: Macmillan, 1972), especially chapter 4, 'Innovation and Social Change'.

11. J. Law, 'The Development of Specialties in Science: The Case of X-ray Protein Crystallography', pages 123-151 below.

12. This treatment of science derives from the tradition set by Robert Merton. Critical analyses of the Mertonian tradition are given by B. Barnes and R. G. A. Dolby, 'The Scientific Ethos: A Deviant Viewpoint', *European Sociology* 11 (1970) 3-25; and R. D. Whitley, 'Black Boxism and the Sociology of Science', *The Sociological Review* Monograph 18 (1972) 61-92.

13. W. O. Hagstrom, *The Scientific Community* (New York: Basic Books, 1965). The basis of Hagstrom's approach is that of 'exchange theory', hence the concentration on publications as the dominant feature of the scientific enterprise.

14. Mulkay, *The Social Process of Innovation,* 34-36.

15. *Ibid.,* 33. To quote Mulkay, 'In particular there is a close resemblance between Kuhn's paradigms and what I have called "cognitive and technical norms"'. On the whole, the term cognitive and technical norm seems preferable to that of paradigm for two reasons. Firstly, it leaves empirically open the degree to which the basic assumptions of particular research communities are connected. Secondly, use of the term 'cognitive *norm*' emphasises the similarity between radical innovation and social nonconformity; it draws attention to the part played by social mechanisms in controlling the emergence of new ideas.

16. *Ibid.,* 8.

17. Hagstrom, *The Scientific Community,* 211-13.

18. G. H. Daniels, 'The Process of Professionalization in American Science: the Emergent Period 1820-1860', *Isis* 58 (1967) 151-65. The contact with professionalization was suggested to me in reading B. Wynne, *Sociology of Science — Unit One* (Leeds: Project SISCON, 1974).

19. J. J. Keevil, *Medicine and the Navy, 1200-1900* (London: E. and S. Livingstone, 1957) I, 119.

20. An introduction to the history of medicine is given in C. Singer and E. A. Underwood, *A Short History of Medicine* (Oxford: Clarendon Press, 1928, 1962).

21. K. Lloyd and J. L. S. Coulter, *Medicine and the Navy, 1200-1900* (London: E. and S. Livingstone, 1961) III, 336-7.

22. D. MacDonald, *Surgeons Twoe and a Barber — being Some Account of the Life and Work of the Indian Medical Service, 1600-1947* (London: Heinemann, 1960).

23. P. D. Curtin, *The Image of Africa* (London: Macmillan, 1965) 361; see also remainder of chapter 14.

24. MacDonald, *Surgeons Twoe, passim.* The IMS's proudest boast was the large number of fellowships of the Royal Society awarded to its members — 31 before 1890. These were for research in botany, zoology, ornithology and philology. The minor medical reputation it made for itself was made almost exclusively in surgery.

25. R. Ross, *Memoirs* (London: John Murray, 1923) 40.

26. H. H. Scott, *A History of Tropical Medicine* (London: Edward Arnold, 1939) 3-7.

27. Much of this section is based on P. Manson-Bahr, *Patrick Manson: The Father of Tropical Medicine* (London: Nelson, 1962), and P. Manson-Bahr / A. Alcock, *The Life and Work of Sir Patrick Manson* (London: Cassell, 1927).

28. J. K. Crellin, 'The Dawn of the Germ Theory', pp. 57-76 in F. N. I. Poynter (ed.), *Medicine and Science in the 1860s* (London: Wellcome Institute for the History of Medicine, 1968).

29. This theory proposed that disease always struck at the cellular level. See W. H. McMenemey, 'Cellular Pathology, with special reference to the influence of Virchow's teachings on medical thought and practice', pp.13-44 in: Poynter (ed.), *Medicine and Science in the 1860s.*

30. W. D. Foster, *A History of Parasitology* (London: E. and S. Livingstone, 1965) 4 *et passim.*

31. Manson-Bahr, *Patrick Manson,* 39.

32. *Ibid.,* 61.

33. On late nineteenth-century British imperialism see B. Semmel, *Imperialism and Social Reform* (London: George Allen and Unwin, 1960); E. J. Hobsbawm, *Industry and Empire* (London: Weidenfeld and Nicolson, 1968; Penguin Books, 1969); M. Barratt-Brown, *After Imperialism* (London: Heinemann, 1963); A. P. Thornton, *The Imperial Idea and its Enemies* (London: St. Martin's Press, 1959); A. P. Thornton, *Doctrines of Imperialism* (London: John Wiley, 1965); R. Owen / B. Sutcliffe (eds.), *Studies in the Theory of Imperialism* (London: Longmans, 1972).

34. R. V. Kubicek, *The Administration of Imperialism* (Durham, NC: Duke University Press, 1972).

35. The notion of 'exceptionalism' is developed in P. D. Curtin, *Imperialism* (London: Macmillan, 1972) xiii *et passim.* 'Closely as imperial theory was bound up with the main lines of Western thought, it was also something of a side issue. Its application lay outside of the Western world itself, and Europeans had a chronic tendency to regard the non-West as an exception to the social, historic and economic patterns they detected in their own society. Non-Europeans were exotic by definition, and they might well behave in curious and unexpected ways. In addition, the social and political goals held out for the empire overseas were rarely identical with those of the metropolis theorist.'

36. Hobsbawm, *Industry and Empire,* 150.

37. Kubicek, *The Administration of Imperialism,* chapter 6, and Curtin, *Imperialism,* 361.

38. There was, of course, a great deal of truth in this view. White men had no immunity to many tropical diseases and the unusual diets most colonialists ate tended to undermine health. There was, however, a growing incidence of disease amongst indigenous people due to the introduction of new diseases, changes in diet, changes in social organization, etc. In time the better sanitary and dietary arrangements of the European colonialists led them to enjoy better health than indigenous peoples. See C. C. Hughes/J. M. Hunter, 'Disease and Development in Africa', *Social Science and Medicine* 3 (1970) 443-493.

39. B. Kidd, *Control of the Tropics* (London: Macmillan, 1899); first published as a series of articles in *The Times,* 1898.

40. H. Johnston, 'Discussion on the Possibility of Acclimatization of Europeans in Tropical Countries', *British Medical Journal* (1898) i, 1168.

41. *Ibid.,* 1169.

42. P. Manson, 'The Necessity of Special Education in Tropical Medicine', *Lancet* (2 October 1897) 842-845.

43. Quoted in Manson-Bahr / Alcock, *Manson,* 217.

44. Only London and Liverpool set up schools of tropical medicine. The Universities of Edinburgh, Oxford and Cambridge offered diplomas in tropical medicine during the first decade of this century.

45. Manson-Bahr, *Patrick Manson,* 62. See also letters to *British Medical Journal* (12 December 1898) 1846; (28 December 1898) 1953.

46. Manson-Bahr / Alcock, *Manson,* 212.

47. Kubicek, *The Administration of Imperialism*, 143. The following extract from Chamberlain's speech at that dinner nicely catches the association of science and Empire: 'The man who shall successfully grapple with this foe of humanity and find the cure for malaria, for the fevers desolating our colonies and dependencies in many tropical countries and shall make the tropics livable for white men . . . will do more for the world, more for the British Empire, than the man who adds a new province to the wide Dominions of the Queen'.

48. *The Times*, 28 December 1898, letter from Drs. Curnow, Anderson and Turner of the Dreadnought Hospital.

49. W. Broadbent, 'Letter to Seamen's Hospital Society', *British Medical Journal* (10 December 1898) 1763.

50. *The Times*, 15 December 1898.

51. G. D. Searle, *The Quest for National Efficiency* (London: Blackwell, 1971) chapter 2, especially pp. 37-44. The army hospital at Netley closed in 1904 and many Army Medical Officers subsequently took courses at the London School of Tropical Medicine.

52. See Manson-Bahr, *Patrick Manson*, 124.

53. *Ibid*. This was the observation of St Bartholomew's Hospital.

54. See especially letters from Oswald Baker (IMS) 21 December 1898, and from Sidney Hodges (Wesley Missionary Society), 23 February 1899.

55. P. Manson-Bahr, *The History of the School of Tropical Medicine in London, 1899-1949* (London: London School of Hygiene and Tropical Medicine, no. 11, 1956). In June 1899 a small Liverpool School of Tropical Medicine opened, financed by local commercial interests led by the West African merchant, Alfred Jones. The School was based upon the Physiology Department of University College, Liverpool and the Southern Hospital.

56. 'Editorial', *Journal of Tropical Medicine* 1 (1898) 2. Bale and Sons, and Daniellson, the publishers of the journal, were an important plank in British colonial imperialism. In 1905 they began printing a semi-popular journal entitled *Tropical Life* devoted to tropical agriculture, mineral resources and colonial economic development in general.

57. P. Manson, 'The Need for Special Training in Tropical Disease', *Journal of Tropical Medicine* 2 (1899) 57-62.

58. A reminder of this interest is still with us today in the title of Britain's foremost cancer research age,cy — the Imperial Cancer Research Fund. The Imperial designation comes from comparative work done by British doctors in the 1900s on the relative susceptibilities of the tropical native and the European to cancer. It seems that the doctors thought that cancer was a disease caused by maladaptation and that the observed low incidence of cancer amongst tropical natives was due to their being more in harmony with their environment than were Europeans. Consequently, all Colonial Medical Officers had to report cases of native cancers to the Colonial Office in London to allow for the compilation of comparative statistics.

59. Manson-Bahr, *Patrick Manson*, 98.

60. Kubicek, *The Administration of Imperialism*, 149.

61. Ross, *Memoirs*, 179; on his Diploma of Public Health (taken in 1889) see pages 83-84.

62. *Ibid.*, parts III and IV.

63. R. Ross, *Mosquito Brigades and How to Organize Them* (London: Philip, 1902).

64. *Ibid.*, 75.

65. The notion of 'theories of science for development' is developed in my D.Phil. thesis, 'Science and Colonial Imperialism in the Development of the British Colonial Empire, 1895-1940', in preparation for the University of Sussex.

66. For details see C. Forman, 'Science for Empire, 1895-1939' (unpublished Ph.D. thesis, University of Wisconsin, 1941), part I.

67. C. Parkinson, *The Colonial Office from Within, 1909-1945* (London: Faber and Faber, 1949) 48.
68. Kubicek, *The Administration of Imperialism,* 153.
69. *The Times,* 16 March 1901. Chamberlain, it was reported, 'confessed that he trembled at the budget which would be produced and there might be a reaction in consequence of attempting too much'.
70. Ross, *Memoirs,* 436.
71. R. Ross, *Memories of Sir Patrick Manson* (London: Harrison Pamphlet, 1930) 22-23.

J. D. DE CERTAINES

La Biophysique en France:
Critique de la Notion de Discipline Scientifique

Sociologiquement, la biophysique existe; on en parle, on utilise le terme pour se différencier par rapport à d'autres chercheurs, pour nommer des institutions, pour qualifier des enseignements, etc. Pourtant, nul n'est capable de la définir, de préciser sa situation épistémologique. 'La biophysique est comme ma femme, aurait dit un jour Katchalsky, je ne sais pas la définir mais je la reconnais bien.'[1] Cette boutade exprime bien sa situation actuelle: on reconnaît relativement bien la biophysique (existence sociologique) mais on ne peut réussir à la définir (existence épistémologique).

Peut-on dans ce cas conserver l'appellation de 'discipline'? Le vocabulaire forgé pour rendre compte des divisions de la science du XIXe siècle est-il encore valable pour décrire les secteurs de recherche constituant les éléments dynamiques de la 'science-se-faisant' dans cette seconde moitié du XXe siècle? Si la biophysique n'est pas un cas pathologique dans la science d'aujourd'hui, son étude doit constituer une bonne introduction à la remise en question de la notion de discipline.

Il ne s'agit donc plus d'étudier la naissance d'un domaine repérable mais, autour et à propos d'une appellation de plus en plus utilisée, de parcourir une page d'histoire, débordant sur l'actualité, de la science en France dans la complexité de ses rapports internes comme de ses liens avec les autres pays. Après une 'reconnaissance' de la biophysique en France, refusant toute frontière artificiellement imposée à l'objet de cette reconnaissance ou à sa méthode, je proposerai quelques orientations pour la recherche d'une nouvelle conceptualisation plus apte à rendre compte d'une science qui ne se laisse plus découper en disciplines comme au siècle dernier.

RECONNAISSANCE DE LA BIOPHYSIQUE EN FRANCE

Qu'est-ce que la biophysique? Une réponse fréquente, surtout chez les biologistes moléculaires (et l'on verra pourquoi), est: 'La biophysique n'existe pas.' Quand cette affirmation vient du titulaire d'une chaire de biophysique ou du directeur d'un important laboratoire officiellement spécialisé en biophysique, on ne peut s'empêcher de relever une contradiction flagrante: comment des chercheurs peuvent-ils simultanément bénéficier de l'existence institutionnelle d'une 'discipline' en en étant le titulaire d'une chaire ou le directeur d'un laboratoire et nier son existence en lui refusant un contenu épistémologique? Quel lien existe donc entre l'existence sociologique et l'existence épistémologique de ce que l'on nomme encore discipline?

Certains, prudents, présentent la biophysique comme un 'secteur vague'; d'autres, évoquant la déception ressentie par beaucoup de participants au récent congrès international qui s'est tenu à Moscou, disent: 'C'est un moyen de réunir dix mille personnes n'ayant rien de commun à se dire, sauf en petits groupes d'une centaine.' Parmi ceux qui acceptent de risquer une définition, on a deux options assez divergentes:

— première définition: la biophysique est l'application des techniques physiques à la biologie; elle constitue ainsi le support technologique de la biologie moléculaire
— deuxième définition: la biophysique est la physique des systèmes biologiques, c'est-à-dire une tentative de comprendre les phénomènes biologiques dans les lois de la physique et, éventuellement, en contribuant à renouveler la physique elle-même.

Ces deux définitions impliquent des attitudes contradictoires; pourtant, dans un même numéro spécial sur la biophysique de la revue *Physique et chimie,* à une page d'intervalle, G. Champetier donne la première définition et R. Wurmser la seconde.[2]

Il apparaît donc vain de chercher un contenu précis au mot *biophysique* mais, dans la mesure où ce mot fonctionne, servant à nommer des institutions, permettant à certains chercheurs de s'identifier, de se reconnaître ou de s'exclure, on peut tenter l'inventaire des institutions ou des groupes qui, d'une façon ou d'une autre, portent cette étiquette commune.

Cette 'reconnaissance' de la biophysique en France ne doit pas masquer la diversité des objets 'reconnus'; au contraire, on doit s'interroger sur la signification de l'existence d'une appellation unifiante (ici, le terme *biophysique*) alors que les groupes usant de cette appellation contestent et même refusent toute identification entre eux. Pour faciliter cette reconnaissance, je distinguerai un peu arbitrairement deux grandes catégories de biophysiciens: les scientifiques et les médicaux (au sens où les facultés des sciences sont distinctes de celles de médecine).[3]

La biophysique médicale

En 1958, les Journées médicales de Bordeaux sur le thème 'Les Méthodes biophysiques appliquées à la médecine et à la pharmacie', ont été la première réunion de biophysiciens en France. Introduisant le volume commémoratif de ces journées le doyen Sigalas a formé le voeu qu'il constitue le premier numéro des 'Annales françaises de biophysique' qui n'existaient pas encore.[4] Déjà à cette époque, une table ronde annuelle des isotopistes, accueillant nombre de biophysiciens même non isotopistes, préparait la voie à la Société française de physique médicale et biologique qui fut fondée fin 1964 et qui devint en 1967 la Société de biophysique et de médecine nucléaire, l'appellation *médecine nucléaire* ayant été rajoutée pour permetttre l'affiliation à la Fédération internationale de médecine nucléaire. Cette société compte actuellement parmi ses membres près de 80% d'isotopistes mais sa revue est beaucoup plus ouverte sur les différents domaines attribués à la biophysique.

Il existait pourtant depuis longtemps une discipline de physique médicale qui avait au XIXe siècle une signification proche de physiologie humaine et qui devint, avec les progrès de la physique, synonyme du terme *biophysique* qui lui succéda progressivement vers 1960. Si l'on reprend l'histoire de cette physique médicale depuis un siècle, on peut découvrir plusieurs strates successives:

— au XIXe siècle, l'optique dominait la physique médicale du fait de l'immédiateté du phénomène physique et donc de l'évidence du problème de physique posé aux médecins
— puis les progrès de l'électricité ont amené du point de vue fondamental le développement de l'électrophysiologie (avec DuBois-Reymond, Helmholtz, etc.) et du point de vue des applications l'électrocardiographie, l'électroencéphalographie, et l'électromyographie
— les rayons X, connus depuis la communication de Röntgen à la Société physicomédicale de Würzburg en 1896, polarisent vers 1930 l'attention de la majorité des physiciens médicaux
— depuis 1950, ce sont les isotopistes qui occupent la majorité des postes de physiciens dans les facultés de médecine.

Si l'on regarde maintenant le devenir de ces secteurs de recherche, on constate que la biophysique les a successivement pris en charge, à leur sortie de la physique pure pourrait-on dire, pour les développer jusqu'à la constitution de secteurs indépendants échappant aux biophysiciens: l'électrophysiologie est entre les mains des physiologistes; l'électro-cardiographie entre les mains des cardiologues; le microscope électronique est l'instrument des cytologistes; la radiologie a pris son indépendance; la médecine nucléaire tend actuellement à en faire autant. Chacun de ces domaines a laissé sa trace en quittant la biophysique, ce qui explique l'hétérogénéité et le gonflement excessif de ses programmes d'enseignement. Mais surtout, chaque départ constitue une crise qui contraint les biophysiciens restant à rechercher un domaine nouveau.[5] Dans cette évolution, la biophysique apparaît donc comme une discipline de passage, lieu d'innovation puis de maturation, très peu d'institutionnalisation, et échappe de ce fait au modèle habituel des disciplines scientifiques; il est difficile de situer de telles disciplines de passage dans l'histoire et la géographie des disciplines connues. C'est à un autre type d'analyse des secteurs de recherche, à une autre conceptualisation qu'il faut recourir pour dépasser ces différences.

Actuellement, le secteur nouveau de la biophysique médicale semble être le génie biologique et médical (GBM). En 1967, se tient à Tours sous la présidence de A. Fessard le premier congrès français d'électronique médicale et de génie biologique. Dès 1966, la Délégation générale à la recherche scientifique et technique (DGRST) avait engagé une action concertée de GBM qui devait durer cinq ans et faire évoluer 'le contexte initial désolant de carence technologique'.[6] Très vite, le GBM devait se présenter à son tour comme une discipline indépendante.[7]

On peut faire deux remarques à propos du GBM. La première concerne le rôle de l'instrumentation. Prenons par exemple le problème des capteurs: les crédits accordés au GBM ont permis d'en mettre au point un certain nombre (pression, débit, endoscopie, etc.), souvent sans relation avec les problèmes scientifiques à résoudre. Ces capteurs ont permis l'accumulation de données dont on ne savait pas très bien quoi faire. On eut alors parfois recours à l'informatique, remède miracle, pour exploiter ces données trop nombreuses et mal sélectionnées; le résultat fut souvent un problème inextricable, infiniment plus complexe que s'il avait été abordé sans surenchère de moyens instrumentaux. Néanmoins, l'apparence scientifique de pareilles démarches était garantie par le caractère sophistiqué du matériel utilisé. On peut ainsi s'interroger sur le rôle du prestige accordé au matériel dans la reconnaissance par la communauté scientifique des secteurs nouveaux de recherche. L'autre remarque porte sur les contraintes exercées par l'industrie sur la recherche publique: il est logique pour l'industrie de s'intéresser plus au GBM que, par exemple, à la photosynthèse. Est-ce suffisant pour expliquer la reconversion de la physique médicale dans le GBM? En termes plus généraux, quel est le rôle joué par la politique économique de la recherche (par exemple, une politique de démantèlement de la recherche fondamentale trop coûteuse et de privatisation des secteurs à sauvegarder du fait de leur rentabilité à court terme) dans l'évolution des secteurs de recherche et dans leur droit à une existence institutionnelle?

Cette succession d'orientations (optique, électrophysiologie, radiologie, médecine nucléaire, GBM) fait aussi ressortir le balancement continuel entre les deux pôles de la physique médicale[8]:

— service théorique et technique d'autres disciplines médicales confrontées à des problèmes de physique auxquels les médecins sont en général mal préparés (électronique médicale, informatique médicale, médecine nucléaire)
— recherche fondamentale spécifique (au niveau de l'organisme, cellulaire, subcellulaire ou moléculaire).

Pour les groupes de chercheurs, ces deux pôles correspondent à la division entre hospitaliers et fondamentalistes:

— les hospitaliers sont ceux chez qui domine la vocation médicale. La biophysique est pour eux une technologie au service de la clinique. Leur formation proprement physique est en général moins importante que celle des fondamentalistes auxquels ils reprochent de vouloir imiter les scientifiques sans en avoir les moyens.
— les fondamentalistes sont ceux pour qui la recherche fondamentale est première. Obligés d'assurer une présence à l'hôpital depuis la réforme du plein temps, ils ne le font souvent qu'avec réticence.[9] Se voulant physiciens bien que travaillant en milieu médical, ils ont souvent une position assez inconfortable et risquent le rejet simultané des vrais physiciens et des médecins praticiens. Pour leurs publications, ils doivent utiliser deux réseaux différents, des revues scientifiques où ils parlent la langue du physicien et des revues médicales où, comme le disait l'un d'eux, ils prennent 'le langage de *France-Soir*' pour être compris de leurs collègues praticiens. Un certain nombre de fondamentalistes sont des physiciens ayant fait leur médecine sur le tard pour des raisons de recherche ou de carrière car le conservatisme du milieu médical s'oppose à l'accès de non-médecins à des postes universitaires importants, même dans les disciplines fondamentales; l'assistance publique se reconnaît une mission de recherche, mais de recherche avec un petit *r*.

Entre ces extêmes, le cas le plus fréquent est un dosage variable de médecin et de physicien qui fera parfois apparaître le biophysicien comme 'un être hybride ayant sacrifié la moitié de ses études médicales à la physique et la moitié de ses études de physique à la médecine,' avec le risque de n'être qu' 'un monsieur qui parle de médecine aux physiciens et de physique aux médecins'. C'est l'homme d'une double culture, l'homme de la pluridisciplinarité, celui qui peut passer les frontières linguistiques entre savoirs. . . S'exprimant ainsi, on débouche sur un vocabulaire peu rigoureux dont la fonction principale me paraît être de masquer notre incapacité à analyser le phénomène d'hybridation des disciplines: qu'est-ce qu'une culture scientifique? Qu'est-ce qu'une barrière linguistique? Qu'est-ce que la pluridisciplinarité? Peut-on analyser des secteurs hybrides d'aujourd'hui avec le vocabulaire servant à décrire les disciplines d'autrefois?

La biophysique 'scientifique'

La biophysique 'scientifique', sans être plus unifiée que ne l'est la physique médicale, représente ce que l'on pourrait appeler le 'noyau dur' de la biophysique, et ceci pour deux raisons:
— toute recherche 'scientifique' est considérée comme fondamentale par les médecins.
— c'est surtout aux 'scientifiques' que l'on doit la remontée de la biophysique au niveau moléculaire et c'est le moléculaire qui donne le ton à toute la biologie actuelle, non sans parfois un peu d'impérialisme: l'ironie d'Edgar Morin tombait juste quand il parlait de 'l'Evangile selon Sainte Molécule' qui soutient la religion des plus éminents biologistes.[10] Ainsi les médecins suivent-ils les 'scientifiques' sur la voie qui doit leur permettre, selon une expression de Leriche 'd'écrire l'histoire de la maladie avant le stade anatomique.'[11]
Parler de noyau dur, c'est poser la question des origines, des caractéristiques, du rôle d'un secteur de recherche considéré comme modèle épistémologique pour d'autres secteurs. Quelles sont les raisons objectives ou subjectives qui font reconnaître une science comme dure? Si l'on fait le lien entre l'existence de sciences considérées comme plus dures que d'autres et l'existence d'une hiérarchie de disciplines héritée d'Auguste Comte, on est conduit à une question voisine qui est celle de l'origine, des justifications et du rôle (épistémologique mais aussi sociologique et politique) d'un système hiérarchisé des branches du savoir tel qu'il survit fortement en France.[12]

Même si l'unanimité sur une définition de la biophysique demeure impossible, une certaine conscience d'existence spécifique a permis un début d'institutionnalisation. Des sociétés de biophysique existent en Hollande depuis 1932, aux Etats-Unis depuis 1956, au Japon depuis 1960, et en Angleterre depuis 1961. En France, il n'existe pas à proprement parler de société de biophysique chez les scientifiques mais un Comité national de biophysique, chargé de l'organisation de rencontres et de représentation internationale, a été fondé par l'Académie des sciences dans sa séance du 7 mars 1966.

Au niveau international, lors d'une réunion organisée par l'Union internationale de physique fondamentale et appliquée (IUPAP) en 1959, les biophysiciens ont décidé de se regrouper indépendamment des diverses instances internationales existant déjà.[13] Pour préparer ce regroupement, une rencontre a été organisée en 1960 à Amsterdam par la Société hollandaise de biophysique; il en sortit l'idée d'un congrès international qui se tint à Stockholm en 1961 et au cours duquel fut créé l'Union internationale de biophysique fondamentale et appliquée (IOPAB), membre du Conseil international des unions scientifiques (ICSU). En dix ans, du congrès de Stockholm à celui de Moscou, le nombre des participants a été multiplé par dix.

On peut distinguer en première analyse quatre catégories de biophysiciens 'scientifiques' suivant leurs origines: physiologie, biochimie, chimie physique, physique, origines dans lesquelles on retrouve les deux pôles, biologie et physique, différemment dosés.

Les physiologistes

Les physiologistes français sont demeurés longtemps beaucoup moins physiciens que leurs collègues anglo-saxons: aux Etats-Unis, le terme *biophysics* désigne la physiologie. En France, la venue des physiologistes à la physique est assez récente et va de pair avec le passage d'une physiologie au niveau des organes à une physiologie cellulaire puis moléculaire. Cette reconversion se traduit par le développement rapide de certains secteurs de recherche (conduction nerveuse, contraction musculaire, physiologie sensorielle, problèmes de membranes, photosynthèse) et par l'appel à la collaboration de physiciens. On peut penser que ce retard des physiologistes est lié à leur formation biologique française, c'est-à-dire une formation particulièrement pauvre en mathématiques et physique. Ceci pose la question du lien entre la composition des programmes universitaires et le maintien de certaines disciplines sous des formes archaïques; on peut aussi s'interroger sur le rôle de filières universitaires 'cul-de-sac' comme les DUES de chimie-biologie ou de biologie-géologie, qui n'offrent de débouchés ni dans l'enseignement ni dans la recherche et drainent souvent les étudiants considérés comme moins doués qui ne peuvent affronter des études de mathématiques ou de physique.[14]

Les biochimistes

Les biochimistes utilisent maintenant de nombreuses techniques physiques mais cela ne correspond pas pour autant à un tournant vers la biophysique dans la mesure où la perspective reste chimique. La différence entre le biochimiste et le biophysicien est souvent très mal perçue car tous deux utilisent les mêmes appareils. Je voudrais proposer deux exemples pour faire percevoir cette différence.

Supposons un même cours d'initiation sur les protéines fait soit par un biochimiste, soit par un biophysicien. Le chimiste insistera sur la structure primaire en parlant de liaison peptidique, de méthodes chimiques de détermination des séquences ou de synthèse. Le biophysicien portera son attention sur les structures secondaires, tertiaires ou quaternaires, sur les transconformations et sur leur importance en biologie.[15] Considérons maintenant les modèles moléculaires de l'acide désoxyribonucléique (ADN). Le biochimiste utilisera volontiers un 'modèle éclaté' montrant plus clairement les différents composants: sucre, base, radical phosphoryle et l'allure générale de la double hélice. Le biophysicien préférera souvent le 'modèle compact', mettant moins en valeur le détail de la composition chimique mais rendant mieux compte de la forme, du volume de la double hélice, faisant apparaître les sillons où vont pouvoir se loger des protéines.

Les biochimistes français semblent penser beaucoup moins en termes de structure que leurs collègues anglo-saxons; l'histoire de la biologie moléculaire, mettant François Jacob et Jacques Monod après J. D. Watson et Francis Crick, ne souligne pas assez les différences d'approche entre des analystes structuraux, disciples des Bragg, et des généticiens moléculaires. Il n'y a peut-être qu'une nuance mais c'est cette nuance qui me paraît séparer les biochimistes des biophysiciens.

En France, les biochimistes qui perçoivent mal cette différence sont conduits à considérer la biophysique comme un ensemble de techniques au service de la biochimie. C'est pourquoi la biophysique est souvent enseignée dans le cadre des certificats de biochimie comme la partie technologique de ces certificats. Cela explique aussi que les biologistes moléculaires puissent affirmer habituellement que 'la biophysique n'existe pas', réduisant ainsi d'éventuels rivaux en techniciens subalternes à leur service.

Les physico-chimistes

Secteur hybride jouant sur le prestige de la physique auprès des non-physiciens, possédant sa propre société depuis 1908, la chimie physique a été une des principales portes d'entrée de la physique en biologie. Au début, tentative de marginaux n'enseignant qu'en cours libres et travaillant sous diverses étiquettes (chimie, physique, physiologie), la chimie physique des macromolécules d'intérêt biologique s'est peu à peu taillé une place. Jean Perrin y a largement contribué en demandant la fondation de l'Institut de biologie physico-chimique qui sera inauguré en 1931 ; l'IBPC a pu donner refuge à des disciplines ignorées ou du moins n'étant pas encore admise à l'université: e.g., la génétique avec Ephrussi, la biophysique avec Duclaux et Wurmser. En 1946 est créée pour Wurmser à Paris la première chaire de biologie physico-chimique ; Tonnelat, un de ses élèves, lui succèdera en 1961 puis s'installera à Orsay laissant la chaire parisienne à Dervichian, directeur du laboratoire de biophysique de l'institut Pasteur.

L'obstacle a été longtemps la difficulté de traduire les problèmes du biologiste dans le langage du physico-chimiste mais l'introduction de certaines techniques en biologie (microscope électronique, marqueurs radio-actifs, etc.) a permis aux deux types de discours de se rejoindre sur un terrain commun, celui du recours à la physique.

Lorsqu'on parle de biologie physico-chimique, on doit mentionner l'espoir et les questions soulevées par deux grandes 'aventures' de la biophysique actuelle: l'évolution de la thermodynamique et les développements de la quanto-chimie.

La thermodynamique classique, ne pouvant répondre qu'à des situations expérimentales très particulières, était progressivement devenue une discipline négligée, incapable de susciter l'intérêt de la plupart des chercheurs. Katchalsky, Glansdorff, et Prigogine, en allant au delà de la seule considération des états d'équilibre et des évolutions réversibles, ont fait renaître une science jeune, la thermodynamique des processus irréversibles (TPI), riche d'espoirs pour la biologie. La France mit un certain temps à recevoir cette nouvelle problématique mais, malgré l'opposition persistante de certains parmi les plus éminents des biologistes moléculaires, on peut considérer que sa reconnaissance a fortement progressé depuis dix ans.

L'autre aventure qui touche la biophysique est celle de la chimie quantique. La naissance de la mécanique ondulatoire entre 1920 et 1930 a été suivie de peu par son application à l'étude de la liaison chimique. L'extension de la quanto-chimie aux macromolécules biologiques est devenue très vite une perspective ouverte. Hélas, la complexité des calculs et surtout le nombre d'approximations successives nécessaires pour les mener à bien ne laissent guère de place à la quanto-chimie au delà des molécules de la taille du benzène. Les militants de la chimie quantique s'efforcent cependant de maintenir l'espoir et même revendiquent quelques résultats: l'explication par B. Pullman en 1964 de la synthèse de l'adénine obtenue l'année précédente par Ponnamperuma au cours de ses recherches sur la biogenèse ou l'approche par R. Daudel et B. Pullman des problèmes de cancérogenèse.[16] Il faut cependant reconnaître que la plupart des biophysiciens demeurent très réservés, attendant que les promesses des quanto-chimistes soient suivies de résultats suffisamment nombreux.

Les physiciens

La migration de physiciens vers la biologie s'est faite à différentes époques et sur différents thèmes de recherche mais il me semble plus intéressant de regrouper ces migrations, non par leur chronologie, mais par leurs causes politiques, idéologiques, matérielles ou théoriques, en distinguant quand il y a lieu les forces de répulsion qui éloignent les physiciens de la physique des forces d'attraction qui les font venir à la biologie; au plan international, les exemples ne manquent pas.

Les migrations pour des raisons politiques mettent généralement en jeu des forces de répulsion. Le passage de la physique à la biologie n'est qu'un phénomène secondaire dû aux conditions de reclassement dans le pays d'accueil; l'histoire du groupe du phage nous fournit les exemples de Max Delbruck réfugié aux Etats-Unis en 1937 ou de Salvador Luria en 1940.[17] On peut aussi citer l'exemple de Schrödinger réfugié en Irlande au moment où il écrit *What is Life?* Il faudrait s'interroger sur les raisons qui ont permis aux physiciens émigrés avant la guerre de fonder une discipline nommée biologie moléculaire plutôt qu'une autre nommée biophysique.

Les causes idéologiques sont à la fois répulsives et attractives dans la mesure où c'est la différence de valeur entre deux situations qui est motrice. Elles sont très présentes aujourd'hui chez nombre de physiciens las d'améliorer les écrans de télévision, las d'une recherche fondamentale dont les applications ne leur paraissent ni strictement nécessaires ni même parfois bénéfiques. Ils se tournent donc naturellement vers la biologie pour 'servir l'humanité' et sont encouragés à cette reconversion par la publicité, parfois un peu trouble, faite à la recherche bio-médicale auprès du grand public. Cette idéologie de service peut servir à couvrir d'autres motivations moins prestigieuses: 'De temps à autre, rapporte J. D. Watson, au cours d'une réception ou dans un laboratoire, j'entends dire que la résolution du problème du cancer serait un désastre qui supprimerait les crédits qui nous permettent de travailler.'[18] Un autre danger de cette idéologie de service réside dans l'absence d'analyse qui va souvent de pair avec les bonnes intentions; on ne peut oublier que c'est une lettre du pacifiste Einstein qui fit développer les recherches qui conduisirent à Hiroshima et firent naître une crise de conscience mondiale des scientifiques. Que penseront les physiciens, partis en croisade contre le cancer, quand ils auront réussi à contrôler la génétique humaine? Que deviendront les généreux biophysiciens quand ils n'auront plus la justification du cancer?

Les raisons matérielles de migrations de physiciens vers la biologie sont aussi très actuelles: des forces de répulsion viennent de la réduction des crédits accordés à la recherche qui, étant donné les différences entre les besoins suivant les secteurs, touche plus gravement la physique. En effet un chercheur coûte moins cher en biophysique qu'en physique; le biophysicien peut donc survivre plus longtemps à l'étouffement des laboratoires par absence de crédits. D'autre part la biologie, paz le biais de la recherche bio-médicale, peut diversifier ses réseaux de financement en faisant appel à la sensibilité de l'opinion aux grandes maladies et particulièrement au cancer. Moins pauvre relativement que la physique, la biophysique peut donc constituer un pôle d'attraction en période de pénurie.

Par raisons théoriques, j'entends toutes les raisons qui font qu'une discipline n'a plus grand-chose à se mettre sous la dent; dans le langage de Kuhn, je dirais que c'est l'ennui que peut faire naître le *puzzle solving* de la 'science normale'. Cela fut le cas des radio-cristallographes, venus de divers secteurs pour constituer l'école de W. H. Bragg à Cambridge qui devint ainsi, selon F. Jacob, 'la Mecque de l'analyse cristallographique et de la structure des macro-molécules biologiques.' Les plus illustres furent W. T. Astbury, (le créateur du nom de biologie moléculaire) et J. D. Bernal, puis J. Kendrew (myoglobine) et M. Perutz (hémoglobine), enfin J. D. Watson et F. Crick (ADN). D'autres exemples sont les mécaniciens des fluides passant à l'hydrodynamique physiologique, les magnéticiens au bio-magnétisme, les électroniciens au génie biologique.

Un groupe de travail réuni par le CNRS à Paris estimait récemment à

quarante par an le nombre de postes bio-médicaux ouverts à des physiciens en réorientation. En fonction de leur origine et des demandes, les
chercheurs se retrouveront dans l'une des trois activités de la
biophysique:
— recherche appliquée, malgré la traditionnelle répulsion des scientifiques français pour ce qui est technique et le clivage non moins
  traditionnel entre fondamental et appliqué, clivage qui fait apparaître
  comme une déchéance le passage du premier au second
— recherche fondamentale au niveau physiologique
— recherche fondamentale au niveau moléculaire.

La hiérarchie des biophysiciens
Les liens que les différents groupes de biophysiciens vont pouvoir
entretenir entre eux dépendent à la fois de l'origine de leurs membres et
de leur secteur d'activité. Pour comprendre ces liens, il faut au préalable
éclaircir deux questions: l'une sur les rapports entre les niveaux
physiologique et moléculaire, l'autre sur le type de physique mis en
oeuvre par le biophysicien.

   Le progrès des techniques fait qu'actuellement l'observation macroscopique tend à rejoindre l'analyse de structure au niveau moléculaire.
Ainsi par exemple, la contraction musculaire n'a longtemps fait l'objet
que d'une description phénoménologique par les physiologistes; puis
l'évolution des techniques, les microscopes optiques puis électroniques,
les rayons X, l'analyse chimique, ont permis une connaissance structurale
au niveau moléculaire qui rendait compte des observations des
physiologistes. Les recherches sur la conduction nerveuse n'ont pas
encore réussi à achever ce pont entre le phénoménologique et le structural mais on peut penser que l'on y arrivera assez rapidement. Si on ne
peut donc plus opposer comme il y a quinze ans les fonctionnalistes à
l'échelle macroscopique et les structuralistes à l'échelle microscopique, il
demeure que le couple structure-fonction sert souvent à définir la
biophysique: pour les uns, la biophysique est l'étude des structures; pour
d'autres, c'est l'articulation de la structure et de la fonction, cet espace le
plus souvent encore inconnu, qui fait son objet propre. C'est alors seulement que le terme bio-physique se justifie pour désigner la jonction entre
l'étude des structures (physique) et l'étude des fonctions (biologie), mais
cette jonction peut se faire avec différents dosages des divers types de
physiciens (cristallographes, thermodynamiciens, physiciens du solide,
etc.) et de biologistes (physiologistes, anatomistes, cytologistes,
biochimistes, etc.); rendre compte de ce dosage est fort difficile et le

terme biophysicien a le tort d'évoquer une collaboration d'égal à égal, ce qui est rarement le cas. C'est pourquoi certains comme F. Crick préfèrent l'appellation plus générale de "biologie moléculaire":

> Je fus moi-même forcé de me désigner sous le nom de biologiste moléculaire parce que, toutes les fois que des ecclésiastiques curieux me demandaient ce que je faisais, je m'épuisais à leur expliquer que j'étais un mélange de cristallographe, de biophysicien, de biochimiste et de généticien, explication que, de toute manière, ils trouvaient trop difficile à saisir.[19]

Cette remarque montre bien que, face aux subtilités des spécialistes, c'est la nécessité de justifier d'une identité perceptible par les non-spécialistes ou par l'opinion publique qui limite les subdivisions et détermine les appellations. J. Ben-David et R. Collins ont proposé de reconnaître comme disciplines les secteurs nouveaux lorsqu'ils constituaient 'un moyen potentiel d'établir une nouvelle identité intellectuelle et en particulier un nouveau rôle professionnel'.[20] Bien que limitée par l'archaïsme de l'idée de discipline, de nombreux travaux comme celui de Ben-David et Collins ont montré la nécessité, dans l'analyse des secteurs nouveaux de recherche, de dépasser une perspective interne à la science pour prendre en considération les facteurs sociaux qui font qu'un domaine neuf peut être reconnu et qu'une appellation peut être prestigieuse, incomprise, inquiétante, bénéfique ou nuisible.

La deuxième question concerne le type de physique mis en oeuvre par le biophysicien. En effet, il ne faut pas confondre l'utilisation technologique et celle qui renvoie à un niveau théorique. La technologie biophysique met en oeuvre aussi bien les acquis de la physique classique que ceux de la physique la plus moderne. Mais l'utilisation d'instruments dont le principe relève par exemple de la mécanique quantique ne signifie pas grand chose dans la mesure où médecins et biologistes considèrent la technique physique comme une 'boîte noire' dont ils ne connaissent que très grossièrement le principe. Ils emploient d'ailleurs souvent ces appareils bien en-deçà de leurs capacités et cela pose le problème du transfert à des utilisateurs biologistes de techniques mises au point par des physiciens. L'expérience des laboratoires de spectroscopie, d'ultracentrifugation, ou de radiocristallographie tenus par des physiciens auxquels les biologistes apportent leurs échantillons n'a jamais été très concluante car une mesure correcte doit tenir compte du traitement subi par l'échantillon et ne peut être valablement interprétée qu'avec une bonne connaissance des techniques utilisées.

Au niveau théorique, tout le monde s'accorde pour reconnaître que les biophysiciens ne se réfèrent qu'à la 'vieille physique' malgré les efforts de quelques quanto-chimistes. Il y a là un problème d'écart entre disciplines lorsque l'on descend la classification de Comte: un mathématicien s'abaisse en faisant de la physique et l'on connaît l'expression péjorative 'mathématiques pour physiciens'; de même un physicien se dévalorise en faisant de la biologie: Delbruck, refusant de se dire biophysicien, a intitulé une conférence faite en 1949: 'Un physicien se penche sur la biologie'. De même, dans un laboratoire de physique des solides en partielle reconversion, on ne parle pas de biophysique mais on dit la 'biochose' afin de ne pas dévaloriser le mot de physique. Selon G. Stent, aux yeux du groupe du phage, il n'y avait que deux sortes de personnes se considérant comme des biophysiciens: les physiologistes, capables de réparer leur propre équipement électronique et des physiciens de second ordre cherchant à convaincre les biologistes qu'ils sont de premier ordre.[21]

Sachant que cette hiérarchie de Comte va de pair avec la capacité d'une discipline à intégrer une formalisation mathématique, on ne peut éviter de s'interroger sur la place réelle ou mythique des mathématiques en biologie. On peut distinguer sur ce point deux défauts chez les biophysiciens. Le premier est une peur incontrôlée devant toute expression mathématique qui apparaît a priori incompréhensible, ce qui n'est que le résultat de l'image de marque des mathématiques dans l'enseignement français. Le second est un culte mythique des mathématiques qui fait que l'on croit avoir trouvé la vérité dès que l'on a réussi à mettre un résultat en équation, parfois au prix d'un médiocre tripatouillage de formules qui impressionnera beaucoup le profane.

Conformément au modèle de Comte, on peut ordonner les différents groupes de biophysiciens selon l'usage croissant et le prestige des mathématiques dans leurs domaines respectifs:

biophysiciens médicaux hospitaliers
biophysiciens médicaux fondamentalistes
biophysiciens scientifiques d'origine physiologie
biophysiciens scientifiques d'origine biochimie
biophysiciens scientifiques d'origine chimie physique
biophysiciens scientifiques d'origine physique appliquée
biophysiciens scientifiques d'origine physique mathématique.

Par rapport aux secteurs voisins, les biophysiciens se situeront à la fois en fonction de leurs origines propres et d'une image globale de la biophysique qui, actuellement, est plutôt favorable car elle ajoute le prestige de la physique (discipline mathématisée, placée très haut dans la classification de Comte, riche de succès théoriques et pratiques ayant impressionné le grand public: l'atome, la conquête de la lune, le transistor, la télévision, l'ordinateur) à celui de la biologie qui compense les aspects inquiétants de la physique par sa vocation de lutte contre les maladies.

Pour situer un domaine de recherche, il ne suffit pas de parler des rapports internes entre ses membres, ou de ses relations avec ses voisins, il faut aussi, dans bien des cas, préciser ses capacités d'accueil de secteurs de recherche non reconnus mais qui constituent cependant son champ d'expansion potentiel. Il y a là deux niveaux de reconnaissance: le premier est celui de la communauté scientifique, par nature assez hostile à ce qui pourrait perturber son ordre et sa hiérarchie. Après avoir connu le succès, A. Szent-Györgi remarquait:

> Une découverte doit, par définition, présenter une variante avec les connaissances existantes. J'en ai fait deux dans ma vie. Toutes deux avaient été rejetées d'emblée par les papes en la matière. Si j'avais prévu ces découvertes dans mes demandes de crédit et si ces mêmes autorités avaient eu à en juger, les décisions qu'ils auraient prises sont évidentes . . . Le problème est d'importance, en particulier actuellement où la science s'affronte avec un des mystères de la nature, le cancer, qui pourrait bien requérir des approches entièrement nouvelles.[22]

L'autre niveau de reconnaissance dépend de la détermination des frontières entre science et non-science et, dans la mesure où la science incarne en Occident la rationalité, des frontières entre raison et déraison. Il existe en effet aux frontières de la biophysique reconnue, des sujets tabous, par exemple la perception extra-sensorielle qui pourrait être une des questions ouvertes de la biophysique sensorielle. De même, depuis Mesmer au XVIIIe siècle, le sens commun lie occultisme et bio-magnétisme, ce qui rend tout à fait inconvenant de s'interroger en France, contrairement à l'URSS ou aux USA, sur les effets biologiques des champs magnétiques.

La biophysique existe-t-elle?

Après cette rapide reconnaissance de la biophysique en France, de ses problèmes et de ses espoirs, une certaine impression de confusion doit se dégager: elle recrute un peu partout, récupère toutes les techniques, importe et exporte des idées, s'engage dans de nombreuses voies sans lien apparent entre elles. Elle est partout et nulle part. Elle apparaît comme un lieu de convergence des incertitudes épistémologiques et des problèmes sociologiques. Les facteurs sociaux semblent plus qu'ailleurs venir y troubler la limpidité et la pureté d'une science qui se voudrait objective. Ses nombreuses définitions ne peuvent être que contradictoires. La clef de cette situation doit, à mon sens, se trouver dans une autre question: la biophysique constitue-t-elle maintenant une discipline?

Un certain horizon de questions présentes dans le champ de la science depuis un siècle, l'existence d'une appellation administrativement reconnue et utilisée, un début d'institutionnalisation (laboratoires, sociétés, colloques, chaires d'enseignement) pousseraient à répondre oui. Le caractère non-homogène du groupe des biophysiciens, la possibilité pour chacun de prétendre à une autre identité que celle de biophysicien (qui est souvent seconde), l'absence de contenu clair, de méthodes vraiment spécifiques, le fonctionnement difficile des rares institutions qui existent, la grande perméabilité des frontières suffiraient à justifier une réponse négative.

Oui? Non? La possibilité d'une alternative fait naître la question de l'opérationalité du concept de discipline pour rendre compte des secteurs de la recherche d'aujourd'hui: ne cherche-t-on pas, en s'interrogeant sur le statut de discipline de la biophysique, à faire rentrer la science actuelle dans un cadre archaïque qui ne lui convient plus.

Je considère pour ma part que la biophysique n'existe pas comme discipline avec toutes les caractéristiques épistémologiques et sociologiques que ce terme implique: elle n'a pas de paradigme bien défini, ne fournit qu'une identité occasionnelle à des gens dont l'appartenance principale est autre, paraît plus lieu de désaccord que facteur d'unité . . . Et pourtant elle existe! Cette contradiction est une sorte de démonstration par l'absurde du fait que le concept de discipline, dans ce cas mais sans doute aussi dans beaucoup d'autres, n'est plus opératoire. Il faut donc tenter de raisonner autrement sur les divisions internes de la science.

ELEMENTS POUR UNE NOUVELLE PROCEDURE D'ANALYSE DE LA DIFFERENCIATION INTERNE DES DISCOURS ET PRATIQUES SCIENTIFIQUES

Deux erreurs me semblent exister dans l'opinion commune que l'on se fait d'une discipline et parfois même se retrouver dans l'analyse des chercheurs.

La première est de considérer que les secteurs de la science naissent puis progressent vers un état de maturité où ils se figent pour l'avenir dans le conservatisme de ce que Kuhn a appellé la 'science normale', elle-même établie dans une sorte d'équilibre quasi-immuable. Ce n'est pas un hasard si les études souvent citées de A. Ihde, N. Mullins, G. Stent, la théorie de Kuhn portent toutes sur la phase de croissance qui conduit une discipline à être reconnue, c'est-à-dire établie dans une maturité dont l'existence même mériterait d'être discutée.[23] Ne faut-il pas plutôt raisonner sur un état permanent de non-équilibre de la science? Le problème ne serait plus alors celui de la naissance des disciplines mais celui de la mouvance systémique de la science actuelle.

La deuxième erreur fondamentale est de considérer qu'il n'y a qu'un niveau de division de la science ou du moins qu'un seul niveau, en général celui de la science comme discours constitué, est déterminant pour induire le système de cloisonnement. Or la science n'est pas savoir pur, elle est ensemble de professions, d'institutions, de réseaux oraux ou écrits de circulation de l'information; elle est aussi objet d'enseignements, facteur économique de plus en plus important, support de l'idéologie technocratique. Il faut donc une analyse différenciée selon chaque niveau possible dans la mesure où chacun a ses propres cloisonnements internes qui ne correspondent pas nécessairement à ceux des autres.

La science comme système composé en état stationnaire de non-équilibre

Il n'existe plus de phases stables, de disciplines en équilibre de maturité comme a pu l'être par exemple la zoologie pendant des siècles. La 'science normale' de Kuhn est un état aussi fugitif que la 'science extraordinaire'; la 'révolution scientifique' devient permanente et les paradigmes se succèdent sans interruption. On ne peut pas prétendre pour autant que la créativité, l'innovation, le renouvellement permanent sont devenus habituels, que les paradigmes se succèdent rapidement dans un continuel jaillissement de théories et foisonnement de techniques. On doit seulement constater que les divers secteurs de recherche sont en mouvance continuelle les uns par rapport aux autres, ce qui est relativement nouveau, du moins à cette échelle. Le mouvement brownien des idées, des théories, des questions s'amplifie. Ces secteurs élémentaires s'unissent entre eux pour constituer ce que l'on appelait autrefois des disciplines et ces unions sont en renouvellement constant. Les divisions internes de la science ne sont plus perceptibles que de façon instantanée et on ne peut plus se fonder sur leur observation fugitive pour comprendre l'organisation cognitive et sociale de la recherche.

Je voudrais proposer un modèle théorique de cette situation que

j'emprunterai à la physique: l'analyse en termes de disciplines me paraît
être à une conceptualisation actuellement opératoire ce que l'ancienne
thermodynamique est à la thermodynamique des processus irréversibles.
Dans la thermodynamique classique, le principe de Boltzmann (évolution d'un système isolé vers un état d'équilibre) pourrait constituer un
modèle de toutes les études, en général assez internalistes, faisant s'ar-
rêter l'évolution des disciplines à une phase stationnaire censée corres-
pondre à un état d'équilibre. Si cet équilibre, comme le montre l'exemple
de la biophysique, n'existe plus dans la science d'aujourd'hui, il faut
changer de modèle.

On se trouve donc contraint dans l'étude des éléments constitutifs de la
science à opérer une remise en question analogue à celle qu'a dû faire
l'école de Prigogine pour introduire la thermodynamique en biologie:
'Pour situer les structures biologiques, écrit Prigogine, il semble essentiel
de s'écarter du principe d'ordre de Boltzmann et de tenir compte de ce
que les phénomènes biologiques caractéristiques se déroulent loin d'un
état d'équilibre thermodynamique.'[24]

Mais tout n'est pas en déséquilibre de la même façon: dans la société, la
recherche scientifique occupe une certaine place qui n'évolue que lente-
ment du fait du cadre relativement rigide que constituent les contraintes
économiques et sociales. Les techniques (e.g., microscopie, spectroscopie, radiocristallographie, analyse chimique), les objets d'investigation (e.g., virologie, bactériologie, cytologie) ont une certaine stabilité
par nature: l'usage du microscope est très répandu mais il s'agit toujours
de microscopie; de même, les immunologistes, généticiens, biophysiciens
moléculaires et d'autres peuvent s'intéresser au virus pour des raisons
très diverses, le virus n'en reste pas moins ce qui définit la virologie.

Ce que l'on appelle discipline n'est que l'arrangement instable des cellules élémentaires que sont chaque technique, chaque objet, chaque
théorie. L'ensemble de ces arrangements fugitifs, du fait des contraintes
externes, peut constituer une totalité apparemment stable. La nouveauté
de la science actuelle en ce domaine est que les arrangements des cellules
élémentaires sont beaucoup plus complexes et variables qu'ils ne l'étaient
dans les disciplines reconnues au XIXe.

On peut donc, du point de vue de la stabilité, distinguer trois niveaux
systémiques (voir tableau à la page suivante). Selon l'hypothèse de
l'équilibre local formulée par Prigogine en 1947, un système qui n'est pas
dans son ensemble en équilibre peut être considéré comme la juxtaposi-
tion de sub-systèmes élémentaires qui chacun pour sa propre part se
trouve en équilibre thermodynamique interne. De même par exemple, la

	niveaux systémiques	analogie en thermodynamique
méta-système	la recherche scientifique	état stationnaire de non-équilibre
système	les 'disciplines'	non-équilibre
sub-système	cellules élémentaires de constitution des secteurs de recherche: objets, méthodes	cellules élémentaires en équilibre thermodynamique interne

biophysique qui dans son ensemble n'est pas en équilibre et ne peut donc être analysée comme une discipline stable, est l'ensemble des combinaisons variables que l'on peut réaliser à partir des cellules élémentaires stables que sont chaque technique physique, chaque objet biologique. On s'explique ainsi que l'analyse soit impossible au niveau des disciplines.

Le méta-système qu'est la recherche scientifique est, pour prendre le vocabulaire de la nouvelle thermodynamique, en état stationnaire de non-équilibre, ce qui revient à dire que la recherche scientifique dont les éléments constitutifs (les disciplines) varient rapidement, n'est pas de ce fait en équililibre mais que les contraintes externes (sociales, économiques, politiques) la maintiennent dans un état stationnaire de non-équilibre.

L'irréductibilité des niveaux de division interne entre eux

L'université a produit un certain découpage de la science en matières d'enseignements. Le CNRS a son découpage en sections. Chaque institut, chaque centre est cloisonné selon des critères propres en laboratoires, équipes distinctes . . . On pourrait aussi diviser la science, par exemple, selon les sujets de recherche ou les réseaux de publications, mais ces diverses divisions ne se correspondent plus entre elles.

Au XIXe siècle, ces différents découpages de la science se recouvraient approximativement pour constituer un certain nombre de disciplines aisément différenciables: un enseignant de zoologie, par exemple, avait fait sa thèse en zoologie, était titulaire d'une chaire de zoologie et dirigeait un laboratoire de zoologie. Actuellement la situation est bien différente: un chercheur en cancérologie, par exemple, peut avoir une maîtrise de physique, un troisième cycle de biophysique, travailler avec des immunologistes dans un centre de recherche médicale, enseigner la biochimie dans une faculté des sciences, publier dans des revues scientifiques ou médicales, appartenir à une section du CNRS où il sera isolé. Les différents découpages ne se recouvrent plus, les appartenances se diversifient et de ce fait deviennent moins rigides: la division en disciplines ne rend plus compte de la réalité des situations.

Parmi les découpages observables aujourd'hui dans la science en France, on peut citer: le découpage universitaire (UER,[25] titres des maîtrises, certificats, unités de valeurs), celui des grandes institutions de recherche (par exemple, les sections du CNRS), celui des sujets de recherche (découpage grossier: par exemple, le cancer, la conduction nerveuse, la contraction musculaire; découpage plus fin: les virus oncogènes, les récepteurs synaptiques, la structure moléculaire de l'actomyosine), celui des applications (thérapeutiques: cardiologie, cancérologie, neurologie; industrielles: pharmacie, GBM, industries agricoles ou alimentaires), celui des sociétés savantes, celui des réseaux oraux ou écrits, officiels ou officieux, de circulation des informations scientifiques, celui des centres et instituts, celui des chercheurs selon leur statut professionnel (secteur public ou privé, titulaires, contractuels, ou vacataires).

On pourrait probablement énumérer d'autres découpages de la science à tel ou tel niveau mais cette énumération ne constituerait que la phase initiale d'une reconstruction conceptuelle qui devrait être suivie par:
— une étude particularisée de chaque découpage dans son état actuel et en suivant le processus de sa formation historique
— une analyse du type de relation existant entre les divers éléments à l'intérieur de chaque découpage
— la reconstitution du champ résultant de ces divers découpages, compte tenu de l'importance relative de chacun d'eux
— l'analyse des relations existant entre les divers niveaux de découpage.
Serait ainsi élaborée une compréhension de la dynamique des secteurs de recherche intégrant les divers niveaux épistémologique, sociologique, économique et politique, et ne faisant plus appel à l'idée caduque de discipline. La science apparaît ainsi dans toute sa complexité organisationnelle. Pour en établir la socio-dynamique, il suffit de choisir un facteur transformant et de voir comment il agit dans le temps selon chaque niveau. Un certain nombre de lois devraient ainsi apparaître, comme par exemple:
— Pour un stimulus donné, les effets ne se répartissent pas également sur chacun des niveaux de découpage: par exemple, la croissance de la biologie moléculaire transformera le champ de la biologie en agissant sur le découpage des sujets de recherche mais ne modifiera pas le découpage par statut professionnel des chercheurs.
— Même si les effets à deux niveaux différents étaient identiques, ils n'apparaîtraient pas à la même vitesse; chaque niveau a sa résistance

propre au changement.

— Toute transformation de l'un des niveaux modifie les conditions d'évolution des autres niveaux.

— Même si un niveau reste découpé comme avant l'action du stimulus, il peut se produire un changement de prestige entre ses divers éléments.

— Chacun de ces niveaux, outre l'influence des autres niveaux, sera soumis à diverses pressions externes à la science: contraintes de l'industrie, pressions politiques, influence de l'opinion publique sensible à l'attribution d'un prix Nobel, au cancer, aux problèmes écologiques. Ce ne sont donc plus seulement des sujets de recherche, des titres, des centres, des finalités qu'il faudra prendre en considération mais aussi les représentations sociales de ces sujets, titres et centres. Ainsi le fait que la biophysique jouisse d'une représentation sociale plutôt favorable peut expliquer le nombre des demandes d'emploi par des biophysiciens; ce nombre en effet ne correspond pas à une particulière régression de la biophysique mais au seul fait que chimistes, biochimistes, physiologistes choisissent cette appellation plus prestigieuse et plus rare pour avoir des chances de trouver du travail.

— Pour reconstituer la dynamique de l'ensemble d'un secteur de la recherche, il faut tenir compte de l'importance relative de chacun des niveaux: les niveaux *objectivement* les plus importants sont ceux dont les modifications ont le plus de conséquences sur les autres niveaux; le niveau *subjectivement* le plus important sera celui que les chercheurs utiliseront prioritairement pour se définir. Par exemple, un même chercheur pourra se définir comme cancérologue (sujet de recherche) au CNRS (statut professionnel) dans une équipe de biophysiciens (méthode) ou bien comme biophysicien travaillant en cancérologie dans un centre du CNRS.

La recherche de ces lois, la construction conceptuelle correspondante, à refaire pour chaque niveau, ne vise pas à mettre au point une gigantesque combinatoire permettant de jouer avec les facteurs, internes ou externes, expliquant l'évolution des divisions de la science, mais à forger un instrument d'analyse opératoire alors que les discours en termes de discipline semblent de plus en plus inadéquats pour décrire, expliquer et donc éventuellement transformer.

Cette ébauche d'orientation pour une nouvelle conceptualisation reste très insuffisante; elle me semble cependant permettre de renoncer à la recherche de plus en plus vaine de rangs bien dessinés, identifiés, nommés, de dépasser le simplisme du cloisonnement en disciplines sans pour autant abandonner le souci d'une compréhension opératoire des secteurs de la recherche scientifique actuelle dans leur synchronie comme dans leur diachronie. Alors seulement on pourra dire comment la biophysique existe sans exister, est une discipline sans cesse naissante et qui ne verra jamais le jour; son intérêt est d'être en cela un modèle de la science qui renaît des cendres de disciplines apparemment immuables mais qui pourtant ne fonctionnent plus comme telles.

J. D. de Certaines, Service de Biophysique, Université de Rennes, UER Claude Bernard, bd du Professeur L. Bernard, 35000 Rennes.

J. D. DE CERTAINES a fait ses études en biologie et sciences humaines aux universités de Paris VI et VII, Dakar, Nantes, et à l'Ecole pratique des hautes études. Il a travaillé plusieurs années comme sociologue au Sénégal et en France. Actuellement il est assistant de biophysique à la faculté de médecine de Rennes.

NOTES

1. Les citations sans précision d'origine sont extraites de 40 entretiens avec des biophysiciens, scientifiques ou médecins, réalisés en 1972-1973 dans 19 équipes de recherche différentes.
2. 'La biophysique', *Physique et chimie* no. spécial (1970) (Revue de l'ESPCI de Paris).
3. 'Facultés': avant la mise en application de la Loi d'orientation de l'enseignement supérieur de 1968 qui a créé les nouvelles universités.
4. *Colloque de biophysique,* Journées médicales de Bordeaux, octobre 1958 (Paris: Sedes, 1961).
5. Dans les travaux sur la naissance des disciplines on a beaucoup étudié les crises sous l'angle de la résistance des domaines constitués mais pas assez sous l'angle plus positif de leur renouvellement.
6. 'Génie biologique et médical', *Le Progrès Scientifique* no. spécial de mars (1972).
7. 'Une nouvelle discipline: le génie biologique', *Atomes* 245: juillet-août (1967).
8. H. Atlan, *Biophysics in a Medical School* (polycopié 1972).
9. La réforme du plein temps a obligé tous les enseignants titulaires des UER (voir note 25) médicales à avoir une fonction hospitalière représentant la moitié de leur charge.
10. E. Morin, *Journal de Californie* (Paris: le Seuil, 1970).
11. Cité par P. Bacques, *Introduction à la médecine moléculaire* (Paris: Maloine, 1972).
12. On peut se demander si la réponse proposée par F. Jacob pour rendre compte de l'hétérogénéité des discours scientifiques est suffisante:
    Dans le monde vivant comme ailleurs, il s'agit toujours d''expliquer du visible compliqué par de l'invisible simple', selon le mot de Jean Perrin. Mais dans les êtres comme dans les choses, c'est un invisible à tiroirs. Il n'y a pas une organisation du vivant, mais une série d'organisations emboîtées les unes dans les autres comme des poupées russes. Derrière chacune s'en cache une autre. Au delà de chaque structure accessible à l'analyse finit par se révéler une nouvelle structure, d'ordre supérieur, qui intègre la première et lui confère ses propriétés (*La logique du vivant* (Paris: Gallimard, 1970) 24).
13. 'International Organization of Biophysics', *Nature* 200: December (1963) 1141-42.

14. DUES: Diplôme universitaire d'études scientifiques qui sanctionne les études scientifiques du 1er cycle, durant les deux premières années d'université. Le lecteur intéressé par ce problème pourra consulter le livre de M. de Saint-Martin, *Les fonctions sociales de l'enseignement scientifique* (Paris: Mouton, 1970).

15. Une transconformation est un changement de conformation moléculaire (structures supérieures à la structure primaire) induisant en général des modifications fonctionnelles et constituant donc le domaine privilégié des biophysiciens moléculaires.

16. R. Daudel, *Théorie quantique de la liaison chimique* (Paris: Presses universitaires de France, 1971) 143-150 et 165-69.

17. Dans le cas de Delbruck la migration semble n'avoir fait qu'accélérer un passage à la biologie, notamment sous l'influence de Bohr dont il avait été l'élève. En effet, dès 1935, donc deux ans avant qu'il n'émigre aux Etats-Unis, Delbruck avait publié avec Timofieff-Ressovsky et Zimmer un article sur la mutation et la structure du gène. Cf. P. Thuillier, 'Comment est née la biologie moléculaire?' pp. 111-141 in: *Jeux et enjeux de la science* (Paris: Laffont, 1972).

18. J. D. Watson, 'Biologie moléculaire et cancer', p. 144 in: J. W. Fuller (ed.) *Responsabilité biologique* (Paris: Hermann, 1974).

19. G. Stent, *L'avènement de l'age d'or* (Paris: Fayard, 1973) 49.

20. J. Ben-David/R. Collins, 'Social Factors in the Origins of a New Science: the Case of Psychology', *American Sociological Review* 31 (1966) 452.

21. Stent, *L'avènement de l'âge d'or.*

22. Texte reproduit dans le supplément *Informations de la Semaine des Hôpitaux* du 21 novembre 1972.

23. A. J. Ihde, 'An Inquiry into the Origins of Hybrid Sciences: Astrophysics and Biochemistry', *Journal of Chemical Education* 46: 4 (1969) 193-196; N. C. Mullins, 'The Development of a Scientific Specialty: the Phage Group and the Origins of Molecular Biology', *Minerva* 10:1 (1972) 51-82; Stent, *L'avènement de l'âge d'or,* première partie: 'Grandeur et décadence de la biologie moléculaire'; T. Kuhn, *La structure des révolutions scientifiques,* 2ème éd. (Paris: Flammarion, 1972).

24. I. Prigogine, 'La thermodynamique de la vie', *La Recherche* 3:24 (Juin 1972) 547-562.

25. UER: Unité d'enseignement et de recherche. C'est la structure primaire de l'université définie par la Loi d'orientation de l'enseignement supérieur du 12 novembre 1968.

JOHN LAW

The Development of Specialties in Science:
the Case of X-ray Protein Crystallography

INTRODUCTION

In Britain in the late twenties and thirties, a small number of the growing community of X-ray crystallographers chose to study the structure of protein molecules, despite the obvious technical difficulties of this work and the scepticism of many of their colleagues.[1] The problem raised by this minority choice is discussed in the light of a number of sociological distinctions which offer a means for analysing intellectual change in scientific specialties. Specialties are seen to change over time, both in terms of the work undertaken by the member specialists, and in terms of their interaction network characteristics. Mullins has advanced a general theory of specialty development, in which changes in social structure are correlated with intellectual and theoretical developments.[2] Despite Mullins' use of Kuhn's work, the former concentrates less on the development of *ideas* (although these are to some extent discussed) than on the changing network characteristics of a specialty over time.[3] Mullins' hypothesis is stimulating, but it requires further specification and empirical validation.[4]

This paper discusses the intellectual structure of a scientific specialty in greater detail.[4] In the light of this discussion, a distinction is made between what are called 'technique', 'theory', and 'subject matter' specialties. This distinction is quite compatible with Mullins' theory, but supplements it by paying greater attention to cultural factors. It suggests that 'mature' specialties will vary in important respects, and it considers the nature of solidarity in both mature and immature specialties. Finally, the theory has implications for the way in which specialties move from immaturity to maturity, although these implications are not discussed in detail here.

THE CULTURAL STRUCTURE OF SCIENTIFIC SPECIALTIES

T. S. Kuhn has argued that the actions of scientists in all mature sciences are directed by a 'paradigm'.[5] The paradigm is a scientific achievement that has been accepted by a substantial group of scientists, and is used by them as a basis for their scientific work. It is both a 'received achievement' and also offers opportunities for what he calls 'articulation' — that is, cultural development. Although Kuhn does not see the paradigm as being reducible to a set of norms and rules, such norms or rules can usually be extracted from it, and form, together with the exemplary concrete achievements, a guide for future scientific action. The paradigm is thus open-ended, and there is always work for the scientist to undertake. Kuhn calls this process of articulation 'normal science'. Periods of normal science are interrupted by major conceptual revolutions (such as the Copernican revolution, or development of the quantum theory) when old theoretical frameworks are overthrown, and new ones established. In this paper the discussion is restricted to the case of normal science, although the process of intellectual institutionalization is also mentioned.

Kuhn characterizes science as a set of paradigm-sharing communities. This accords with the views of other historians and sociologists who argue that decisions about what constitute acceptable additions to scientific knowledge (and hence acceptable scientific action) are made largely within those small groups of research workers who are sufficiently well in touch with one another's work to understand, criticize and develop it.[6] Hagstrom calls such interacting groups at a common research front 'specialties', and the term is used in the same sense here. It is clear from Kuhn's work that within a normally operating specialty, scientists will interpret each other's works in terms of a paradigm, and judge it by criteria implicit in that paradigm; it follows that acceptable research actions in a specialty are limited. Thus both theories and methods deal with limited sets of phenomena. Under normal science conditions, the only problems which may be tackled are those to which the theory and methods apply. In any specialty there will be a class of problems that is *permissible* (because those problems are held to be within the compass of current theory and methods), and a much larger class that is *impermissible.* However, Kuhn himself does not make a systematic distinction between those problems that are seen as merely *permissible,* and those that are thought of as *important, urgent,* or *pressing.* He does not deal in general terms with areas of work, methods, or theories, that are thought of as *highly preferred,* and those that are *less highly preferred.* [7] However, it will be shown that an understanding of the structure of such more or less preferred areas, methods, or theories, allows the sociologist to distinguish between different types of paradigm-bound specialties, and specialties at different stages of intellectual development.

The research actions of a scientist may therefore be classified in two respects (or along two 'axes') by his colleagues — permissible/impermissible, and preferred/less preferred. Once it is deemed permissible, a piece of work may be seen as lying anywhere along the latter axis. To a large extent, different factors determine whether a piece of work is seen, on the one hand, as permissible or impermissible and, on the other, as more or less preferred. This study of protein crystallography permits some of the causes and consequences of the application of this second distinction to be worked out in a case study.

In order to distinguish between the two 'axes' consider a simple model where the actor interacts with both members and non-members of his own specialty (see figure 1). His decision about what constitutes permissible work is made exclusively through interaction with members of his own specialty, for they alone have the ability to judge the competence with which the actor makes use of shared theory or methods. However, his decision as to what constitute the preferred types of work is made in interaction with a much wider range of actors. This is because such a decision depends both on the importance of the work if it is successfully completed, and an estimate of its difficulty. The importance of the work depends on the views of significant others both inside and outside the specialty. Assessment of the difficulty is a more technical problem, however, which can in general only be judged by specialty members: while very difficult work may be highly rewarded if it is successful, it will not constitute a preferred type of work if specialty members judge that the chances of success are very low indeed. Thus, while the two axes are linked, the permissible/impermissible judgment is made by a more restricted range of actors than the preferred/less preferred decision. This has important consequences for both the direction of cultural change in the specialty, and the new areas brought under investigation.

Few specialties are as discrete and culturally unified as the model below implies. Nonetheless, the basis for solidarity within many specialties in real life, as well as in such a model, can be thought of as mechanical.[8] In science, mechanical solidarity may be defined as the development and maintenance of relationships which depend on shared standards and exemplars, and hence on a relatively high degree of consensus about theory and method. In the thirties, X-ray crystallography approxi-

FIGURE 1. *Factors Affecting the Scientific Actor's Choice of the Type of Work Undertaken*

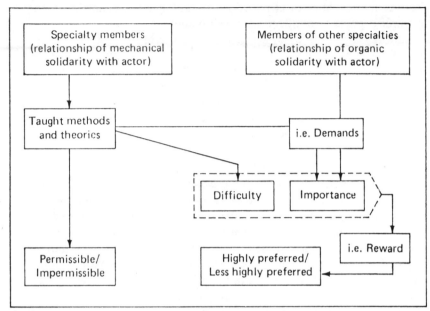

mated to a specialty whose members were held in relationship to one another on a basis of mechanical solidarity. Thus they used broadly the same theories and methods, passed innovations round the community, and fiercely objected to what they felt were deviant developments in crystallographic methods.

The interaction of protein crystallographers with interested non-crystallographers developed, in the first instance, on a basis of organic solidarity. In science, organic solidarity may be defined as an aspect of the division of labour in which scientists come into relationship with one another because one performs services which the other cannot easily carry out for himself. Thus, in the thirties, X-ray crystallographers found that their technique could be applied to a wide range of different crystals. Organic chemists, metallurgists, mineralogists, and protein chemists all at various times made use of the results of X-ray crystallographic investigation, and developed relationships with crystallographers that can broadly be defined as organic. Data presented below shows that certain non-crystallographers working on proteins thought that the investigation of proteins by means of X-rays was extremely important. If the model presented above is correct, then the appeals of such non-specialists were most likely to be listened to when they called for work which, in crystallographic terms, was neither 'too easy' nor 'too difficult' — for work, which, in other words, stretched the available techniques to their limits, but was none the less likely to be successful. In general, crystallographers worked on organic or inorganic molecules, or on metals. A few crystallographers, however, concentrated on proteins, which many of their colleagues thought presented virtually insoluble technical problems.

X-RAY CRYSTALLOGRAPHY

A Brief Background

X-ray crystallography is a technique used to determine the three-dimensional molecular structure of substances that can be wholly or partly crystallized.[9] Generally speaking, the more complicated the molecule, the less easy it is to determine its structure. This means that proteins (which have molecular weights of many thousands) are very difficult structures to solve.

X-ray diffraction was invented by a German physicist, von Laue, in 1912, but its potentialities for crystal structure determination were most systematically developed in Britain by W. H. and W. L. Bragg (father and son), who each headed a major school of X-ray crystallography between the wars.[10] W. H. Bragg was head of a school at University College, London, and then, after 1923, at the Royal Institution. The workers in this group concentrated on the structures of organic crystals, while W. L. Bragg and his group (which was located until 1937 at the Manchester University Physics Department) concentrated on inorganic structures. Before the First World War it was a major feat to solve the very simple structure of rocksalt, but after 1918 the workers in these two schools developed the technique and applied it to structures of increasing complexity.

The Braggs trained a number of important students, and some of these went on to set up their own schools of X-ray crystallography in Britain.[11] Almost all British X-ray crystallographers in the thirties were either the Braggs' pupils, or their pupils' pupils. Most of these workers contributed to the fields of organic, inorganic, and metal crystallography. A few — notably Astbury, Bernal, and at a much later date, W. L. Bragg — became interested in the structure of proteins.

TABLE 1. *Some Important Students and Collaborators of W. H. Bragg*

1921-1928	W. T. Astbury
1922-1927	K. Lonsdale (also 1932-)
1923-1927	J. D. Bernal
1924-1926	A. L. Patterson
1926-1928	J. M. Robertson (also 1930-)
1927-1929	E. G. Cox

TABLE 2. *Some Important Students and Collaborators of W. L. Bragg*

1919-1936	R. W. James
1923-	A. J. Bradley
1936-	H. Lipson
1934-1936	I. Fankuchen
1937-	M. Perutz
1965-	D. C. Phillips

The work on proteins started in Britain in the late twenties. Introduced to the problem of fibre structures by W. H. Bragg in 1926, Astbury left the Royal Institution in 1928 to become a lecturer in Textile Physics in the Department of Textile Industries, University of Leeds.[12] In partial collaboration with wool chemists, he started an energetic X-ray and chemical study of the structure of the fibrous protein, keratin.[13] Bernal left the Royal Institution in 1927, and moved to the Cavendish Laboratory, Cambridge. He did work on various molecules, both organic and biological, and began serious work on the structure of crystalline protein in 1934.[14]

Therefore, by 1934, two crystallographers — Astbury and Bernal — were working on proteins. Together with some of their pupils they were the only British crystallographers who did important work on proteins in the thirties — a monopoly that was in large measure maintained until the fifties. The most important protein crystallographers, together with an indication of master-pupil relationships, are shown in figure 2.[15]

While the overall size of the British crystallographic community was small in the thirties (perhaps numbering less than fifty university researchers), only about half a dozen members chose proteins as a major object of study. The other crystallographers worked on increasingly complicated organic molecules, on inorganic crystals (including minerals), and on metal structures. A full understanding of their chosen

FIGURE 2. *The Most Important British Protein Crystallographers, indicating Master-Pupil Relationships*

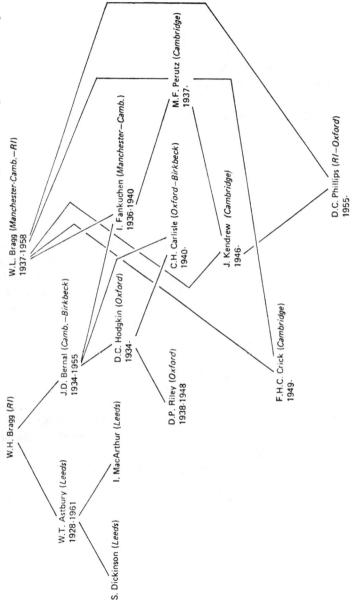

Key:

All the above, with the exception of W. H. Bragg worked on proteins; approximate dates of interest in proteins are given under each name; lines indicate approximate master-pupil relationships; main locations of work are indicated after each name. This list includes all important crystalline protein crystallographers in Britain before 1950.

subject matters is beyond the scope of this paper. The protein crystallographers alone will be considered, and their choice of subject matter alone will be discussed. What pressures did the crystallographers feel that led them either to work on, or to avoid, proteins? To answer this question it is necessary to have some knowledge of the considerable technical difficulties in protein crystallography.

Perceived Technical Problems in Protein Crystallography in 1939

In the thirties a number of major technical problems lay between the crystallographers and successful protein structure determination.[16] These can be summarized as follows:

The Preparation of Satisfactory Crystals
Many protein crystals are unstable and require special conditions. Until the work of Bernal in 1934, no good diffraction photographs of single crystals had been obtained, and it was one of Bernal's major triumphs that he was able to show that if he took diffraction pictures while the crystals were suitably humid, the photographs revealed the existence of detail right down to the atomic level.[17] Even after 1934 it was not easy to obtain good diffraction pictures, such were the difficulties of handling crystals, and the lengths of exposures required.[18]

The Phase Problem
This is central to X-ray crystallography. In order to determine the structure of a crystal from its diffraction effect, it is necessary to know not only the intensities and positions of the refracted beams, but also their relative phases. There is no direct way of measuring these. Many methods have been used to get round this difficulty. In early days trial-and-error methods were used, working from postulated models; but this was only possible with quite simple crystals, since the chance of successfully guessing the structure of a complicated molecule was obviously very remote.

In the middle thirties an American crystallographer, A. L. Patterson, developed a method which partially avoided the phase problem by using the intensities of the reflected beams alone. While this method worked well for simple crystals, and crystals that contained a few heavy atoms, it did not help greatly in situations where crystals were very complicated. So although this method made pretty diagrams which were the subject of much controversy in the late thirties, many workers felt that it was not satisfactory as a direct means of solving protein structures.[19]

In the late thirties Bernal proposed two methods of evading the phase problem, both of which involved the Patterson method. They depended on the fact that it was possible to alter the intensities of reflections by taking X-ray pictures of crystals that varied slightly in certain respects only. Bernal hoped that this variation would be sufficient to indicate the phases of some of the reflections. The first method was the 'swelling and shrinking' method, which was used with relative lack of success for many years by Perutz. The second was the 'isomorphous replacement method'. This method, which was quite well known to organic crystallographers in the thirties, involves taking X-ray diffraction pictures of crystals identical in shape and molecular structure (i.e. isomorphous), but differing in that in one case a heavy atom is present, while in another case it is absent (or replaced by a further heavy atom). If the crystals are strictly isomorphous, then the positions of the diffracted beams do not alter, and only the intensities vary. Through study of these variations the phase contributions of the heavy atoms can be determined, and from this the phases of the reflections can be deduced. This method was proposed as a possible solution to the phase problem not only by Bernal, but also by Robertson, in 1939, although it was not used by Perutz until 1954.[20]

The Problem of Making Accurate Intensity Measurements of Large Numbers of Reflections
Proteins give many more X-ray reflections than small crystals, and although relatively accurate methods of intensity measurement were available in the thirties, the sheer numbers of reflections made the methods inadequate. This problem was only solved after the war through the work of Kendrew and Phillips.

The Problem of Data Handling
With thousands of reflections to be measured and processed, data handling and calculation problems became very considerable. This fundamental problem was solved in the fifties with the development of electronic computers.

Interpretation of Results
In the thirties it was not clear whether a protein electron density map would be interpretable, even when one was finally calculated.[21]

Thus, in 1939, the perceived problems of protein crystallography were very considerable. Each of these problems arose as a direct or indirect result of the immense size of even the smallest proteins, compared with other crystals being studied at the time. It is therefore not surprising that some crystallographers were pessimistic about the outcome of this work, and were unwilling to work in the area themselves.[22]

Technical Solidarity in the X-ray Crystallographic Community

Despite the special difficulties of working on proteins, the basic methods used were common to the entire crystallographic community. Although other workers had also specialized in particular crystal types, and there was always some adaptation of methods to cater for special conditions, none the less the basic crystallographic methods were uniform across the community. Thus, the work of the protein crystallographers depended on several crucial developments that had not been made in connection with proteins. (See figure 3). For example, all protein work used various adaptations of Fourier methods which were well known in the whole community, and had been developed primarily by W. L. Bragg and his collaborators in their work on minerals. One such adaptation, and a crucial one, was the Patterson method mentioned above. Patterson was not a protein crystallographer. Again, it was Robertson, an organic crystallographer, who most systematically developed the heavy atom and isomorphous replacement methods. While certain contributions (such as Bernal's work on wet proteins) were specifically developed in the context of protein crystallography, most of the basic routines and methods were common to the entire crystallographic community. Strong evidence for the fact that methods were widely shared and the object of great interest throughout the community, can be seen from the controversy which followed the deviant Patterson diagram interpretations and theories of protein structure advanced by the mathematician, D. Wrinch. Both W. L. Bragg and J. M. Robertson, neither of whom were protein workers, published criticisms of Wrinch's method. Bragg's contribution is particularly interesting, underlining the technical solidarity of the community. He wrote:

> Letters on the interpretation of Patterson Fourier syntheses (vector maps) have recently appeared in *Nature*. Is not the claim made or implied in these letters, that a new method of interpretation has been discovered, due to a misapprehension concerning the existing methods of crystal analysis?
>
> [That scattering matter is grouped in characteristic ways and hence makes Fourier methods soluble] has been the basis of crystal analysis

FIGURE 3.   *Some 'Critical Path' Contributions to the Solution of Protein*
Structures

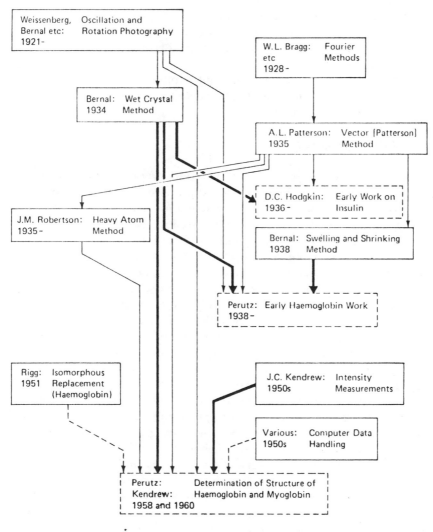

Key:

━━━━━━   Technical contributions from crystallographers working on proteins
────────   Technical contributions from crystallographers not working on proteins
─ ─ ─ ─   Technical contributions from non-crystallographers

for the last twenty-five years, and is so well known that it is generally taken for granted and not specifically referred to in recent work. . . .

Exaggerated claims as to the novelty of the geometrical method of approach and the certainty with which a proposed detailed model is confirmed are too likely, at this stage, to bring discredit upon the patient work which has placed the analysis of simpler structures upon a sure foundation.[23]

In addition, the general lack of deviant published work is in itself evidence for the existence of standards, both internalised and rigidly enforced through informal channels.

The Protein Community

In the thirties, therefore, there was a crystallographic community which included workers who chose to work on proteins. In addition, however, there was also what will be called a 'protein community'. This is defined as that group of scientists who were interested in proteins from the structural, chemical, and genetical points of view, and who were in contact with scientists from other disciplinary backgrounds who were also interested in such questions. Astbury, Bernal, and a few of their followers, were active in both the protein and the crystallographic communities, and in fact they were the only active members of both.

As the argument concerns the actions of certain protein crystallographers and their interaction with non-crystallographers, no systematic analysis of 'protein community' membership and its intellectual origins is required here. It is sufficient to state that for a period of time protein crystallographers were in contact with other protein workers who were *not* crystallographers. This can be demonstrated in a number of ways. For example, there were three cross-disciplinary meetings in 1938: the so-called 'Klampenborg' meeting; the Cold Spring Harbor Symposium on Quantitative Biology (on protein chemistry in 1938); a Royal Society discussion on the protein molecule.[24] The first of these was a small elite meeting with about a dozen participants, two of whom, Astbury and Bernal, were X-ray crystallographers, and there were also quantum physicists, cytologists, geneticists, and an embryologist. At this meeting the chemical nature of the gene was discussed (it being thought that the gene was probably largely made of protein). At the second meeting (which was much larger) there were scientists from many different disciplinary backgrounds. Astbury attended this meeting, as did a German fibre crystallographer, K. H. Meyer; D. Wrinch (the British mathematician mentioned above in connection with her unpopular theories on protein structure) was also present. Both Astbury and Wrinch played an important role at the meeting, presenting papers, and taking a vigorous part in many of the discussions. The third of these meetings, which was also fairly large, was dominated by physical chemists, X-ray crystallographers, and protein chemists.[25] Astbury, Bernal, and Hodgkin were the three British crystallographers who read papers, while Meyer and Boehm, X-ray crystallographers from Germany, also spoke. In addition, Wrinch read a paper.

Thus at these meetings certain crystallographers were in touch with biochemists and physical chemists. In addition to such formal meetings there was a small informal group of British scientists called the 'Theoretical Biology Club' which met in the thirties. The members of this group, which was cross-disciplinary, were interested in biology at a molecular level. They were Joseph Needham (embryologist), J. D. Bernal (crystallographer), Dorothy Wrinch (mathematician), Max Black (philosopher), C. H. Waddington (embryologist), J. H. Woodger (philosopher), Woodger's wife, Eden Woodger, and B. P. Weisner (zoologist).[26]

Bernal and Astbury were thus both active in the protein community. Hodgkin was also in contact with scientists from other backgrounds. She knew Wrinch, attended the lectures of both F. G. Hopkins and J. Needham, was friendly with N. W. Pirie, the virologist, and knew of the ideas that were being put forward in the Theoretical Biology Club at the time.[27]

Fankuchen was also a member of the protein community. He collaborated with Bawden, Pirie, and Bernal in 1936 in a paper on plant viruses and with Bernal alone in 1941 in a paper where the authors make a complete review of the work on virus structures, citing (among others) Bawden, Pirie, Eriksson-Quensel (physicist), Stanley (protein chemist), and Wyckoff (crystallographer).[28]

Attitudes to Protein Crystallography

It has been shown that a number of crystallographers developed an interest in the structure of proteins in the thirties. This group expanded, both by the addition of students and, to a very limited extent, by migration (see note 70, below), in the late thirties and forties. In the forties a number of crystallographers worked on proteins, but in different ways and with differing emphases. It is convenient to characterize attitudes to this work under seven headings, by referring to key workers or groups.

M. F. Perutz was a student of W. L. Bragg, Bernal, and Fankuchen in the late thirties. He and his post-war collaborator, J. Kendrew, developed a direct crystallographic approach to the proteins, hoping to improve methods to a point where success would be achieved.

The titles and contents of Perutz' papers indicate that his approach was almost always *crystallographic.* His papers, which are briefly described below, nearly always involve the study of haemoglobin using technqiues from crystallography — the use of Patterson analyses, difference Pattersons, swelling and shrinking methods, and so on.[29] The first, written jointly with Bernal and Fankuchen in 1938, gave unit cell dimensions and molecular weights of haemoglobin and chymotrypsin.[30] The second (1939) was on the absorption spectra of haemoglobin; the third and fourth papers (1942) presented two-dimensional Patterson projections for met- and oxyhaemoglobin.[31] Further papers in 1946 and 1947 dealt with wartime work on the swelling and shrinking of haemoglobin, and this subject was developed in a paper published in 1949, when he advanced an hypothesis that the interior of the molecule contained rod-like areas of high electron density.[32]

The use of Patterson projections was important in this work, although it did not lead to a solution until used in conjunction with heavy atom analysis. Thus, W. L. Bragg has written:

> For a long time the idea that the molecule contained some kind of regular structure of protein chains, which would give a strongly defined character to a Patterson synthesis was a guiding star which encouraged the investigations. As events turned out, it was a false star.[33]

Perutz continued to work on the swelling and shrinking method until 1954, when he became aware that the isomorphous replacement method might be possible in haemoglobin. From 1954 until 1960 he worked on a 5·5Å resolution map of haemoglobin, and in 1968 a 2.8Å resolution map was published.[34] His collaborator, Kendrew, was the first to structure a crystalline protein, myoglobin, in 1957.[35]

Perutz' approach was direct, first by means of Patterson methods and the swelling and shrinking method and later by means of heavy atom replacements. While he had contact with non-crystallographers, these contacts did not lead him to use non-crystallographic techniques, as can be seen from a study of his published papers. Sometimes the contacts with outsiders were important, but for crystallographic reasons:

> I was sent a set of reprints from A. Rigg who was working at Harvard,

who had made a mercury compound of haemoglobin and showed that it was still physiologically active. I jumped at this immediately. . . . These papers had been in the *Journal of General Physiology* which I would not normally have read. They were sent because I had been working on sickle cell anaemia which Rigg was interested in.[36]

Perutz did not believe that solving the structure of the proteins would be easy. Indeed, at the beginning, he did not even formulate it as a possibility:

Little was known about proteins, their shape was not known. Others were doing work on their sedimentation rates, and their viscosity, and the question arose as to whether X-ray analysis might be of any use. Certainly, at the beginning, I did not think of solving the complete structure.[37]

His persistence is interesting, because many crystallographers looked upon protein work with considerable scepticism. Kendrew, speaking about his arrival in Cambridge to join Perutz after the war, has said:

Max [Perutz] had been on this thing for a very long time, he started before the war, and really, it's incredible actually, how persistent that man's been in following this thing through, very much further than the rest.[38]

Kendrew went on to note how doubtful many crystallographers were about the chances of success of this work, and Perutz has also noted that most crystallographers were still sceptical even after the first heavy atom replacements were prepared.[39]

Dorothy Hodgkin also advocated and worked on an exclusively crystallographic approach to the full protein molecule.[40] But her strategy was to develop skills and techniques by applying them to a range of non-protein molecules of gradually increasing difficulty. Thus, she has said:

My own idea about how to make progress was to do simpler things first, but I have never at any time completely stopped work on insulin. I held it by me while trying out methods of structural analysis on simpler molecules — the sterols, penicillin — but I suppose that I always saw the structure of insulin as a goal.

Hodgkin has not discussed the scepticism of most crystallographers towards the work on proteins, and this may be because she was less exposed to these doubts, working as she was, with spectacular success, through a series of simpler molecules.[41] She never lost faith that the structures of the proteins would be determined because she could see that the methods were always developing. Her main interest was in developing the heavy atom method, partly because, unlike Perutz, she was never diverted on to the swelling and shrinking method, which was clearly unsuitable in the case of insulin. Her attitude to non-crystallographers was clear:

> Of course we were interested in other work on proteins, but we really did feel that nothing except X-ray analysis would give us what we wanted. The kind of information that was wanted was the organisation of the molecules, and X-ray crystallography was the only way we were going to get it.

J. D. Bernal believed that a direct crystallographic approach to the proteins was possible but that to achieve success it would be necessary to develop certain methods (notably computing and photography). This belief was mixed with another — that it was important to use all possible sources of information, no matter what their disciplinary origin, in order to elucidate the structure of the proteins. Bernal was, however, very interested in crystallography and the advance of knowledge through crystallographic techniques. Thus even when he concentrated most strongly on proteins, he none the less did other crystallographic work.

Bernal outlined his approach in a lecture given at the Royal Institution in 1939.[42] Here he pointed out that three relatively new methods — centrifugal, electrical, and X-ray — had provided much new data on protein structures. Up until that point X-ray diffraction had been most useful in disproving hypothetical structures, but unless the phase problem could be solved it was not clear how it could make a more positive contribution. He mentioned the swelling and shrinking and isomorphous replacement techniques as two possible ways of getting round the phase problem and concluded with an appeal for more cross-disciplinary collaboration:

> The picture thus presented is far from being a finished or even a satisfactory one. The crucial fact that requires elucidation is the precise mode of folding or coiling of the peptide chains, and for this we may have to wait for some considerable time, until the technique of X-ray and other methods have been advanced much further than at present. The problem of the protein structure is now a definite and not unattainable goal, but for success it requires a degree of collaboration between research workers which has not yet been reached. Most of the work on proteins at present is unco-ordinated; different workers examine different proteins by different techniques, whereas a concentrated and planned attack would probably save much effort which is now wasted, and lead to an immediate clarifying of the problem.[43]

But although Bernal supported the development of cross-disciplinary collaboration, his own writing on the relationship between protein chemistry and X-ray crystallography was not always consistent. With hindsight he was to write:

> By 1940 it was clear that a successful attack on the complete protein structure could be made, but there were still many difficulties. Two modes of attack suggested themselves: the first was a straightforward X-ray crystallographic study of crystalline protein, using all the techniques of an advanced crystal analysis. Computers were not available for this until much later, in the mid-1950s. The second was a model-building method based on an exact knowledge of the structure of amino acids and smaller peptides themselves and an attempt to build up the protein a priori and then check the structure by X-ray methods. I remember very well discussing the problem with Pauling just before the war. He was in favour of the second method, which I thought indirect and liable to take a very long time.[44]

Thus, Bernal thought that a direct crystallographic approach to protein structure allied to other chemical and physical methods, was the best way of ensuring success. It is possible that he held this view because he believed, or at least hoped, that the structure of proteins would turn out to be relatively simple and regular.[45]

His feeling about the direction in which protein crystallography should move was clear. After the war his approach was described in the following words:

> Professor Bernal took the view, in the light of early experience, that a direct attack using existing methods alone would be futile, but that what was needed was a thoroughly well-prepared and long-term approach, bringing to bear on the problem new methods which would themselves require new research to develop. The two chief needs at that time seemed to be the improvement, on the one hand, of experimental techniques and, on the other, of methods of computation. The first called for the development of more powerful X-ray tubes capable of being used for very small crystals and also for improved methods of detecting and measuring the diffracted X-rays. The second called for new and rapid methods of reducing enormous masses of data obtainable from complex crystals, particularly proteins, and for shortening the exhausting work of deducing the structure from them.[46]

Thus, at least in the post-war period, Bernal sought to develop crystallographic methods — and this was true despite his interest in collaboration with workers from other disciplines. He was always first and foremost a crystallographer, as can be seen from the other crystallographic work carried out in his laboratory after 1945. This work was often of practical application, including X-ray studies of cement and concrete formation, coal oxidation, flour structure, and fuel ash.[47]

The attitudes of Perutz, Bernal, and Hodgkin to protein crystallography were not in all cases mutually exclusive. They probably appear more distinct in the above account than in fact they were, and it is doubtful whether they should be seen as having viewpoints that were seriously incompatible. Their views, and particularly that of Bernal, may be contrasted with those of the American X-ray crystallographer and structural chemist, Pauling.

Linus Pauling exercised considerable influence on protein crystallography in the USA and particularly in his own institution, the California Institute of Technology. He argued that the best way to make progress was to carry out crystallographic studies of the component parts of proteins, and he thought that the direct approach of Perutz, Hodgkin and Bernal was unlikely to succeed.[48] He appears to have advocated this approach partly because of his background in structural chemistry, which led him to place much more reliance on model building than any of the British crystallographers. Bernal has written:

> Pauling was shocked by the freedom with which the X-ray crystallographers of the time, including particularly Astbury, played with the intimate chemical structure of their models. They seemed to think that if the atoms were arranged in the right order and about the right distance apart, that was all that mattered, that no further restrictions need to be put on them.[49]

Pauling's approach was fruitful in that from this study he developed his hypothesis for the structure of the alpha-helix. In the end however, important though this was, it was by direct crystallographic methods of the sort originally envisaged by Bernal that the structures of the crystalline proteins were elucidated.

W. T. Astbury took yet another approach to protein crystallography. Unlike Bernal and the others, he reached a point in the development of his interests at which he could no longer be called, first and foremost, a crystallographer. He did not abandon the use of crystallography, but began to make major use of other methods in his work, and started to look upon himself as a 'molecular biologist'. The reason for this almost certainly lies in his choice of subject matters — crystalline techniques did not allow for the complete elucidation of the structure of fibrous proteins because those proteins could not be rendered into completely crystalline form. Furthermore, this fact was evident from a very early stage. Although Astbury at no point explicitly called himself a molecular biologist, his general attitude is revealed in the 1951 Harvey lecture:

> The name 'molecular biology' seems to be passing now into fairly common use, and I am glad of that because, though it is unlikely I invented it first, I am fond of it and have long tried to propagate it. It implies not so much a technique as an approach, an approach from the viewpoint of the so-called basic sciences with the leading idea of searching below the large-scale manifestations of classical biology for the corresponding molecular plan. It is concerned primarily with the *forms* of biological molecules, and with the evolution, exploitation, and ramification of those forms in the ascent to higher and higher levels of organisation. Molecular biology is predominantly three-dimensional and structural — which does not mean, however, that it is merely a refinement of morphology. It must of necessity enquire at the same time into genesis and function.
>
> I think that it might be worthwhile explaining how I myself, classified primarily as a physicist, came to find myself in this galley — how I 'discovered' molecular biology, if you like.[50]

In the course of the above lecture he mentioned several 'molecular biological' techniques in relation to a discussion of work on rheumatoid subcutaneous nodules. The idea was to 'correlate findings of four methods: (a) classical histology; (b) X-ray diffraction analysis; (c) electron microscope; and (d) microbiochemistry; the whole in relation to clinical observations besides'.[51]

Astbury worked until 1945 in the Department of Textile Industries at the University of Leeds. In 1945 he was made Professor of the newly formed Department of Biomolecular Structure. While he was proud of this name, he would have preferred it to have been called the Department of Molecular Biology.[52]

Astbury's move towards molecular biology can also be seen in the titles of his papers. He wrote no papers on biological molecules before 1928, and only two non-biological papers thereafter. While crystallography was the most important technique in his early work, electron microscopy also became important in the forties. He wrote many papers from 1929 onwards on the theory of protein structure, and although these in part rest on crystallographic data, their contribution is normally at a more general level, and they use data from various sources.[53]

On several occasions Astbury outlined the special difficulties of fibre crystallography. For example, in 1935 he opened an important paper with such a discussion and suggested that best progress must depend on the interpretation of X-ray photographs in relation to other chemical and physical data.[54] It is clear from other quotations that he valued collaboration with chemists and others from different disciplinary backgrounds.[55]

Crystallographers who were not themselves working on proteins also had a variety of attitudes to this work. Many thought that the technical problems were so great that it was better to stick to simpler molecules. This attitude was fairly common in the forties and early fifties. At the same time, there was undoubtedly some support and encouragement from certain crystallographers. Thus J. M. Robertson, a leading organic crystallographer who never worked on proteins himself, suggested in 1939 that heavy atom replacement might be a possible method of determining the structure of proteins.[56] He also maintained a small amount of protein work in his department at Glasgow in recent years, so he cannot be counted among those whom Phillips, a leading protein crystallographer of the fifties and sixties, called the 'scoffers'.[57]

It is not possible to tell from the available data whether Robertson's attitude was widely shared. However, in the post-war period, many non-protein crystallographers were certainly doubtful about the work on proteins. Frank expressions of such scepticism are not easily discovered, now that the protein structures have been determined. However, Phillips, discussing a decision he made in 1954 to join a team of protein workers at the Royal Institution, recently noted:

> Many of the professional crystallographers were extremely sceptical about the whole business. They regarded it as a complete waste of time. If any of the protein crystallographers made a mistake, then there was much jeering. I was aware of this feeling because Howells, the other PhD student at Cardiff, had gone to join Perutz. In the US I found that there was more scepticism — and I got to know Harker at Brooklyn and his work on ribonuclease, and I found that he was also being jeered at. So I suppose that I began to regard protein as a sort of challenge, and when Bragg's letter arrived, I took the offer up.[58]

This scepticism has also been mentioned by Perutz and Kendrew, and even W. L. Bragg, who was a staunch supporter of the work of Perutz and Kendrew, judged this work in 1947 as having 'a chance of success indistinguishable from zero'.[59] Kendrew remembers that even Fankuchen, who worked on proteins in the prewar period, became openly sceptical after the war, although he was quick to admit that his scepticism had been mistaken when the structure of myoglobin was determined in 1958.[60]

The scepticism did not have much effect on the extent of professional communication between the protein workers and other crystallographers. Phillips has noted:

> I went on going to scientific meetings. I went to the IUC International Meeting at Paris in 1954, but I didn't go to the one in Montreal in 1957 — I suppose that might be a sign of being a little more cut off. By the 1960 meeting at Cambridge we had results, and the scoffers were silenced. And I certainly went on going to the X-ray Analysis Group meetings at London — and there was certainly general exchange of techniques and views. I don't think we were really cut off.[61]

Similar attitudes have been expressed by Hodgkin.[62]

A final set of attitudes towards protein crystallography were expressed by *non-crystallographers interested in protein structure.* Some non-crystallographers attached great importance to this work. Thus, Needham wrote in 1936: 'Of the new means of heightening our acuity of vision, the most powerful is without doubt the use of X-radiation. . . .'[63] Svedberg, the physical chemist, in his opening address to the 1938 Royal Society discussion on the protein molecule, wrote:

> X-ray analysis of protein crystals and semi-solid protein deposits in living organisms has yielded results of the highest importance for the elucidation of the structure of the protein molecule.[64]

Finally the virologist, F. C. Bawden, wrote in 1942:

> Of the many techniques introduced into research on viruses during recent years, none has aroused more interest than those of the crystallographer. The value of these techniques in such work is amply shown by three recent papers by Prof. J. D. Bernal and Dr. I. Fankuchen.[65]

Several empirical points have been made in this narrative:
— A brief summary of the development of X-ray crystallography in Britain has been given, and it has been shown that a sub-set of the crystallographic community concentrated its attention on the study of proteins in the thirties. This sub-set was small and in some ways atypical.
— Technical problems of protein crystallography have been described, as these were perceived in 1939. Solution of some of these problems was

held to be especially difficult, so that while it can be argued that protein crystallographers were using techniques that were 'permissible', they were also, for many of their colleagues, doing a 'non-preferred' type of work.
— Evidence of mechanical solidarity in the X-ray community, and in particular between some protein crystallographers and certain other crystallographers, has been presented.
— It was suggested that some protein crystallographers participated in what was described as a 'protein community'.
— An account of the variety of approaches, attitudes, and stratagems of those who took up protein crystallography has been given; additionally, the attitidues of some of those, both crystallographers and others, who did not, were outlined.

DISCUSSION

The protein crystallographers were constrained in their use of techniques by their relationship (essentially one of mechanical solidarity) with the crystallographic community. That is to say, they tended to sanction the use of 'outside' techniques. Several of them pioneered acceptable crystallographic innovations (Bernal, Perutz, Hodgkin) and they all made use of crystallographic techniques. Again, with the exception of Astbury, none of them made important use of non-crystallographic techniques. The X-ray methods tended to remain stable or to show relatively direct development (see figure 3) and when Wrinch, a worker peripheral to the crystallographic community, proposed a deviant development of the Patterson method, this innovation was strongly criticized in print by leading members of the crystallographic community. The very absence of any deviant use of methods can be seen as evidence for the strong basis of mechanical solidarity in the community. It was through such technical and mechanical solidarity that the definition of 'permissible' and 'impermissible' in the crystallographic community was developed.

The protein crystallographers were rewarded by the protein community for successful work in structuring, or providing clues to the structure of proteins. Clearly, these rewards would no longer have been forthcoming if they had abandoned their work on proteins. The relationship (one of organic solidarity in the first instance) was one of the factors affecting their definition of the preferred types of work. In addition, however, other members of the crystallographic community, through their own estimate of what was too difficult or too easy in crystallographic terms, contributed their definitions to the perceptions of what was preferred. It has been shown that there was a wide range of opinions among other crystallographers about the advisability of working on proteins. While some thought that such work was feasible, others, particularly in the forties and fifties, seem to have felt that it was likely to prove a waste of time. In a sense then, for many in the crystallographic community, protein work was very much 'non-preferred'.

The dominant theme in the history of British X-ray crystallography has been the consistent development of methods and their application to more and more complicated crystals. Thus the primitive methods used by W. L. Bragg before 1914 were only capable of solving the structures of very simple molecules — those with one parameter.[66] More sophisticated methods were developed during the twenties, thirties, and forties, to deal with more complicated molecules. By the late thirties, structures with about a hundred parameters were being determined but the proteins, with thousands of parameters, were more difficult again.

However, all the protein crystallographers, with the possible exception of Astbury, were centrally concerned with the development of crystallographic methods. Perutz, perhaps the most optimistic, developed swelling and shrinking methods as far as possible before having his attention drawn to the isomorphous replacement method. Both these methods can be seen as articulations of the central standards of X-ray crystallography, depending as they do on Fourier methods and Patterson syntheses.[67] In Kuhnian terms, the central standards can be seen as constituting exemplary procedures for deriving structures from diffraction patterns. As such they related to conditions for taking diffraction readings, and conditions for moving from photographs to structures. In their simplest abstracted form they constituted symbolic generalizations such as Bragg's Law, and rules for taking account of factors such as temperature effects and intensity measurements.[68] The problem for Perutz was to develop and apply available law sketches and exemplars to situations beyond the routine. The process can be traced in the papers mentioned above.

Hodgkin, unlike Perutz, developed methods in relation to easier problems with simpler molecules. This involved a similar extension of symbolic generalizations through the development of new and revised exemplary applications to situations that were novel in certain respects. Bernal, whose appreciation of the problem was in some important ways similar, also sought to develop methods. Pauling's attitude, unlike any of the three just mentioned, was that it was best to use existing exemplary procedures in X-ray crystallography to determine the structures of component parts of the proteins. Once having determined the structures of these parts, he proposed to apply existing exemplary procedures developed in physical chemistry to build models of whole proteins.

Thus Bernal, Hodgkin, and Perutz were all crystallographers who worked in relation to crystallographic standards to develop and articulate the standards in order to solve protein structures. Even Pauling's approach was in part crystallographic. The three British crystallographers all therefore maintained relationships with the rest of the X-ray crystallographic community (on the basis of mechanical solidarity), as well as relationships (on the basis of organic solidarity) with some members of the protein community. For Astbury however, this relationship with other crystallographers was not so easy to maintain. This was partly because of the nature of the subject matter that he studied. If crystalline proteins constituted a permissible area of work for X-ray crystallographers, then fibrous proteins verged on the impermissible. Thus Bernal, remembering Astbury's move to Leeds in 1928, wrote:

> I remember at the time how shocked some of us were at Astbury going into this completely complex and very mundane field. We felt that it was very premature — let us find the structure of regular things first before we tackle the irregular ones.[69]

As might be expected, Astbury was enthusiastic about interdisciplinary communication and the use of all possible approaches to protein structure. He came to use other techniques (notably electron microscopy) and no longer thought of himself primarily as a crystallographer, but rather as a molecular biologist. It is suggested that Astbury, unlike the other crystallographers, became primarily attached to a barely permissible subject matter and through it to the protein community. Although he continued to use X-ray crystallography, this wawas only one of a number of different possible techniques. The inadequacy of X-ray crystallographic methods by themselves to determine the structure of the fibrous proteins was certainly one of the most important reasons for this change. Another important factor was that his colleagues, protein chemists and others, came from wide and varied backgrounds.

All of the above workers, through their interaction with the members of the protein community, received positive sanctioning or 'rewards' for their contributions to knowledge about the structures of proteins.

In the crystallographic community, the basis of mechanical solidarity rested on the correct application of a sophisticated technique to the solution of crystal structures. In this sense, despite the fact that there was some subject differentiation within the specialty, most X-ray crystallo-graphers had no necessary attachment to a particular kind of molecule.[70] In other specialties (perhaps the phage group at an early stage, and almost certainly the protein community discussed above), the basis of solidarity may rest on a concern about a specific subject matter or problem, which may be studied by means of several techniques.[71] It may be legitimate for the practitioner to learn to apply new methods. (The case of Astbury obviously springs to mind.) In yet other specialties (for example German physics in the twenties) commitment to and the development of theory may be the main object, and the relevant subject matters and techniques may change from time to time.[72]

It is now possible to distinguish between three different types of spe-cialty. A *technique-* or *methods-based specialty* (of which X-ray crystallography is an example) constitutes an interacting group of scientists, whose solidarity rests on the basis of shared scientific gadgetry and its development. Misuse of the method is liable to result in severe nega-tive sanctioning for the deviant, while preferred subject matters are defined only indirectly in relation to the strongly held methodological standards. Only those exemplars which can be employed in relation to the gadgetry are used. *Theory-based specialties* are defined in terms of a shared formalism — members are those whose main standards concern theory and its development, and exemplars relating to various gadgetries and problems will arise out of that central concern with theory. *Subject matter specialties* have as members those who work on a particular subject matter or problem. Members of such a specialty are prepared to use a variety of techniques and theories, none of which may be preferred, in general.[73]

Theory- and methods-based specialties constitute communities where the basis of solidarity is mechanical. They depend on received achieve-ments, which are sufficiently well specified to constitute a reasonably clear guide to action. In Mullins' scheme they represent specialties at either 'cluster' or 'specialty' stage, but not earlier. Subject matter special-ties arise on a basis of organic solidarity. They depend, that is, on the identification of a shared problem, and hence correspond most closely to Mullins' 'network' stage of specialty development.

CONCLUSION

This paper has attempted to demonstrate that detailed analysis of conceptual change indicates that important differences may exist between specialties. These differences affect the manner in which theory and methods are chosen and developed. The next research problem that suggests itself is to explore the way in which a mechanical basis of solidarity is established (or alternatively not established) in a specialty.

The data in this paper offer certain clues. The 'protein community', for instance, was an apparently subject-based specialty. It seems that its members sought to determine the structure and function of proteins and of the genetic material. That is, they sought to establish successes or exemplary standards on which to base further work on proteins. It can thus be argued that the members sought to convert the basis of their solidarity from organic to mechanical. They did this by discussing each others' work, trying to see its relevance for their own problems, encouraging and rewarding those who made contributions from other specialties, and by seeking successes in the common area. Had these successes been available, then the conceptual basis for a new theory- or methods-based specialty would presumably have been available (and a serious conflict for those who were members of both the protein and crystallographic communities might have arisen).[74] We must now concentrate our efforts on understanding the process of negotiation that occurs in such problem-based specialties. Under what conditions are such negotiations successful? How is it that some specialties achieve maturity on a basis of shared methods and others on a basis of shared theories? To answer such questions, further detailed conceptual and social analysis is required.

John Law, Department of Sociology, University of Keele, Keele, Staffordshire ST5 5BG.

JOHN LAW read sociology at Cardiff and received his Ph.D. degree from the University of Edinburgh Science Studies Unit in 1972. Following a period as Simon Marks Research Fellow at the University of Manchester, he has since 1973 been a lecturer in sociology at the University of Keele. His current research includes work on the sociology of twentieth-century sedimentology.

NOTES

This article has already appeared in *Science Studies* 3 (1973) 275-304.
    1.   I would like to thank the following for advice, assistance, and material help: Mr S. B. Barnes, Dr A. P. M. Coxon, Dr D. O. Edge, and Dr T. R. Elsdale of the University of Edinburgh; Mr D. French of Lanchester Polytechnic; Dr M. J. Mulkay of the University of York; Dr N. C. Mullins of Indiana University.

I would also like to thank those crystallographers and molecular biologists who consented to be interviewed, and those who read early drafts of this paper.

The research was supported by a grant from the SSRC and was carried out at the Science Studies Unit, University of Edinburgh, and the Department of Sociology, University of Manchester.

2. N. C. Mullins, 'The Development of a Scientific Specialty: the Phage Group and the Origins of Molecular Biology', *Minerva* 10 (1972) 51-82.
3. T. S. Kuhn, *The Structure of Scientific Revolutions* (University of Chicago Press, 1970).
4. Mullins applies his scheme to ethnomethodology in a paper in *Science Studies* 3 (1973) 245-273.
5. Kuhn, *The Structure of Scientific Revolutions*.
6. See for example: W. O. Hagstrom, *The Scientific Community* (New York: Basic Books, 1965); D. J. de Solla Price, *Little Science, Big Science* (New York: Columbia University Press, 1963); D. Crane, 'Social Structure in a Group of Scientists: A Test of the "Invisible College" Hypothesis', *American Sociological Review* 34 (1969) 335-352 and *Invisible Colleges* (University of Chicago Press, 1972).
7. With the exception of anomalies, which are by definition problems of urgency and importance.
8. K. J. Downey, 'The Scientific Community: Organic or Mechanical?', *Sociological Quarterly* 10 (1969) 438-454. Although there are obvious similarities between Downey's use of the terms 'mechanical' and 'organic' and their use here, there are also differences. Thus it is not accepted here that divisions between disciplines constitute a mechanical segmentation, and it is suggested that specialties may have either a mechanical or an organic basis of solidarity. For a classic discussion of 'mechanical' and 'organic' solidarity, as these terms are traditionally used in sociology, see E. Durkheim, *The Division of Labour in Society* (New York: Free Press, 1964), especially chapters 2 and 3.
9. For a general history of X-ray crystallography see the excellent *Festschrift* volume: P. P. Ewald (ed.) *Fifty Years of X-ray Diffraction* (Utrecht: International Union of Crystallography, N. V. A. Oosthoek's Vitgeversmaatschappij, 1962).
10. See tables 1 and 2.
11. See tables 1 and 2.
12. Reluctant to go at first, Astbury was under some pressure from W. H. Bragg to take up this post. Bragg evidently did not share the scepticism of many of his junior colleagues about X-ray work on fibres.
13. For a detailed account of Astbury's career see J. D. Bernal, 'William Thomas Astbury', *Biographical Memoirs of Fellows of the Royal Society* 9 (1963) 1-35.
14. For an account of early work on crystalline proteins see D. C. Hodgkin / D. P. Riley, 'Some Ancient History of Protein X-ray Analysis', p.15ff. in: A. Rich / N. Davidson (eds.) *Structural Chemistry and Molecular Biology* (San Francisco: Freeman, 1968).
15. This figure must take the place of a detailed discussion of the social relationships, institutional locations, and numbers working on proteins in the thirties and forties.
16. I am indebted to several crystallographers for advice about this section.
17. J. D. Bernal / D. Crowfoot, 'X-ray Photographs of Crystalline Pepsin', *Nature* 133 (1934) 794-795.
18. Another problem concerning the preparation of crystals appeared at a later date, when it became necessary to prepare isomorphous derivatives; but this was not a problem that seriously concerned workers in the thirties.
19. See for example the correspondence which appeared in *Nature* in 1939, which is discussed further below: W. L. Bragg, 'Patterson Diagrams in Crystal Analysis', *Nature* 143 (1939) 73; J. D. Bernal, 'Vector Maps and the Cyclol Hypothesis', 74; J. M. Robertson, 'Vector Maps and Heavy Atoms in Crystal Analysis and the Insulin Structure', 75.

20.   This method was used successfully by Perutz and Kendrew in the late fifties.
21.   This problem turned out to be illusory, as interpretation proved to be much easier than expected.
22.   Important technical contributions to the solution of protein structures are indicated diagrammatically in figure 3.
23.   Bragg, 'Patterson Diagrams in Crystal Analysis'.
24.   See C. H. Waddington, 'Some European Contributions to the Prehistory of Molecular Biology', *Nature* 221 (1969) 318-321; *Cold Spring Harbor Symposium on Quantitative Biology* 6 (1938); 'Discussion on the Protein Molecule', *Proceedings of the Royal Society A* 170 (1939) 40-79.
25.   The following gave papers: physical chemists: G. S. Adair, J. F. Danielli, E. Gorter, K. O. Pedersen, F. J. Philpot, J. St. L. Philpot, P. A. Small, T. Svedberg; X-ray crystallographers: W. T. Astbury, J. D. Bernal, G. Boehm, D. Crowfoot (Hodgkin), K. H. Meyer; protein chemists: K. Linderström, A. Neuberger, S. J. Przlecki, H. H. Weber; immunologists: E. Holiday, J. Marrack; mathematician: D. Wrinch. (This classification is according to the nature of the paper contributed.)
26.   This list of names is deduced from the dedication (in initial form) given to the members of the Theoretical Biology Club by J. Needham in his book *Order and Life* (New Haven: Yale University Press, 1936).
27.   Interview with D. C. Hodgkin, 26 November 1970.
28.   F. C. Bawden / N. W. Pirie / J. D. Bernal / I. Fankuchen, 'Liquid Crystalline Substances from Infected Plants', *Nature* 138 (1936) 1051-1052; J. D. Bernal / I. Fankuchen, 'X-ray and Crystallographic Studies of Plant Virus Preparations', *Journal of General Physiology* 25 (1941) 111ff.
29.   Perutz has also published a handful of papers on one of his hobbies — glaciology.
30.   J. D. Bernal / I. Fankuchen / M. F. Perutz, 'An X-ray Study of Chymotrypsin and Haemoglobin', *Nature* 141 (1938) 523-524.
31.   M. F. Perutz, 'Absorption Spectra of Single Crystals of Haemoglobin in Polarized Light', *Nature* 143 (1939) 731-733; 'X-ray Analysis of Haemoglobin', *Nature* 149 (1942) 491-494; 'Crystal Structure of Oxyhaemoglobin', *Nature* 150 (1942) 324-325.
32.   M. F. Perutz, 'The Composition and Swelling Properties of Haemoglobin Crystals', *Transactions of the Faraday Society* 42B (1946) 187ff; J. Boyes-Watson / E. Davidson / M. F. Perutz, 'An X-ray Study of Horse Methaemoglobin', *Proceedings of the Royal Society A* 191 (1947) 83-132; M. F. Perutz, 'An X-ray Study of Horse Methaemoglobin II', *Proceedings of the Royal Society A* 195 (1949) 474-499.
33.   W. L. Bragg, 'First Stages in the X-ray Analysis of Proteins', *Reports on Progress in Physics* 28 (1965) 1-14.
34.   M. F. Perutz *et al.*, 'Three Dimensional Nourier Synthesis of Horse Oxyhaemoglobin at 2.8Å Resolution', *Nature* 219 (1968) 131-139.
35.   J. C. Kendrew *et al.*, 'A Three Dimensional Model of the Myoglobin Molecule Obtained by X-ray Analysis', *Nature* 181 (1958) 662-666.
36.   Interview with M. F. Perutz, July 1970.
37.   *Ibid.*
38.   In the BBC TV programme, 'The Prizewinners', 11 December 1962.
39.   M. F. Perutz, 'The MRC Unit for Molecular Biology', *New Scientist* 271 (1962) 208. There are two points to be remembered about this scepticism. Firstly, crystallographers had good reason to be sceptical until 1954, considering the known technical difficulties. Secondly, none of the 'second generation' of protein crystallographers were physicists or crystallographers by first training. Perutz, Kendrew and Hodgkin were all chemists, and Kendrew (speaking in the BBC radio programme, 'Masters of Science', 8 July 1969) has suggested that in his case initial ignorance of the technique was good as it prevented him from seeing all the difficulties.
40.   Much of the data in this section is taken from an interview with D. C. Hodgkin,

26 November 1970.
41. She was awarded a Nobel Prize for her work on vitamin B-12.
42. J. D. Bernal, 'Structures of Proteins', *Nature* 143 (1939) 663-667.
43. *Ibid.,* 668.
44. J. D. Bernal, 'The Pattern of Linus Pauling's Work in Relation to Molecular Biology', p. 372ff in: Rich / Davidson, *Structural Chemistry and Molecular Biology.*
45. See for example Bernal, 'Astbury', 23.
46. *Nuffield Foundation Report of Grants Made During the Ten Years April 1943-March 1953* (Oxford 1954) 106.
47. D. C. Hodgkin, 'Birkbeck, Science and History', First Bernal Lecture, 23 October 1969.
48. See for example his opening remarks in L. Pauling / R. B. Corey / H. R. Branson, 'The Structure of Proteins: two Hydrogen-Bonded Helical Configurations of the Polypeptide Chain', *Proceedings of the National Academy of Sciences* 37 (1951) 205ff.
49. Bernal, 'Astbury', 23.
50. W. T. Astbury, 'Adventures in Molecular Biology', *Harvey Society Series* 46 (1951) 3ff.
51. *Ibid.,* 35.
52. See 'William Thomas Astbury' p. 354ff. in: Ewald, *Fifty Years of X-ray Diffraction*; W. T. Astbury, 'Molecular Biology or Ultrastructural Biology?', *Nature* 190 (1961) 1124.
53. A relatively complete list of Astbury's papers is given at the end of Bernal, 'Astbury'.
54. W. T. Astbury / W. A. Sisson, 'X-ray Studies of the Structure of Hair, Wool and Related Fibres III — The Configuration of the Keratin Molecule and the Orientation of the Biological Cell', *Proceedings of the Royal Society A* 150 (1935) 533-551.
55. W. T. Astbury / S. Dickinson, 'X-ray Studies of Myosin', *Nature* 137 (1936) 909-910.
56. Robertson, 'Vector Maps and Heavy Atoms'.
57. Interviews with J. M. Robertson, 18 December 1970, and D. C. Phillips, 21 October 1970.
58. *Ibid.*
59. Perutz, 'The MRC Unit for Molecular Biology'; Kendrew in 'The Prizewinners' and 'Masters of Science'; W. L. Bragg, 'The X-ray Analysis of Biological Molecules', Address to the Lisbon Academy of Sciences (Lisbon, 1963).
60. Interview, 28 June 1970.
61. Interview, 21 October 1970.
62. Interview, 26 November 1970.
63. Needham, *Order and Life,* 142.
64. T. Svedberg, 'Discussion on the Protein Molecule', *Proceedings of the Royal Society A* 170 (1939) 40-56.
65. F. C. Bawden, 'Crystallography and Plant Viruses', *Nature* 149 (1942) 321-322.
66. In crystallography, the number of parameters indicates the number of atoms in the molecule whose positions are not determined by symmetry considerations. This number is therefore a guide to the difficulty of a structure determination.
67. In this discussion Kuhn's later vocabulary is used.
68. Kuhn, *The Structure of Scientific Revolutions,* 183.
69. Bernal, 'Astbury', 7.
70. Kendrew was an exception, having been brought to crystallography via an interest in proteins. He notes (personal communication) that for him crystallography was simply a tool — the tool that he judged would be the most effective in determining the structure of the proteins. Once having chosen crystallography, however, he notes that:
    It was obviously necessary to stick to the technique of choice. The technique in this case being a sophisticated and complex one, it was clearly an advantage to put all one's eggs in one basket. The fact was that *no* other technique showed any hope of

providing the kind of three-dimensional information that was wanted; to spend time on any other techniques would simply have been time wasted and a diversion from the real task in hand.

71.   See Mullins, 'The Phage Group'.

72.   The difference between German and British crystallography was always very striking. In Britain most people working on crystallography sought to develop more sophisticated methods and solve difficult structure types. In Germany crystallography was much studied while it cast light on the structure of the atom and other fundamental physical problems. It became much less popular when it was no longer relevant to physical problems. See for example: H. Mark, 'Recollections of Dahlem and Ludwigschafen', p. 605ff in: Ewald, *Fifty Years of X-ray Diffraction.*

73.   This is not dissimilar to the distinction that Pantin makes between 'restricted' and 'unrestricted' sciences. See C. F. A. Pantin, *The Relations Between the Sciences* (Cambridge University Press, 1968) 18.

74.   It should be noted, however, that no necessary progression from subject matter to theory- or methods-based specialties is entailed here. Indeed, the protein community, at least between the wars, emerged with no overall successes.

M. J. MULKAY/D. O. EDGE

Cognitive, Technical and Social Factors in the Growth of Radio Astronomy

THE EMERGENCE OF RADIO ASTRONOMY

Physicists first began to show an interest in extra-terrestrial radio emission towards the end of the last century.[1] In 1873 Maxwell had demonstrated that light waves were not the only form of electromagnetic radiation and that there must be a wide range of wavelengths on both sides of the optical spectrum. Fourteen years later Hertz was the first to observe the radio waves predicted by Maxwell. Within a few years of Hertz's discovery several attempts were made to detect radio emission from the sun, on the assumption that the brightest source of visual light could reasonably be expected to emit on radio wavelengths as well. These attempts, which continued throughout the 1890s in Europe and America, were entirely unsuccessful, owing to the crudity of available techniques. These failures appear to have deterred others from entering the field. It also seems likely that physicists decided not to pursue the matter further because they accepted Planck's radiation theory, which was announced in 1902 and from which it was calculated that extra-terrestrial radio emission would be undetectable. Whether these were the only reasons we cannot be sure, but it is clear that no further investigation took place in this area for the next thirty years.

In 1930, the Bell Telephone Company asked Jansky, one of their employees, to identify the sources of the static which interfered with radio-telephones. Using an antenna designed specially to locate the direction in which radio waves originated, Jansky found that, apart from local sources of static such as thunderstorms, his equipment recorded an unidentified steady hiss static. After more than a year of detailed study, he concluded that this was caused by radio emission from the Milky Way. This meant that our own galaxy was, in some way, a source of observable radio waves. The discovery of 'cosmic static' was quickly published and widely publicised by Bell Telephones. But there was no response from the academic community and in 1935 Jansky was told to turn his attention elsewhere. His work was not, however, entirely ignored. For Reber, an American radio engineer, decided that Jansky had made an important discovery and, in his spare time, Reber built equipment to measure and map the celestial distribution of the cosmic static. Unlike Jansky, Reber actually made personal contact with professional optical astronomers and, by the early 1940s, had interested several of them in his results. At this point, however, the world war temporarily stopped astronomical research in the US and elsewhere. After the war, despite the continued activity of Reber, the expansion of investigation into celestial radio emission was much slower in America than in several other countries, in particular, Australia and Britain. The reasons for this are complex. But of particular importance were certain technical innovations and discoveries arising from the development of radar in Britain during the war, and the formation there, after the war, of research groups whose members were specially well equipped to use the new techniques in order to follow up the discoveries.

Those mainly responsible for the wartime discoveries were Hey and his colleagues at the Army Operational Research Group. Hey's job was to study the reports on the operation of all army radar equipments, to identify sources of interference and, indeed, to investigate anything which might impede the effectiveness of Britain's radar. In fulfilling this task Hey made three quite unexpected observations each of which, after the war, was taken up by other physicists who had been engaged in the development of radar within the British Telecommunications Research Establishment (TRE). The first of these discoveries was the detection of radio emission from the sun.[2] The second achievement was the detection of radar echoes from meteor trails. Hey's third major observation was of a localised region of radio noise in the direction of Cygnus. This was the first discrete source of radio emission, apart from the sun, to be observed. It was the first 'radio star', as the sources were termed (misleadingly, as it turned out) at that time. Of these discoveries, only the third was in any way related to the prior work of Jansky and Reber.

At the universities of Manchester and Cambridge research groups were set up shortly after the war into which were recruited men with knowledge of the radio techniques evolved in the course of the development of radar at TRE. Blackett, head of the Department of Physics at Manchester, and Ratcliffe, head of the Radiophysics Group at the Cavendish

Laboratory, Cambridge, sought out promising young scientists that they or their colleagues had known or heard of in TRE. Although Hey's discoveries were common knowledge within these groups, it appears that initially both Blackett and Ratcliffe were mainly concerned with continuing the kind of research they had been engaged in during the 1930s. But some of the young physicists involved, building upon the work of Hey rather than that of Reber or Jansky, came to create within a few years an entirely new field of investigation which, by the late forties, was being referred to as 'radio astronomy'.[3] The pattern of development at Manchester and Cambridge, the two main centres of radio astronomy in Britain, was somewhat different.

Blackett's department of physics at Manchester was centrally concerned with the study of cosmic rays. During the war Blackett had worked out, along with the young physicist Lovell, that it might just be possible to detect cosmic ray showers by means of radar techniques. By the early months of 1946 Lovell and several of his wartime colleagues had joined Blackett's department and had begun to pursue this problem at the Jodrell Bank site. Quite soon, however, they came to realise that the radar echoes they were receiving were not from cosmic ray showers but from meteors. Thus, although the radar observation of cosmic rays proved to be more difficult than had originally been estimated, the same techniques, it soon appeared, were eminently suitable for the study of meteors. Accordingly the small research group at Jodrell Bank quickly abandoned cosmic rays in favour of this more fruitful line of inquiry, which was already being followed up by Hey and his colleagues.[4]

Systematic investigation of meteors by visual and photographic techniques had always been hampered by clouds and moonlight, and by the impossibility of making daytime observations. These difficulties, however, were irrelevant to radar techniques. Thus the work on meteors at Jodrell Bank expanded rapidly as the physicists there discovered that more and more observations, often of the geometrical kind usual in optical astronomy, could be made with a flexible application of electronic techniques. The rate of publication increased quickly; for example, one paper was published in 1946, nine in 1948, and eleven in 1951. Almost all of these early papers were on meteors. By 1948-9 those working at Jodrell Bank, although trained as physicists and although starting from a physics problem (i.e. cosmic rays) had become centrally concerned with problems which they recognised to be astronomical. Consequently, throughout the late 1940s, they published increasingly in astronomical journals and participated more and more in the professional activities of the community of optical astronomers.

So far we have seen that the emergence and early growth of radar meteor astronomy at Manchester was due to such factors as: the formation of a group of researchers with a similar scientific background but without a strong commitment to existing lines of investigation; the stimulus of Hey's discovery of radar echoes from meteors combined with the failure to observe cosmic rays; the gradual recognition of a whole series of related astronomical problems which, largely for technical reasons, were unresolved; and the availability of technical equipment and skills suitable for further investigation of these problems. In addition, there was the crucial factor of sponsorship. Perhaps partly because research into cosmic rays was declining in interest, Blackett provided enthusiastic support for the new venture. This was a critical factor in the whole affair. Blackett helped the young physicists in a great variety of ways; for example, by furnishing them with money, by following their work in detail and facilitating its publication, by promoting their entry into the Royal Astronomical Society (RAS), and by using his wide range of contacts to recruit research personnel, so that the group could grow very rapidly to twenty-one persons by 1951.

By the early 1950s, although the number of researchers and the output of research reports continued to grow at Jodrell Bank, the proportion of meteor papers began to fall. This decline continued throughout the fifties until, by the early 1960s, meteor research had ceased at Jodrell Bank. This change in intellectual focus seems to have occurred mainly as a result of a decline in the perceived significance of the problems remaining in the meteor field, in comparison with other available avenues of research. In the field of meteors the researchers at Jodrell Bank had come to concentrate on the problem of whether or not the sporadic meteors, that is, those which do not arrive in showers, were of interstellar origin or were confined to the solar system. By the early fifties, Lovell and his colleagues had helped to show, to the satisfaction of most participants in this research network, that the latter view was correct. After this, interest in meteors at Jodrell Bank began to decline and quite different problems attracted the attention of new entrants to the group. In particular, work started on a second of the lines of inquiry which had been opened up by Hey, that of 'radio stars'. This area of research was already being developed at Cambridge.

The events leading to the emergence of radio astronomy at Cambridge were similar in several respects to those at Manchester. Ratcliffe, the leader of the radio physics group at Cambridge, re-formed his group after the war mainly with ex-members of TRE. Within his unit a small sub-group soon evolved, in this case under the immediate leadership of the young physicist Ryle. Ryle and his immediate colleagues decided explicitly not to join Ratcliffe and the other radio physicists in conventional ionospheric research, essentially because they thought that all the interesting problems in the latter field had already been solved. They decided instead to follow up Hey's discovery of radio emission from the sun, using techniques and skills derived from their work on radar, and with Ratcliffe's full support. Because they were part of an established university department, they were guaranteed access to graduate students and, as a result, their group was able to grow steadily in size, even before science students in general knew of the existence of this new area of study.

There were, however, several differences between developments at Manchester and Cambridge. Ryle's sub-group was, for example, closely linked with the parent unit for several years and its members' work on radio emission from the sun was seen as being closely related to that of their colleagues on the earth's ionosphere and on radio propagation in general. This contrasts with the geographical separation of Lovell's group on the Jodrell Bank site and their pursuit of astronomical problems which were scientifically unrelated to the cosmic rays with which the main department was concerned. A second difference between the two sub-groups arose from the fact that radar techniques were unsuitable for study of the sun without considerable modification.[5] It was impossible, therefore, for the Cambridge group, unlike that at Jodrell Bank, simply to use existing techniques. There was consequently an early concern at Cambridge with devising new radio (rather than radar) techniques, specifically to measure radio emission from relatively small celestial sources, namely, sunspots. These initial technical differences were to have important long term consequences for the intellectual development and social structure of the two groups.

From 1946 to 1949, all the work of the small group under Ryle was concerned with the physics of radio emission from the sun and was published in physics journals. After 1950 the proportion of solar papers declined rapidly and results were published increasingly in journals of astronomy. This change in the direction of research was due to two complementary developments. On the one hand, research on the sun was coming to appear less and less promising. The problems in this area were becoming increasingly intractable. On the other hand, the same radio techniques that were used on the sun were applied successfully at Cambridge and in Australia to the observation of 'radio stars', the first of which had been discovered by Hey. This led, by the early fifties, to the identification of a number of discrete radio sources which did not coincide with visual stars. This discovery revealed an area of research previously unexplored, which could be investigated only by those competent in radio methods. During the early 1950s the Cambridge group, led by Ryle, transferred its major research effort to the new field.

By the early 1950s, then, both these groups of physicists had evolved partially overlapping interests in clearly astronomical issues. Their members had also begun to publish regularly in astronomical journals, to attend meetings of the RAS, and to communicate informally with optical astronomers. It was, in fact, at this time that the term 'radio astronomy' came into common use in the scientific community. Thus, some six to seven years after the end of the war, the new field of radio astronomy was becoming generally recognised as a definite area of scientific endeavour; its practitioners had built up distinct research groups in two British universities; and regular patterns of recruitment were becoming established. Contributions had been made to solar physics and to meteor astronomy; and new techniques had been developed, particularly at Cambridge. At that time, however, although the new discipline had a distinctive name as well as established research groups and regular publication outlets, it had no paradigmatic achievements. Rather its members were faced with several broad areas of investigation, for example: what were the 'radio stars'? How were they distributed? Was the radio emission from our galaxy simply the composite emission from radio stars or was there also emission from interstellar gas? As yet, no coherent intellectual framework had been developed to deal with such problems; nor were techniques available which could resolve them. These technical and intellectual developments were to require many more years of sustained inquiry.

THE BRANCHING OF NEW AREAS OF INQUIRY

Until the late 1940s the growth of radio astronomy occurred intermittently. In the 1890s a number of physicists were prepared to look for celestial radio emission and, if they had been successful, it seems likely that a slow but cumulative growth would have been set in motion. But the necessary techniques were lacking and theoretical developments soon appeared which made further empirical research seem unprofitable. By the 1930s techniques had improved to such an extent that Jansky could make his accidental discovery. However, this development took place outside the academic community, whose members were no longer prepared to take an interest in this line of exploration. Thus there followed another decade of inactivity, even though techniques were available and the essential first discovery had been made. Academic scientists became actively interested only after they had been taken out of the universities into research on radar. This wartime experience was crucial to the development of radio astronomy because it produced further technical developments, because it involved academically reputable physicists in repeating the work of Jansky and Reber and in making further related discoveries, and because it led to the formation of self-recruiting research groups in Britain and Australia, whose members knew of these discoveries and were competent to pursue them.

Once the British and Australian groups began to publish during the late 1940s, demonstrating the existence of a new area of investigation, scientists in other countries started to enter the field. By the mid-1950s an international research community had emerged, with groups in France, Canada, Holland, Italy, Japan, USSR and elsewhere. During the fifties, the growth of radio astronomy in the USA was particularly marked. Nevertheless, developments in America lagged behind those in Britain and Australia and, indeed, were dependent on personnel recruited from these two countries. In 1960, for example, there was roughly one British or Australian radio astronomer active in America for each native American worker. This fact alone is indicative of the importance for the growth of radio astronomy of the formation of groups derived from radar research — a development which occurred in Australia as well as in Britain, but did not occur to the same extent, or with the same impact, in the USA.

Accompanying the emergence of an international community of radio astronomers during the 1950s, there was a remarkable intellectual expansion which is represented in the figure. An obvious feature of this figure is the proliferation of relatively distinct lines of research. Clearly we cannot even sketch such a complex development here in its entirety. We shall, therefore, give merely a brief account of research into discrete radio sources (coded J-N in the figure) in order to exemplify certain important features of the overall pattern. The work in this area was dominated, until well into the fifties, by the groups at Cambridge, Jodrell Bank and Sydney, Australia.[6]

During the late 1940s a number of guiding questions began to crystallise in this field. At the most general level, these questions were: what

Main Lines of Development in Radio Astronomy, showing Emergence of New Areas

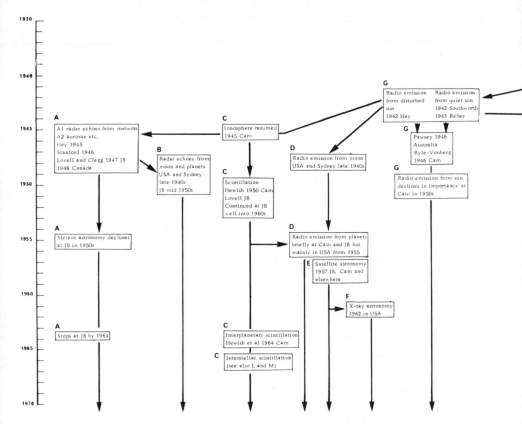

Note: Special prominence is given to work at Jodrell Bank (JB) and Cambridge (Cam).

kinds of objects are the radio stars? How are they distributed in space? To what extent, if at all, do they coincide with visual stars? What are the physical processes which produce the radio emission? These questions were attempts to define an area of ignorance, attempts to specify what kinds of information were needed in a field where very little was known. Each of these broad questions, in practice, found expression in a range of more concrete, subsidiary questions which, in the early stages, were closely linked with problems arising from radio research on the sun and

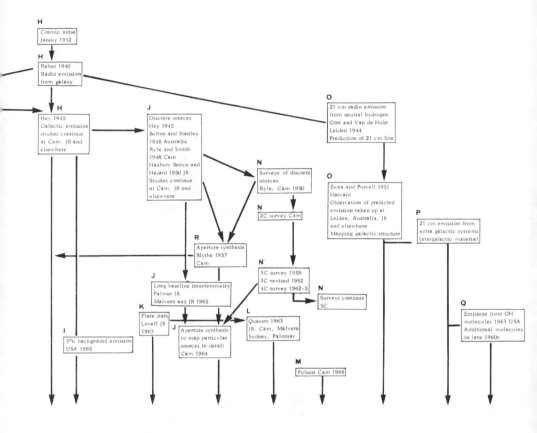

the galaxy. For example, it had been suggested, before the discovery of discrete sources, that the diffuse radio emission from the plane of our own galaxy (the Milky Way) originated in interstellar gas. Once discrete sources were observed it became necessary to ask: is galactic emission, perhaps, the sum of radiation from a large number of separate 'radio stars'? But if this was so, to what extent did these radio stars resemble the sun which was itself a source of radio waves? The answer to this seemed to be that the radio stars had to be immensely more powerful at radio wavelengths, yet much less powerful at visual wavelengths. Thus it was suggested that our galaxy might well contain as many (previously unsuspected) radio stars as it did visual stars; that there might, indeed, be an 'invisible universe' as yet unexplored. By means of such speculations participants tried, at the time, to reconcile the information available on radio stars with what was known about the sun and about galactic emission.

Initially the attempts to answer the guiding questions produced highly ambiguous results which could be, and were, interpreted in widely different ways. Gradually, however, certain of these issues came to be more clearly defined and the study of discrete sources emerged as a fairly distinct line of research. Of special importance in bringing this about was the identification of several radio sources with particular visual objects. During the 1940s the Australian workers claimed the identification of three sources — the Crab Nebula and two extragalactic nebulae — but these claims were not universally accepted, mainly owing to the crudity of the radio positions. Observations at Jodrell Bank in the early 1950s demonstrated that nearby 'normal' galaxies are radio sources. By late 1951, the Palomar optical astronomers, Baade and Minkowski, felt justified in using time on the 200 inch telescope to search for the two brightest radio sources (Cassiopeia A and Cygnus A), on the basis of more accurate positions derived at Cambridge. The results, confirmed during 1952, established the first agreed identifications, and helped to remove doubts over previous claims. These results, and other related work, made possible by technical advances which produced a marked improvement in the accuracy with which radio sources could be located, led in the period 1952-4 to a revision of a number of widely held views. It quickly became accepted, for instance, that many of the radio sources were not *stars* after all. For those that had been optically identified were either nebulosities within our own galaxy, such as the distinctive Crab Nebula, or they were external galaxies, some of them highly unusual, such as radio source Cygnus A, which appeared to coincide with two galaxies in collision. Thus by this time, although no detailed answers were available to the initial guiding questions, there was general agreement among the radio astronomers involved, as well as those optical astronomers who were interested, that the radio sources were astronomically and, perhaps, cosmologically significant and worthy of further detailed investigation, and that their study should be pursued in large measure separately from that of the sun and the galaxy. There were, however, many possible kinds of observations which could be made, only a small proportion of which could be carried out in any one research group. Consequently, all the groups working in this field were forced to make a choice, in the light of the limited amount of information then available, as to what kind of research programme would be most scientifically productive.

Faced with this situation, the two British groups made notably different choices. At Jodrell Bank, it was decided to concentrate on detailed studies of the radio emission from our own and nearby galaxies, and on measuring the diameters and fine structure of the more intense radio sources. This research programme did not depend on any specific view of the nature of the unidentified sources. The data which would be gathered, it was assumed, would be valuable no matter what the sources eventually turned out to be. At Cambridge an observational programme began in the early fifties. It relied on the technical exploitation, through successive generations of arrays, of principles of spaced aerial design — beginning with simple interferometers and developing later into what became known as 'aperture synthesis'. This technical programme was originally intended to provide a comprehensive catalogue or map of radio sources. The value of such a map was also independent of any particular conception of the sources. It would, however, facilitate further optical identifications and thereby improve the likelihood of establishing the nature of the radio sources. In addition, knowledge of the distribution of radio sources could be used to make inferences about the large-scale structure of the universe.

The scientific objectives of the research programmes on discrete sources of radio emission initiated at Cambridge and Jodrell Bank in the early fifties were relatively simple. The technical problems which they entailed, however, were highly complex. Thus progress throughout the 1950s was slow and directly dependent on technical developments. It was, in fact, not until the early sixties that a professional consensus was first achieved in relation to the radio sources. By this date, after one major false start and a bitter controversy, the technical principles for mapping radio sources had become established and hundreds of sources had been reliably catalogued.[7] At about the same time, during the early sixties, there appeared to be growing agreement as to the nature of the radio sources. Although many of them had been identified with several kinds of extragalactic visual objects, varying from 'normal' galaxies to 'galaxies in collision', these visual objects had all been known or anticipated previously and their emission of radiation at radio wavelengths, although unsuspected before the arrival of radio astronomers, could be explained by the application of known physical principles. It began to look, therefore, as if the research objectives formulated in the early fifties would be realised without giving rise to any major scientific revelation. In 1963, however, work by radio and optical astronomers on particular sources led to the accidental discovery of quasars, an apparently new type of celestial object, radiating energy at a quite unexpectedly high rate. The quasars quickly became the focus of a new field of inquiry and the source of astrophysical and cosmological problems which are still far from solved. Subsequently, in 1968, radio research on quasars gave rise, again quite accidentally, to the discovery of pulsars and to the formation of another major research network. Thus the lines of inquiry in this field diversified during the sixties. The original interest in simply cataloguing sources and measuring their diameters declined; and was replaced by an increasing concern with the astrophysics of the sources themselves and with exploring the nature of entirely new kinds of objects.

Many of the original questions which guided research into the nature of the discrete radio sources now have agreed answers. It is established that the majority are extra-galactic. It is known, by optical identification, what kinds of objects they are. It is also agreed, with some precision, just how they are distributed over the sky. Similarly the original problems concerning the relation between discrete sources and radio emission from the galaxy and from the sun have been resolved. In addition , elaborate and reliable technical methods have been evolved to provide copious data on the sources and their characteristics. Thus there has been, broadly speaking, a movement from vaguely-conceived problems and imprecise techniques towards precise instrumentation, clearly-conceived problems and solutions, and an increasingly firm intellectual consensus among those engaged in the field. At the same time, the researches undertaken to resolve the original problems have recurrently generated new, often totally unexpected, areas of investigation. So, as the major problems have been resolved in one area, interest has tended to focus on new areas where the process of defining, solving and uncovering further problems has been repeated. This branching of fields of inquiry and new research networks, exemplified here in relation to the work on discrete radio sources, has been typical of the growth of radio astronomy in general, as can be seen from the figure.

DISCOVERY AND COMPETITION

With only one exception (coded O), the main lines of research shown in the figure began with the chance observation of an unexpected but striking phenomenon. Similarly, most of the subsidiary developments shown in that figure, such as quasars and pulsars, have arisen through serendipity. In the very early years, these discoveries were made accidentally as advanced electronic techniques were used to achieve practical objectives. In later years the development of new techniques has continued to be an important factor in revealing unanticipated phenomena, although increasingly these techniques have been developed with purely scientific goals in mind. Furthermore, in most recent discoveries an important role has been played by widely shared astronomical expectations, some of which are specific and precise while others are relatively general and indefinite, against which unexpected observations appear with clear significance. The response to such discoveries, however, whether or not they involve widely shared astronomical assumptions, is never uniform throughout the research community of radio astronomers. Thus the two British groups, although working since the late forties within the same broad area of study, have responded quite differently to the series of major discoveries occurring in radio astronomy. This is so because, when each group is faced with the choice of following up a discovery or leaving its pursuit to others, its eventual decision is influenced by several factors, the effects of which tend to vary from one group to another.

In the first place, when a new area of investigation is revealed, the members of separate groups often assess its potential scientific significance quite differently. During the 1960s, as an increasingly firm picture of the radio-optical universe became established, major differences in assessments of scientific importance probably diminished. Nevertheless, there have been and still remain differences between the two British groups in terms of research strategy. From the early fifties to the early sixties there was a deliberate concentration at Cambridge on comprehensive surveys of radio sources, to elucidate problems of their nature and distribution; this defined a major 'theme', accounting for about half the Cambridge publications in this period. At Jodrell Bank a wider range of research topics was developed, with no such obvious, single theme. In addition, those at Jodrell Bank who were concerned with the same range of scientific problems as the Cambridge group tended to adopt, as part of an explicit strategy, a more piecemeal approach. Thus those at Jodrell Bank made use of a multi-purpose telescope to gather various kinds of detailed information about particular sources, on the assumption that in the long run they would be able to arrive, in a manner which could not yet be specified, at general conclusions about the nature of radio sources. At Cambridge, in contrast, it was a basic premise that specific instruments should be devised to produce reliable source counts which, as well as providing an essential overall map of the radio universe could be used as the basis for cosmological conclusions. The two groups differed, then, not only in the range of problems which they attempted to tackle, but also in their approach to those specific fields of research in which their interests overlapped.

Such research strategies are developed in conjunction with particular kinds of techniques. Once a strong commitment has been made to specific technical equipment, the nature of this equipment limits future strategy. It is clear that the problems which are taken up by a particular group are by no means *solely* determined by the nature of the techniques which are available. For example, it was possible for the physicists returning to Jodrell Bank and Cambridge after the war to pursue quite distinct lines of investigation, despite their common technical background in TRE and their use of wartime radar equipment. However, once a group has made an extensive investment in a large-scale technique, the future research strategy and the choice of further areas of study are thereby constrained. Furthermore, not only are techniques and research strategies interdependent, but perceptions of the scientific importance of particular problems are also closely related to the nature of the techniques available. For instance, the two groups responded differently to the detection of radio emission from neutral galactic hydrogen (i.e. the 21 cm spectral line, coded O in the figure) in 1951. At Cambridge no active interest was taken in this new area. In part this was because the leaders of the group, although recognising that this line of research could well produce valuable information about the nature of the galaxy, thought that this was scientifically insignificant compared with what could be gained by single-minded study of the radio sources. The structure of the galaxy was a long-standing astronomical problem and was, therefore, judged by the Cambridge group to offer fewer opportunities for significant scientific advance than the entirely new radio sources. But this judgment was made at a time when the group was developing its highly specialised techniques for source counts, techniques which were unsuitable for work on the hydrogen line, and from which its leaders had no intention of being diverted. The situation at Jodrell Bank was quite different. The group there had already divided into two main teams, one concerned with radar research on meteors and the other with radio research on sources, and had begun to plan the construction of a multi-purpose 'dish' which could cater for the divergent needs of these teams. Moreover, the explicit strategy of encouraging a diversity of lines of inquiry was beginning to form. Consequently, the response at Jodrell Bank to the emergence of the new field was to create another team which could use the multi-purpose telescope to pursue one more line of investigation.

It seems that research strategy, technical resources and judgments of scientific importance have been closely inter-related, both at Cambridge and Jodrell Bank, in such a way that it is impossible to say that any one of these factors is the primary determinant of the direction in which research develops. Judgments of importance tend to be made in relation to a group's technical equipment; yet technical development itself depends on the group's research strategy which, in turn, is conditioned by perceptions of scientific significance, and in particular the judgments of the group leaders. As a result of the interdependence between these factors the two British research groups, having entered radio astronomy from different directions, have continued to develop along distinct lines in their use of techniques, in their areas of interest and in their overall strategies. However, our account so far of the factors influencing the direction in which research develops is undoubtedly incomplete. In particular, we have not considered the impact of competition.

The fundamental requirement of the researcher's role is that he should produce reliable information which is both interesting and original. The strong emphasis on originality means that most scientists are eager to avoid being anticipated by those working in the same area. Consequently, when several researchers are engaged on very similar projects, competition for priority of publication is likely to ensue. Most of our respondents admitted the existence of competitive pressures in radio astronomy, both between individuals and between groups. For various reasons, however, these pressures do not always lead to outright competition. *Within* the British radio astronomy groups, where those involved have similar scientific interests and make use of common equipment to deal with the same body of research problems, there are undoubtedly occasions when researchers compete to establish their sole right to pursue a particular problem or set of related problems. Yet open competition within groups is usually averted because those involved are in sufficiently close contact to perceive when they are encroaching unduly on another's specialty and because they are, consequently, able to develop and make evident to their colleagues their own distinctive interests and skills. At the same time, the development of varied but complementary skills and interests are promoted by the senior scientists in both groups, who adopt a policy of allocating new entrants to distinct, although often related, problems. As a result of such specialisation, the level of intra-group competition is low and the level of active collaboration, particularly among group veterans, is relatively high.

The relationships within and between groups appear to be determined by similar factors. In the same way that individual researchers are concerned and encouraged to select problems which are not too close to those of other group members, so research groups tend to avoid areas where work by other groups is well advanced. The adoption of such a policy of avoiding duplication, and thereby avoiding competition, has been one important factor promoting differentiation between the two main British radio astronomy groups.[8] For instance, one reason why Cambridge undertook no work with radar techniques was that Jodrell Bank had quickly gained a commanding lead in this area. Similarly the radio astronomers at Manchester never seriously considered taking up the distinctive approach to both techniques and radio source problems that had defined the major theme of the Cambridge group. This explicit concern with avoiding duplication of research interests has not been confined to Jodrell Bank and Cambridge. For example, other smaller groups which have entered radio astronomy in Britain in the fifties and sixties, have tended either to focus on those problem areas which the two main groups had ignored or to add distinctive data on those problems by the use of complementary techniques. However, it is only the two major groups which, because of the scale of their activities, have *collaborated* in planning research programmes so that overlap between the activities of the two groups is kept to a minimum. Cooperation of this kind, of course, limits the possibilities for collaboration in joint research projects. It is not surprising to find, therefore, that there are few published papers which members of the two groups have written together nor that the level of mutual citation is low, that is, about one citation in ten.

Our respondents stressed that the absence of research projects shared by the two groups did not mean that there was little cooperation of other kinds. There has been a continual exchange of technical information, an appreciable transfer of research personnel (mainly from Cambridge to Jodrell Bank) and occasional use of the other group's equipment. In addition there has been cooperation since the early fifties in allocating funds, in protecting radio frequencies, in regulating the general development of the discipline, and, as we have seen, in planning research programmes. The existence of these types of cooperation as well as the effective differentiation of research interests has reduced the likelihood of outright competition between Cambridge and Jodrell Bank, although there has been intermittent concern over priority and occasionally strong published criticism of the work of members of the other group. Furthermore, all our respondents admitted the existence of rivalry between the two groups. But, they stressed, it was 'friendly rivalry' and, indeed, the British groups never have been involved in a prolonged or bitter dispute. The maintenance of friendly rivalry has been due firstly to the fact that the two groups began by developing notably different techniques and interests and, secondly, to the fact that by the time their interests were beginning to converge they were able to communicate well enough to ensure that no major research overlap occurred.

Two further features of the social organisation of radio astronomy in Britain work to reduce competitive pressures, namely, the concentration within the large, well-established groups of research into major problem areas, combined with a highly centralised system of government funding.[9] During the last two and a half decades radio astronomy has become a 'big science', in which the more important lines of inquiry are open only to those groups with sufficient expertise to develop the complex techniques required and with sufficient scientific repute to attract extensive financial support from government and industry. The existence of a research oligopoly in radio astronomy, by which access to the requisite equipment is limited to a small number of groups, is particularly evident in the UK, where unlike the USA, the number of observatories has remained virtually unchanged since the early fifties. There are, of course, good technical reasons for maintaining such an oligopoly. For instance, as large-scale, costly equipment becomes essential for further advance, it becomes necessary to concentrate expenditure on a few telescopes, rather than spending the limited resources available on a greater number of smaller and cheaper but relatively unproductive items. This line of reasoning had, by the mid-sixties, become the official policy of the Science Research Council and provided the guiding principle for the distribution of research funds. Some of those outside the main groups saw this policy as expressing the interests of the established groups rather than the needs of an expanding discipline. But it is clear that the support by government of major new groups attempting to set up costly equipment and to organise extensive research programmes would tend to hold back development within the established groups, whose members had already demonstrated their ability to make important scientific contributions. Nevertheless, the fact remains that in British radio astronomy, the existence of a complex research technology combined with the centralised formulation of research policy and the centralised distribution of funds, do appear to limit the possibility of competition and to make it difficult for new groups to enter the field.

The growth of radio astronomy, then, has been characterized by a proliferation of new lines of inquiry. Most of these new departures have been set in motion by the chance observation of quite unexpected phenomena. Every discovery offers unanticipated opportunities for further research and discovery. Faced with these opportunities, radio astronomers do not respond uniformly. Each group comes to concentrate on different lines of inquiry and within groups individual researchers concern themselves with a limited range of problems and techniques. The commitment by groups and individuals to particular kinds of research depends on their assessment of a complex set of related factors, for example, the scientific importance of the area relative to other available problem areas, its suitability in relation to their research strategy, the possibility of devising techniques capable of resolving the problems involved, the technical preparedness of the group, and also the threat of competition. A group takes up a particular line of inquiry, not only when its leaders perceive the problems to be important and solvable, but also when they believe that the group has a technical advantage over potential competitors.

Research groups tend to avoid competition by concentrating, whenever possible, on techniques and problems which are not the main focus of interest elsewhere. Once one group has achieved a clear lead in a particular field, other groups tend to choose different areas rather than face duplication of effort and open competition. Thus the tendency to avoid competition leads groups to move quickly into new fields, such as quasars and pulsars, which appear important and where no group has established an outstanding lead. In this way competition contributes to the proliferation of areas of active research in radio astronomy, whilst the growth of new areas and the development of new techniques provide outlets for those in unfavourable competitive situations. As a result, active disputes occur only sporadically and the relations between groups are characterised by a spirit of rivalry which is often sufficiently mild to allow regular technical cooperation. Such cooperation may well be particularly evident in countries like the UK, where there are few research groups in radio astronomy and where the established groups exert considerable influence upon funding and research policy.

THE SOCIAL STRUCTURES OF THE GROUPS

As research into radio astronomy proceeded throughout the 1950s and 1960s, the two major British groups came to develop quite different internal structures. Whereas the Cambridge group became functionally differentiated in such a way that a high level of overall group integration was maintained, the Jodrell Bank group became differentiated into a loose federation of largely autonomous teams, each of which was concerned with a distinct subject area. The formation of such teams at Jodrell Bank made it possible for that research station to pursue a somewhat wider range of independent research topics than at Cambridge. Nevertheless, the research careers of members of Jodrell Bank, each of whom was confined to one specialised team, had noticeably less diversity than those of their Cambridge counterparts.

Evidence of these differences in group structure is plentiful. First let us look at the incidence of co-authorship among those authors at Cambridge and Jodrell Bank who had a hand (alone or otherwise) in three or more papers, and who joined their respective groups before the end of 1960. Some co-authorship combinations are impossible; the criterion we used was that two authors could not co-author if both had not been in the group together for more than one year. The integrating role of Ryle stands out from the co-authorship data on Cambridge; he maintains an active colleagueship with all the other senior workers there. Otherwise, there are some prominent pairings at Cambridge, but no stable teams. The data is clearly consistent with a high degree of research interaction throughout the group. In contrast, the co-authorships among radio authors at Jodrell Bank indicate relatively cohesive groups around Hanbury Brown, Palmer, R. D. Davies, and Large.

The extent to which the Jodrell Bank research is an enterprise conducted mainly by stable teams is reflected in the lack of single author papers. Of all papers published by members of the Jodrell Bank radio group in the period 1946-1959, 32.9% had a single author: the equivalent Cambridge figure is 60.9%. It appears that the social structure of the Cambridge group allowed considerable scope for the development of individual interests, and a wider freedom of choice of colleague partners. In addition to the differences in the organization of *radio* research at the two centres, there was a major division at Jodrell Bank between those using radio and those using radar techniques. The members of these groupings never published joint papers.[10]

We also examined the extent of possible co-authorship among each group's 'veterans'. Veterans are defined as those who have been in their group for six or more years and had joined the group by the end of 1958. At Cambridge, of eleven veterans, no fewer than six collaborated with half or more than half of the other veterans in the group, and one (Ryle) co-authored at least once with every Cambridge veteran. In contrast, at Jodrell Bank, none of fourteen veterans in the radio group collaborated with as many as half the other veterans. Hanbury Brown, who co-authored most, collaborated with 5 others (46% of the Jodrell Bank veterans). This striking difference is reinforced if we compute the proportion of possible co-authorships which are realised in practice. For the Cambridge group as a whole, this proportion is 25.1%; for the whole Jodrell Bank radio group it is 21.4%. However, when we consider the proportion of realised co-authorships for veterans only, the Cambridge figure more than doubles, to 54.2%; whereas the Jodrell Bank proportion rises to only 23.5%, i.e. still less than that for the Cambridge group as a whole. These figures are clearly consistent with there being a group internally differentiated into teams at Jodrell Bank and a much more integrated group overall at Cambridge.

The picture derived from co-authorship figures is confirmed by citation and other data. Let us consider here only the publication profiles of individual researchers. It might be thought that at Jodrell Bank, with its intentionally 'multi-purpose' instruments, workers would tend to engage in a range of interests, and publish on a variety of topics; whereas at Cambridge, where instruments were usually designed for specific scientific goals, workers would pursue less variable scientific careers. But the opposite is the case. When we compute the proportion of their total papers which individual researchers have published in one specific area of interest, we find that Jodrell Bank produces more publication profiles than Cambridge which are highly focused. Of fourteen veteran radio workers at Jodrell Bank, eight have published 70% or more of their papers within one specific area, whilst one more reaches this figure if his single paper on techniques is re-allocated. At Cambridge, only four out of eleven veterans are so 'single minded'. Detailed examination of papers reinforces the conclusion drawn from this simple comparison of publication profiles and from the other data presented above.

The evolution of markedly different structures within the two groups can be explained in the following way. The group at Jodrell Bank began by exploiting radar techniques which both transmitted and received radio waves. On this basis, a relatively large group developed, committed to radar astronomy. Lovell was the cited, scientific leader of this original group whose initial scientific aims (once the cosmic ray experiment had failed) were concerned with defining meteor orbits and velocities.[11] Within five years, however, developments elsewhere had indicated the exciting possibilities of purely *radio* work, involving the exploitation of receiving systems alone. This possibility could not be neglected, if the Manchester group was to remain competitive. Thus by 1949 a 218 ft. 'dish', which had been built for research into cosmic rays, was adapted for the study of radio emission from the galaxy and from discrete sources. However, the pursuit of radio work was sufficiently distinct from radar work for the two to be beyond the active compass of one scientific leader of what was, by then, a large group (21 persons in 1951, 24 in 1955). Consequently, a separate leader (Hanbury Brown) emerged for radio work and he in turn allowed further independent radio teams to develop during the fifties with their own specific problems and techniques. Meanwhile, the scientific aims of the meteor work were achieved, Lovell was increasingly preoccupied with administering and providing funds for his large unit, and scientific leadership within the *radar* unit was assumed by other workers, with a succession of teams, problems, and specialised techniques.[12] Quite early in this sequence of events, the need for a major instrument, of potential use to the whole group, was perceived. As both radar and radio interests had to be satisfied, a multi-purpose, steerable, large paraboloid was an obvious design choice. *The group therefore became committed, relatively early and irreversibly, to an investment in multi-purpose dishes as the major components of their instrumentation.* Once the first multi-purpose dish was under construction it provided further justification for a research strategy emphasising diversity and for the formation of new teams to take up opportunities for which the forthcoming dish would be particularly suited. Consequently during the 1950s Jodrell Bank became consolidated into subject-based teams which were linked administratively and through common access to the big dish, yet which had distinct scientific interests and which developed and 'owned' their own specialised ancillary equipment.

We have already presented objective data which show that during the fifties, and into the early sixties, research activities within the Cambridge group were more closely integrated than at Jodrell Bank. Four main factors were responsible for this: the concentration on radio techniques at Cambridge; the relatively small size of the group; the direct, participative leadership of Ryle; and the formulation of a focused research strategy. With respect to each of these factors the Cambridge group differed from that at Jodrell Bank. The Cambridge group began with interferometric measurements of radio emission from the sun. For the first four years Ryle and his colleagues published exclusively on this topic. During the next few years there was a transfer of interest away from the sun in favour of discrete sources. This change of focus was led by Ryle who carried with him virtually all the members of his group. Apart from the cogency of the scientific reasons for taking up this new line of research, the change was facilitated by two factors. In the first place, the group was much smaller than that at Jodrell Bank (9 persons in 1951 compared with 21). It was, therefore, much easier for the Cambridge group as a whole to agree about the need to change direction. Secondly, discrete sources could be studied by basically the same radio techniques as had been used for the sun. Thus members of the Cambridge group had no unsuitable technical commitment. Consequently a considerable change of scientific interest took place without differentiation into separate teams. Once the transition had been made, Ryle found himself actively engaged with his colleagues in a research area which was expanding, unlike Lovell whose initial area of research was at this time in decline. Ryle was able, therefore, to collaborate extensively with other group members and to formulate with them a group policy of developing further those interferometric (and, later, synthesis) techniques in the use of which they established a world lead during the 1950s and of applying these techniques to that relatively narrow range of problems for which they were specially suited. As a result of these processes the Cambridge group maintained a considerably higher level of overall integration throughout the fifties and early sixties.

Although the Cambridge group did not divide into subject-based teams, it did evolve during the fifties and early sixties a form of functional differentiation. In the first place a small theoretical group emerged whose members attempted to deal with theoretical problems for the whole group. Similarly a team was formed to provide technical services for the group as a whole. Functional differentiation of this kind has not, in general, developed at Jodrell Bank, where a much more limited theoretical and technical specialisation has occurred within teams. Most Jodrell Bank members owe primary allegiance to the research teams which are broadly defined in terms of scientific problems;[13] any member who then takes up a more general expertise (for example, astrophysical theory, electronic techniques, computing methods) does so in the interests of the task set by his team. He will, primarily, render service to his own team. He can, of course, answer requests and offer advice or help to other teams. But this will, by and large, appear unrewarding, since it is supported by no stable social relations. At Cambridge, in contrast, primary allegiance is to 'the group as a whole' and the pattern of functional differentiation there is linked to the integration of the whole group.[14] However, group structures did not remain entirely stable during the 1960s. At Cambridge, for instance, as the group continued to increase in size, as its techniques became more and more complex, and as the range of its research activities widened, so its differentiation became more obviously subject-based, and the overall integration of the group began to decline. At Jodrell Bank there has been in recent years a movement in the opposite direction. Researchers there during the sixties came to recognise that the existence of autonomous research teams had certain disadvantages. It prevented effective communication throughout the group, it led to unnecessary duplication of ancillary equipment and it fostered inefficient use of the main observational and computing facilities. Consequently, attempts were made to improve communication between teams and to increase technical efficiency by means of regular meetings between representatives of all teams. Thus, although the social structures of the two groups are still significantly different, there has been recently a slight, though definite, movement towards structural convergence.

RADIO ASTRONOMY AND OPTICAL ASTRONOMY

We have described above the formation of a distinct discipline of radio astronomy in the UK and we have traced certain aspects of the discipline's subsequent intellectual and social development. Most radio astronomers, however, no longer regard radio astronomy as a separate area of study. They claim that, although radio and optical astronomy may have been distinct disciplines at one time, they are now indistinguishable. There is much evidence to show that optical astronomy and radio astronomy became closely linked during the fifties and sixties, both socially and intellectually. This interpenetration is clearly exemplified in the absence of a specialised radio astronomical research journal. Yet the integration of these two branches of astronomy is far from complete. Radio astronomers use different research techniques from optical astronomers; they work within separate research units; they seldom publish research reports in collaboration with their optical counterparts; and their discoveries have left unaffected a great deal of optical research.

The first contact between optical astronomers and the early contributors to radio astronomy occurred during the early 1940s in the USA. Both Jansky and Reber were interested for two reasons in the response of optical astronomers to their work: firstly, because they needed help from astronomers to interpret their results; and secondly, because they believed that their work had important implications for astronomical research in general. Jansky, however, made no attempt actively to seek out optical astronomers. He acquired the astronomical knowledge necessary for his research from his colleagues at Bell Laboratories and by consulting basic astronomy textbooks. Reber, in contrast, adopted a much more direct approach. After taking a course in astrophysics he took his results to Yerkes Observatory. The optical astronomers there were, of course, initially rather doubtful about the reliability of the information presented by this unknown amateur. But some of them began to discuss with him the astronomical significance of his results which, from then on, began to appear in the leading American astronomical journal. These results aroused the interest of several astronomers.

In Britain, the first relationships between radio physicists and optical astronomers arose from the work at Jodrell Bank. As soon as the physicists there came to realise that the results they were getting were relevant, not to cosmic rays, but to meteors they began to establish contacts with the astronomical research community. By 1947 they were collaborating with an amateur astronomer and publishing their results in astronomical journals. At the same time they were reading the astronomical literature and developing through practice the skills required in a line of research for which they had not been trained. The majority of the papers published from Jodrell Bank during the late forties were concerned with the geometrical properties of meteor orbits, and were therefore firmly part of the optical tradition of meteor research. This work on meteors led to regular contact with the small number of optical astronomers who were active in the field. Yet, despite the concern with distinctly astronomical problems, the exchange of information with optical astronomers and the direct interaction with optical astronomers in various social contexts, the research group at Jodrell Bank was far from being fully within the astronomical community. In the first place, only a few of its members joined the professional astronomers' scientific society. Secondly, even when meteor research was at its height, much of the effort at Jodrell Bank was devoted to associated problems of physics, problems such as that of measuring the electron density of the ionosphere. Moreover, even the study of meteors was done by reflecting radar pulses off meteor trails in the earth's atmosphere. The use by the Manchester physicists of radar techniques and their concern with the physics of the upper atmosphere prevented optical astronomers from accepting them as full members of the astronomical community. They were generally regarded by astronomers as physicists using a non-astronomical technique to contribute to an area of research which was of only minor astronomical significance. Furthermore, the meteor orbit work at Jodrell Bank declined after the early fifties and upper atmosphere physics came to predominate within the 'meteor astronomy' sub-group. Thus the first contacts in the UK between optical astronomy and radio astronomy, arising out of the physicists' use of radar techniques to study meteors, did not develop into a lasting scientific relationship. Moreover, the convergence of interest in this field among radio physicists and optical astronomers could never alone have led to an extensive integration of the two disciplines, even if the interest in meteor astronomy had not declined; this is partly because the number of professional optical astronomers actively concerned with meteors was very small and also because the other radio groups in Sydney and Cambridge were studying not meteors, but discrete radio sources, galactic radiation and the sun.

The sun had long been an object of study for optical astronomers who consequently had information (for example about sunspots) which the radio physicists knew to be useful. As a result the solar physicists did establish intermittent contact with several optical astronomers during the 1940s. It is clear that, in general, the astronomers were helpful. However, although the International Astronomical Union (IAU) and the International Radio Sciences Union (URSI) had quickly coordinated the work of routine solar radio observations, incorporating the radio data into their regular bulletins, it is clear that there was no great enthusiasm for a more general exchange of information (mainly because radio measures were too crude), and that neither the optical astronomers nor those who were beginning to call their subject radio astronomy conceived of themselves as members of the same discipline. Not only were astronomers sceptical about the astronomical significance of the radio research, but those engaged in this research still regarded themselves, during the late forties, primarily as physicists. This changed as the groups at Cambridge, Sydney and Jodrell Bank became increasingly concerned with detecting and locating discrete radio sources. But the frequency of contact with optical astronomers increased only slowly. The relative lack of communication between optical and radio astronomers at this time is shown by the way in which radio astronomers tended unknowingly to re-invent techniques which have well-established optical analogues (like the transit telescope), to repeat historical errors and to struggle with classical problems, while the basic principles they required were common knowledge among optical astronomers.

In the period around 1950 radio astronomers interested in discrete sources came gradually to approach a few of their optical colleagues more frequently. But at that time radio astronomers were greatly impressed by the almost total lack of connection between radio observations and the visual sky. It did not seem impossible then that there were two separate kinds of celestial objects, each requiring distinct research techniques. The basic scientific problem, therefore, became that of the relationship, if any, between the optical and radio universes. But productive cooperation between optical and radio astronomers over this issue was made difficult by the relative imprecision of radio observations. Thus the dialogue between optical and radio astronomers could be of little benefit to either side until radio techniques were so improved that an unambiguous answer could be given to the question: are any of the radio sources identical with visual objects? Until radio astronomers achieved the necessary technical advance there was no possibility of a cooperative attempt to answer this question. The breakthrough eventually came when Baade and Minkowski were furnished during 1951-2 with sufficiently accurate positions for the strong radio sources in Cygnus and Cassiopeia to make possible clear identification with optical objects. Initially both the optical and the radio astronomers had tended to believe that the radio sources were relatively nearby. However, once the Cygnus source was identified with what appeared to be two distant galaxies in collision, the relevance of radio observations to optical astronomy became readily apparent — at least to those who were intimately involved in this line of research. At Cambridge and at Jodrell Bank these first conclusive identifications were crucial in leading participants to make a considerable and irreversible investment of time, effort and technical resources in the pursuit of problems which were distinctly astronomical.

During the early 1950s a small number of optical astronomers began actively to cooperate with their radio counterparts. But despite such instances of successful cooperation, the techniques used by radio astronomers in the study of discrete sources were still far inferior to those of the optical astronomers. Consequently, the latter were often critical of radio observations and continually exhorted radio astronomers to make their results more precise. In this area of research, therefore, radio astronomy was still very much a distinct and somewhat subordinate branch of astronomical inquiry. But the situation was not uniform thoughout radio astronomy. In particular, a number of optical astronomers were by the early 1950s actively engaged in research into 21 cm. radio emission from galactic hydrogen. There were several reasons for this. In the first place Oort, and other optical astronomers at Leiden, had been involved in the original prediction of 21 cm. emission and in the race to verify it observationally. Moreover, whereas it had long been clear that *optical* techniques were quite unsuitable for mapping the structure of our own galaxy, it was equally clear that the use of radio techniques to map the distribution of galactic hydrogen would prove very useful in achieving this objective — an objective which many optical astronomers regarded as extremely important. Thus Oort and others quickly began to encourage active cooperation between optical and radio astronomers in this field, and accurate maps of galactic radiation at 21 cm. were made during the mid-1950s.

By the mid-fifties a regular exchange of information between optical and radio astronomers had become established both informally and through the journals. The extent of the integration of the two disciplines, however, must not be exaggerated. Some of the radio astronomers we interviewed stressed that optical astronomers did not, at that time, regard them as *real* astronomers. Others emphasised that the intellectual overlap between radio and optical astronomy was still quite small. Similarly, our respondents recalled that only a very small proportion of the subjects discussed at the regular meetings of the RAS during the first half of the 1950s were of interest to them. Gradually, however, optical and radio astronomers came to have more and more in common intellectually and to participate more and more frequently in shared social activities. The Cambridge group, for instance, published predominantly in British astronomical journals from 1955 onwards; in that year seven out of nine research reports and in 1960 all fourteen research papers were published in journals specifically devoted to astronomical topics. The pattern at Jodrell Bank was similar. It is clear from other studies and from the comments of our respondents that astronomical journals could not have been used in this way without widespread approval among optical astronomers of the research being undertaken by radio astronomers.[15] At the same time, radio astronomers were taking a more active part in the formal organizations of the astronomical community. At Cambridge, for example, whereas Ryle was the only Fellow of the RAS in the group from 1950 to 1954, there were five Fellows by 1958 and eleven by 1959. In addition, it had become routine by 1960 for research students in both groups to become junior members of the RAS in preparation for full membership on completion of their Ph.D. Additional evidence of the growing cooperation between representatives of the two branches of astronomy is plentiful. For instance, soon after 1955 the International Astronomical Union began to publish a regular list of lunar occultations of radio sources. Another example is the way in which radio and optical astronomers worked together to define the IAU system of galactic coordinates which was accepted in 1958. Furthermore from 1955 onwards the IAU sponsored joint conferences of radio and optical astronomers on radio problems (following earlier contacts initiated by URSI and Jodrell Bank). Such active cooperation was often undertaken for specific, practical reasons. For instance, the publication of a complete list of occultations and the formulation of an agreed system of galactic coordinates made radio research easier and facilitated the comparison of radio with optical observations. At the same time, regular contact between radio and optical astronomers helped the former by giving them access to tacit astronomical knowledge, knowledge which was not available through the formal channels of communication.

Throughout the fifties radio astronomers continued to depend on their optical counterparts for information which would help them to interpret and to check the accuracy of their own results; and optical astronomers continued to regard their branch of the discipline as technically, and therefore scientifically, superior. However, despite the technical pre-eminence of the optical branch, radio astronomers were becoming increasingly aware of the important contribution which they could make to astronomy and which could not be made by those who lacked their technical skills. This became clear quite early on in the study of the hydrogen line. Similarly, radio astronomers working on discrete sources, although still aware of the great value to them of optical data, were by the second half of the fifties developing research programmes and techniques of inference which would enable them to make important and independent contributions to knowledge about the structure of the universe. The Cambridge group, for example, was producing reliable, large-scale surveys of radio sources by this time and Ryle was using these results to enter into a long-term debate with that sector of the astronomical community concerned with cosmological issues; while at Jodrell Bank, Hanbury Brown and Twiss published several papers on optical theory and were able to apply techniques devised for radio sources to measuring diameters of several visual stars more accurately than ever before.

The growing sophistication of radio techniques, the consequent improvement in the accuracy of radio observations and the increasingly significant scientific contributions of radio astronomy affected the views of both radio and optical astronomers with respect to cooperation. Both sides agreed that, because light waves and radio waves were fundamentally the same except for length, radio and optical research should be complementary. Radio astronomers had been keen almost from the start to draw on the vast accumulation of optical knowledge and to obtain data (for example, measurements of distance) which were not amenable to radio techniques. In contrast many optical astronomers in the early years, although not denying the importance of radio observations in principle, had been deterred by their lack of precision from taking an active interest. But as radio observations became increasingly reliable and precise, so optical astronomers became more and more eager to make use of them. At the same time, the growing confidence of radio astronomers in the accuracy and scientific value of their results led some of them to engage in cooperative research on more equal terms. Out of this cooperation during the early sixties there came the discovery of quasars and the formation of a major field of inquiry in which from the very beginning the contributions of radio and optical astronomers were inextricably bound together. The increasingly accurate positions provided by radio astronomers, combined with the work of the small number of optical observatories which had equipment capable of recording and interpreting the quasar spectra, led to a rush of identifications of radio sources during the years 1964-7. This work brought into broad alignment the optical and the radio universes.

The increasingly close interdependence between radio and optical astronomy has produced important changes in the character of astronomical research. In the first place, radio astronomy has helped to stimulate advances in optical observational techniques. Similarly, the spur of trying to equal the precision of optical methods has helped to promote further technical development in radio astronomy. The second major effect of the advent of radio astronomy has been the regeneration of interest in certain areas of optical inquiry which had become relatively dormant, such as meteors, various classes of stars and galactic structure, the surface conditions and composition of the planets, and also cosmology. Thirdly, radio astronomy has revealed the existence of several classes of object which were previously unsuspected, such as quasars and pulsars, and has led to the formation of entirely new cooperative research networks concerned with these objects. Fourthly, the advent of radio astronomy and the subsequent discovery of remarkable celestial objects has contributed to a marked shift of emphasis during the sixties toward astrophysical problems, such as those of energy generation. Fifthly, radio astronomy has changed certain basic scientific assumptions widespread in the astronomical research community. It has made participants think in much broader terms; for example, that there might be other so far undetected objects which will not necessarily be detected at radio wavelengths. There is a general realisation that the universe is a much more complicated place than had been supposed twenty years ago. This realisation has come very largely from radio astronomy. Finally, some researchers have recently begun to take as their central task the integration of the great variety of separate kinds of observations now being produced, within one consistent astronomical framework.

So far we have stressed that acceptance of radio astronomy by optical astronomers, although sometimes grudging early on, has increased steadily for the last two decades or so, especially as, in recent years, the results forthcoming have become more and more precise, reliable and astronomically significant. Today the research communities of optical and radio astronomy overlap extensively. Radio and optical astronomers belong to the same scientific societies, participate in joint conferences, investigate in many cases the same celestial objects, use equally precise and often complementary techniques, communicate informally and read and cite each others' papers. Yet this seldom leads to collaboration which is close enough to warrant joint publication, in Britain at least. Out of 620 publications from the two major groups up to 1966, only 13 involve collaboration between radio and optical astronomers. Joint research between the two branches of astronomy is infrequent and when it does occur it seldom leads to shared publication. There are several factors which, singly or together, may work to produce this situation. Firstly, it may be that researchers in traditional astronomical departments approach the same phenomena from a perspective somewhat different from that of the radio astronomers and that they prefer generally to present their results separately to an audience whose members share the same perspective. Secondly, it may be that the distinct technical skills of radio and optical astronomers make difficult close collaboration in observational research. There can be little doubt that this is an important factor. The men we interviewed who were still working as radio astronomers, although many of them made use of optical observations in the course of their research, had no detailed practical knowledge of optical techniques. The same is undoubtedly true, *pari passu,* of optical astronomers. Thirdly, partly owing to their use of a distinctive and complex technical apparatus, the British radio astronomy groups have grown up physically and administratively separate from departments of astronomy. This is likely to make active collaboration rather more difficult. Furthermore, it means that, in general, graduate students in these two branches of astronomy are trained in the use of different techniques at separate locations; although radio astronomy students do usually take courses on astrophysics given by optical astronomers and the Royal Greenwich Observatory does run a selective introductory course for potential astronomers of both kinds. A fourth factor may be that of intellectual rivalry. Although there is no evidence of widespread rivalry between radio and other astronomers, in some areas there has certainly been highly critical debate and long-standing intellectual opposition. For instance, the confrontation between Ryle and his colleagues and certain sectors of the astronomical community over cosmological issues, whilst it has been conducted on the whole with academic propriety, has clearly made collaborative research impossible in this field.

We have seen, then, that the merging of radio and optical astronomy is far from total. Organizationally the radio astronomy observatories are distinct units more closely associated with departments of physics than with optical observatories. Furthermore, although there is an extensive exchange of information between optical and radio astronomers, which exerts a considerable influence on the direction taken by research in both these branches of astronomy, particular projects are almost never carried out in collaboration. In addition, it is important to note that a very large proportion of the papers published in astronomy over the last twenty years appear to have remained entirely uninfluenced by the advent of radio astronomy. The proportion of radio and radio-influenced papers published per year in the major British and American journals of astronomy up to 1966 never exceeds 30%. We must be careful therefore not to exaggerate the impact of radio upon optical astronomy. A large section of the astronomical community has continued to pursue traditional problems without giving evidence of having been influenced by the emergence and growth of radio astronomy. Nevertheless, radio astronomy has revitalised areas of optical research which had become almost or completely inactive, by furnishing new observations and by generating new questions. It has also helped to accelerate the further development of optical techniques and it has opened up entirely new areas of investigation to be explored with these techniques. Furthermore, it may well be, as our respondents maintained, that the *most significant* astronomical developments in the last two decades have been in the regions where there has been most cooperation. One striking feature of this development is that, even in those areas where radio astronomy has brought about considerable change in long-established assumptions, there has been no sign of stubborn intellectual resistance on the part of classically trained astronomers, even when the discoveries of radio astronomers have been most challenging and unexpected.

CONCLUDING REMARKS

We have tried in this paper to describe some of the main features of the emergence and growth of radio astronomy, with special reference to the crucial developments occurring in the UK. Much of what we have written above needs to be discussed in the light of current theories about the nature of scientific growth and compared with data from other case studies.[16] This paper is already too long for us to do that here.[17] Such attempts at interpretation must, therefore, be deferred for the moment. In the meantime we hope that other social scientists will be able to make use of the information we have provided.[18]

M. J. Mulkay, Department of Sociology, University of York, Heslington, York YO1 5DD. D. O. Edge, Science Studies Unit, University of Edinburgh, 34 Buccleuch Place, Edinburgh EH8 8JT.

M. J. MULKAY took his B.A. at LSE, his M.A. at Simon Fraser University (Vancouver) and his Ph.D. in sociology at Aberdeen. He is now reader in sociology at the University of York, where he is studying scientific elites and the sociology of knowledge.
D. O. EDGE received his B.A. and Ph.D. degrees from Cambridge, where he specialised in radio astronomy. Following six years as a BBC producer, he has held the post of Director of the Science Studies Unit at Edinburgh University since 1966. He is supervising research into aspects of the development of modern astronomy and physics and has written on the relationships between science and religion, on aspects of 'technological metaphor', and on the philosophy and practice of science education.

NOTES

This article has already appeared in Social Science Information 12:6 (1973) 25-61.
   1.   This paper presents some of the material from an intensive study of the development of radio astronomy in Britain. It is based on data from interviews, from the research literature, from the secondary writings of participants, and from citation and publication analyses. Although some data are presented in the section below on group structure, the detailed evidence for the statements made in this paper will be found in the full study, Astronomy Transformed: the Emergence of Radio Astronomy in Britain (to be published in New York: Wiley-Interscience, 1976) and in the complete research report, 'A Preliminary Report on the Emergence of Radio Astronomy in Britain', University Department of Engineering, Cambridge, vol. I (CUED/A-Mgt. Stud./TR7 1972) and vol. II (CUED/A-Mgt. Stud./TR8 1972). The research was carried out at the Science Studies Unit, Edinburgh, with the help of a grant from the SSRC and at the

University Department of Engineering, Cambridge, with the help of a grant from the Ford Foundation.

2. Similar work by Southworth in America was also known among the British radar workers.

3. The first recorded use in print of this phrase was in 1948.

4. Although Hey made several of the basic discoveries in radio astronomy, he was inactive between 1948 and 1953, owing to the reorganisation of government research establishments. By the time that he re-entered the field, the lead had passed irrevocably to the two university groups.

5. Radar equipment is designed to emit radio pulses which are then reflected back from celestial objects (e.g. the moon) or from atmospheric irregularities (e.g. meteor trails). Radio techniques are designed to receive and record radio emission generated by the celestial phenomenon under study.

6. A much more detailed account of intellectual development is given in Mulkay/Edge, 'A Preliminary Report', I, and in Edge/Mulkay, *Astronomy Transformed.*

7. The controversy which mainly involved the Cambridge and Sydney groups is described in detail in Mulkay/Edge, 'A Preliminary Report', and in Edge/Mulkay, *Astronomy Transformed.*

8. For a general discussion of this process see W. O. Hagstrom, *The Scientific Community* (New York: Basic Books, 1965).

9. See also J. Ben-David, *Fundamental Research and the Universities* (Paris: OECD, 1968).

10. Of a total of 300 papers published by the Jodrell Bank group up to the end of 1965, there are no more than three possible, and relatively unimportant, exceptions to this rule.

11. In this paper, the term 'leadership' refers to active, intimate involvement in the pursuit of research goals, and the resulting provision for colleagues of scientific material (data, techniques, theoretical analysis) which alters significantly the form and content of those scientific activities, the conception of those goals and the means whereby they are to be achieved. This form of leadership is necessarily reflected in co-authorship and citation data. We do not wish to deny that the major component in the leadership of any large scientific group consists of 'supportive' and administrative tasks, the acquisition of resources, and so on; nor that the strategic function involved in such leadership, with crucial decisions on the distribution of resources among the competing interests of group members, can be scientifically creative, involving both a high level of awareness of current research, and a critical expertise in its assessment.

12. This picture is strikingly confirmed, in detail, by both the co-authorship and citation data.

13. The small number responsible for commissioning, operating and maintaining the 'big dishes' forms the only major exception to this rule.

14. High internal cohesion is accompanied by a reputation for excessive secrecy among outsiders. See Mulkay/Edge, 'A Preliminary Report' and Edge/Mulkay, *Astronomy Transformed* for a full discussion.

15. See D. Crane, 'The Gatekeepers of Science', *American Sociologist* 2 (1967) 195-201; J. Ziman, *Public Knowledge* (Cambridge University Press, 1968).

16. See for example, that of T. S. Kuhn, *The Structure of Scientific Revolutions* (University of Chicago Press, 1962); D. Crane, *Invisible Colleges* (University of Chicago Press, 1972); M. J. Mulkay, *The Social Process of Innovation* (London: Macmillan, 1972). Perhaps the best case study at present available is N. Mullins, 'The Development of a Scientific Specialty: the Phage Group and the Origins of Molecular Biology', *Minerva* 10 (1972) 51-82.

17. Preliminary attempts at interpretation are made in Mulkay, *The Social Process of Innovation*; in the paper by G. Nigel Gilbert, pages 187-204 in this volume; in M. J.

Mulkay, G. N. Gilbert and S. W. Woolgar, 'Problem Areas and Research Networks in Science', *Sociology* 9 (May 1975) 187-203; and in D. O. Edge/M. J. Mulkay, 'Fallstudien zu wissenschaftlichen Spezialgebieten' pp. 197-229 in: Nico Stehr (ed.), *Wissenschaftssoziologie*, Kölner Zeitschrift für Soziologie und Sozialpsychologie supplementary vol. 18 (Opladen: Westdeutscher Verlag, 1975).

18.   A much more detailed presentation is available in the research reports mentioned in the first footnote, and in Edge/Mulkay, *Astronomy Transformed*.

G. NIGEL GILBERT

The Development of Science and Scientific Knowledge: the Case of Radar Meteor Research

In recent years it has become clear that a sociological study of academic science should pay attention to the relationship between the social institutions of science and the scientific knowledge which is produced.[1] Yet few empirical studies have tried to illuminate this relationship. By considering in some detail the emergence of one area of research, this paper tries to isolate some of the social and intellectual factors which affect the direction of scientific progress. Particular attention is paid to the growth of knowledge, the web of social relationships in which researchers work and the interaction between these two.

I have chosen to analyse the historical development of a specialty concerned with research into meteors using radar techniques, an area of research which seems in many ways to be typical of scientific investigation.[2] Radar meteor studies began immediately after the second World War and it is therefore probable that many of the significant influences on the course of its development may be similar to those at work in much present day scientific research. Unlike some specialties studied by sociologists, such as molecular biology, radar meteor research did not give rise to unexpected major discoveries, nor did it initiate a radical conceptual reorganisation of its discipline. Consequently, it did not receive any unusual public or scientific recognition. For these and other reasons, we can expect that this area of research is fairly representative of the bulk of normal present day scientific activity.

Although meteors have aroused the curiosity of astronomers for many centuries, it was not until the beginning of the nineteenth century that serious investigations began. Quantitative research using either visual or telescopic techniques proved to be difficult, however, with the result that meteors never became a topic of widespread astronomical interest. But scientists specialising in the physical investigation of the upper atmosphere did begin to take a passing interest in meteors during the early 1930s. These men were primarily concerned with a layer within the upper atmosphere known as the ionosphere. Radio transmission experiments revealed that the ionosphere varied irregularly in density. Some physicists thought that the trail of electrons and ions left behind when meteors passed through the ionosphere was responsible for some of the fluctuations. However, not only was the evidence in support of this hypothesis inconclusive, but there were also many other factors which, it was thought, might plausibly account for the variations.

In 1945, many of the physicists who had been involved in the development of radar during the war were seeking peacetime research posts. Some stayed on at government or military research establishments, continuing to use their wartime facilities and equipment on new problems. Others moved into academic posts. All of them found it necessary to settle on a research programme suitable for peacetime, preferably one based on what they had learned from their experiences in radar research. Some scientists, for example those who were to work at the Australian research centre, the Central Scientific and Industrial Research Organisation (CSIRO), and at Cambridge, England, began research on what was to become known as radio astronomy. Others thought that the radio signals emanating from the sun would repay further investigation.

J. S. Hey, a member of the British Army Operational Research Group (AORG), had become involved with meteors during the war as a result of investigations into the sources of interference in anti-aircraft radar systems, meteors having been suggested as one possible candidate. During the last years of the war and for the first two years of peace, he and his colleagues at the AORG performed a number of pioneering radar experiments on meteor trails. Another British group was led by A. C. B. Lovell. At the end of the war he left the Telecommunications Research Establishment (TRE), where he had been working on radar, to return to the staff of Manchester University. He had obtained a quantity of radar apparatus from the military authorities, which he set up at Jodrell Bank with the intention of using it to study cosmic rays — a subject with which the Physics Department at Manchester had been concerned for some years. He quickly found, however, that the apparatus was unable to detect cosmic rays but that it did pick up reflections which he suspected came from the ionised trails left by meteors passing through the atmosphere. Consequently, he turned his attention to trying to prove the connection between the radar reflections he had observed and the presence of meteor showers. Soon he was joined at Jodrell Bank by other scientists from the TRE who had had similar wartime experience with radar. In addition to these two groups, both of which were deeply involved in early radar meteor research, there was one other in Britain — a military research team concerned with ionospheric physics, which published one paper on meteors. Elsewhere, there were small groups of researchers interested in the effects of meteors on the ionosphere in Canada, the United States and Japan.

Each of the research groups involved in radar meteor research during the post-war years shared three characteristics. Firstly, their members were all physicists by training. Secondly, their members had had previous experience either with radar techniques, as a result of being concerned with development of radar during the war, or with work on the physics of the ionosphere. Thirdly, each group had been able to obtain radar equipment with great ease. A story of Lovell's will illustrate this last point:

During 1946, I acquired much more basic apparatus. I had left many friends in the Air Ministry and a brisk exchange of personal letters with a certain Air Marshal quickly released for me several trailers of radar equipment for which I think I paid a nominal sum of £10, although to buy it in the commercial market would probably have cost half a million.[3]

Many of the research groups which took up radar meteor research were located at military or ex-military establishments where radar had been developed and these had radar apparatus immediately to hand. Other groups obtained their radar through contacts with the military, as Lovell at Jodrell Bank did. No group built its own equipment.

As might be expected, the British researchers began by investigating problems of interest to ionospheric physicists, primarily concentrating on the correlation of ionospheric abnormalities with the passage of meteors. However, the emphasis of their research changed markedly after only a few months. While studying the correlation, J. S. Hey noticed that he seemed to be picking up echoes from only those meteors which passed perpendicularly to the radar beam. This suggested to him that it might be possible to determine the direction of approach of the meteors, and thus the position of the 'radiant', that is the point in the sky from which meteor showers appear to come. Hey also realised that the velocity of meteors could be found, if only rather approximately, with a method similar to that used during the war for finding the velocity of an aircraft. From the point of view of a physicist interested in the physics of the ionosphere, neither the radiant position nor the velocity of a meteor were facts of great significance. However, they were of great interest to members of quite another specialty, meteor astronomy.

Astronomers specialising in meteors were primarily concerned with one longstanding problem, with which they were making little progress. Most meteors entering the atmosphere are not part of a meteor stream, but arrive randomly, from all directions. These are called sporadic meteors. Some astronomers had suggested that sporadic meteors came from interstellar space; others argued that, like shower meteors, sporadics were members of the solar system. The controversy could only be resolved by discovering whether the sporadics followed a parabolic or elliptical path round the sun (implying that they were members of the solar system) or whether they followed a hyperbolic path (implying that they were of interstellar origin). Their paths could be determined only by accurate measurements of both the velocities and the positions of the radiants of sporadic meteors. But at that time the optical techniques of the meteor astronomers were not sufficiently precise to give an unambiguous conclusion to the controversy.

Consequently, meteor astronomers became very interested in the possibility that radar methods might provide more accurate measurements of velocity and radiant position than optical methods could hope to achieve. This interest by an outside group had far reaching effects on the course of radar meteor research. The first response of the radar meteor researchers was to attempt to understand the details of the astronomical problem. According to some of the scientists I interviewed, this involved reading astronomical text books and even listening to programmes on astronomy on the radio. In addition British meteor astronomers were invited to Jodrell Bank, and the radar scientists were invited to meetings of the British Royal Astronomical Society.

As a result, the radar meteor researchers found themselves involved in a change of outlook towards the meteors they were studying. The emphasis previously had been on the effects of meteors on the ionosphere. Now the astronomers were inviting them to consider the speeds and directions of motion of meteors; in particular, the effects on the ionosphere were to be studied in order to learn about meteors. On the whole, the radar experiments were successful. Within three or four years, apparatus had been designed and built to measure velocities and radiant positions with sufficient accuracy to show, fairly conclusively, that sporadic meteors were members of the solar system.

It would have been possible at this stage for the radar meteor researchers to continue to refine their methods in order to achieve greater and greater accuracy. But few new discoveries could be expected to result from these efforts. In fact, almost the only research of this kind to be started after 1953 was begun in Australia and New Zealand, where previously unobserved meteor showers could be studied. Since the possibility of doing research using established techniques at new sites was not one that could be adopted by the majority of researchers, a continuation of radar meteor research necessitated the finding of new problems to solve. The astronomers hoped that the radar workers, having solved one astronomical problem, would go on to solve others, such as the historical origin of meteors.

However, it seemed that radar techniques would be unsuitable for this task. Other possibilities were much more promising. One of these had arisen out of experiments conducted on a large fixed parabaloid aerial which had been constructed at Jodrell Bank to try to observe cosmic rays and meteors. When the aerial became operational, the team at Jodrell Bank found that they were receiving signals from radio sources in Cygnus and Casseiopea. Accidentally, they had built apparatus which would enable them to work on the astronomy of radio sources. At the time, this was an almost unexplored area of research, with good prospects of yielding important results. Moreover, it involved the use of technology similar to that with which they were already familiar from radar meteor work. Consequently, a number of recruits at Jodrell were persuaded to begin investigations of these, and later, of other sources, and research on sources proceeded for some years parallel to research on meteors.[4] However, work on sources relied on radio, rather than on radar techniques. Those who had been working on meteors applied their radar techniques to other topics: for instance, to studies of the upper atmosphere and to attempts to obtain reflections from the moon and planets.

By 1955, radio astronomy had grown at Jodrell Bank to such an extent that it had overwhelmed astronomical studies of meteors. From this date, the number of radar meteor papers published per year dropped steadily and by 1960 work on meteors there had virtually ceased. Hey, the leader at the other important British centre of radar meteor research, had had to give up active research in 1949 when the AORG was disbanded. He moved to the TRE, where he began work on emission from the sun. Later, around 1960, the last of Jodrell's radar meteor scientists moved to the TRE and began work on the development of radar for meteorological purposes. Elsewhere, other directions for research were followed. As the astronomical problem of the orbits of meteors began to be solved interest was renewed in those physical problems which the earliest researchers had begun studying. In addition, new physical problems and research possibilities had arisen during the course of the earlier astronomically orientated research. To give just one example: as a result of the observation of certain long enduring meteor trails it had been shown that the range of the trails sometimes fluctuated, often quite rapidly. When apparatus had been developed sufficiently to make it possible to measure the speed of these fluctuations, it became obvious that they were caused by air currents (i.e. 'winds') in the ionosphere blowing the trail across the sky. This discovery was turned to good use, as it proved to be possible to investigate winds in the upper atmosphere by studying their effect on meteor trails.

Research programmes on the physics of the ionosphere, such as the one on ionospheric winds, were taken up by the majority of research centres working on meteors. In addition, other research groups which had previously concentrated on ionospheric physics, but which had not been particularly interested in meteor research, began to be involved. As a result, the number of radar meteor researchers and the quantity of literature on meteors continued to increase. At the same time meteor research began to be more integrated into the body of ionospheric research. Eventually, meteor research became so interlocked with the rest of ionospheric physics that it is very difficult to distinguish a distinct body of research on meteors after 1960. By this time, researchers considered meteors to be just one phenomenon among many others affecting the ionosphere. Often, meteors were regarded as convenient probes enabling information on the state of the ionosphere to be gathered, as in the example of ionospheric winds just mentioned. It would thus be incorrect to say that meteor research ceased after 1960; rather, it faded imperceptibly into a wider body of ionospheric research.

Looking back on the development of radar meteor research, it is clear that the range and scope of the problems tackled by scientists working in the area grew as time passed. Initially, the focus of interest was on the correlation of meteors with atmospheric abnormalities. As more became known about meteors, further problem areas were opened up. The way in which these new problem areas were revealed often followed a recurring pattern. This pattern can be summarised as follows: first, as part of an established research programme, an experiment was designed to provide data concerning the behaviour of some phenomenon of interest. Often, this data was eventually obtained, but unexpectedly, the apparatus employed in the experiment also provided an opportunity to observe other phenomena. On some occasions, these unanticipated observations proved to be more interesting than the data originally sought. Consequently, the research programme was greatly modified so as to concentrate attention on further exploration of the unanticipated observations. Almost all the examples of radar meteor research I have mentioned so far were begun as a result of this process. To recapitulate: radar observation of ionospheric abnormalities to determine whether they were caused by meteors unexpectedly gave rise to opportunities to measure meteor velocities and radiant positions; Lovell's radar apparatus, intended for observation of cosmic rays, was found to observe meteors; the large parabaloid aerial at Jodrell, intended for studying cosmic rays and meteors unexpectedly turned out to be able to receive radio signals from space; and investigations of meteor trails unexpectedly showed that they could be used to measure ionospheric winds. In each of these cases, the unexpected observation inspired a programme of research which examined the new phenomenon in some detail.

The proliferation of lines of enquiry is one of the most characteristic features of the development of radar meteor research. Almost all significant innovations in the field took the form either of the realisation that hitherto unexamined variables could be measured, or of the discovery of theories which could relate variables previously thought to be unrelated. In either case, the effect of the innovation was to identify a new problem area in which further research would be required. Perhaps surprisingly, the opening up of new problem areas did not proceed more and more rapidly, as I imagine Holton and Price might have suggested.[5] Instead, new problem areas were discovered at an almost constant rate from the beginning of radar meteor research until about 1956; after that date, innovation within the radar meteor area itself ceased, although new problem areas were being opened up in radio astronomy and ionospheric physics.

To see what effect growth in the number of problem areas had on the participating scientists, it is worth examining rather more closely the history of Jodrell Bank, at one time the largest radar meteor research group anywhere in the world. The research at Jodrell Bank can be divided into four principal topics, which participants agree represent fairly the division of work as they saw it. Work on all of the topics began during the late 1940s, but each reached a peak of activity at a different time. Nevertheless, similar patterns of development can be seen in work on each of the four topics.

Each of the topics was begun by a new recruit to radar meteor research, who was directed to a problem area which hitherto had not received much attention. Often, the recruit was helped by suggestions from established researchers about the best methods to use in approaching the new problem area. Each research programme usually involved the construction of new apparatus or the development of a new theory, based to some extent on these suggestions. Over the course of several years, the apparatus and theory were refined and improved by the researcher often with the assistance of a number of research students. The product of the continual improvement of the new techniques and theories was a corpus of interrelated research focussed on the one problem area. Eventually the researcher moved away from Jodrell Bank, or lost interest in meteor research, with the result, in three of the four cases, that as soon as the research students he supervised completed their theses, work on the topic ceased. In one case a new research leader emerged from among the research students working on the topic, and he continued working in the problem area, but changed the emphasis of the research slightly.

Each research 'leader', therefore, was engaged in a developing research programme centred on his particular problem area. Because each of the research leaders focussed on different problems, they were not concerned at being anticipated by other researchers at Jodrell Bank. In other words, there was no competition, among the research leaders.[6] Similarly, there was little competition between Jodrell Bank and other research centres, because each had slightly different equipment and focussed on different problem areas. Interviews confirmed that the scientists at Jodrell Bank had not been worried about competition, and none could cite an instance of being anticipated.[7]

Each scientist was always restricted in the choice of further directions for developing his research. Perhaps the most important restriction was the scientist's limited experience of working in only one problem area. Research outside that area would have involved learning new skills and neglecting the expertise which previously had been carefully accumulated. It was also important for the scientist to ensure that his research was original. His knowledge of other research in the field (after 1948, it seems that all radar meteor researchers except those in Russia knew of each other's work) enabled him to avoid replicating research which had either already been carried out or which was currently in progress. These two restrictions still left the scientist a wide choice. But if he were to receive the reward of recognition, which is a necessary addition to the thrill of making discoveries for most scientists, the work he did had to be of interest to an 'audience' of fellow scientists. For much of the time, the most significant audience for the radar meteor scientists at Jodrell Bank was made up of their immediate colleagues, although during the early years it was augmented by members of the optical meteor astronomy community. The interest of such an audience could only be maintained if the scientist's research programme remained closely related to the research programmes of other meteor researchers. Thus each scientist was limited to following a research programme which differed from that of any other scientist at least to the extent that new findings were likely to be generated and which, at the same time, resembled other research to the extent that the expected results would be of interest to other re-searchers.

Within these constraints, each scientist had a number of possible options. He could be bold, by opening up and establishing a new problem area, as did the leaders at Jodrell Bank. But finding these new problem areas was not easy at any stage and became more difficult with the passing of time. Alternatively, he might be more timid, like the majority of research students at Jodrell Bank who restricted their work to following up and, in some cases, to refining the problems revealed by their leader's research.

Those who did open up new problem areas have now been much better rewarded by the scientific community than those who were only able to work on established problems. All but two of the six research leaders are now professors and had been so appointed by 1966; one of the others died young. By contrast, only two of the nineteen others who had worked on meteors at Jodrell Bank had been appointed to a post more senior than senior lecturer by 1966, although the professional ages of the two groups are not very different. Most of those who did not open up new lines of enquiry left the radar meteor research area shortly after completing their thesis work, to begin research often in quite different specialties of physics. The leaders, however, remained within the radar meteor field for a decade or more and then took up research in closely related fields. The recognition they received from other radar meteor scientists would have been a strong factor in discouraging the research leaders from aban-doning their meteor research to move on to new problems and new fields.

One can see from this account that the growth of knowledge on meteors was related in a complex way to the careers of radar meteor scientists. Only groups with particular past histories began radar meteor research. Researchers who succeeded in opening up new lines of enquiry were rewarded heavily compared with those who were involved only in working within established problem areas. Thus, there was a constant pressure on the researchers to locate new problem areas, with the result that the scope of radar meteor research expanded steadily. Eventually, the problems became so marginal to the original research problems that the research became indistinguishable from the more established specialty of ionospheric physics.

Having traced the growth of radar meteor research, I shall now compare my findings with those resulting from case studies of other areas of scientific research. One such case study is presented by Ben-David and Collins, who have examined the emergence of experimental psychology as a separate discipline in the middle of the nineteenth century.[8] The authors are primarily concerned to show that it is not sufficient to consider only the accumulation of 'fertile' ideas to explain the origin and growth of new areas of research. Consequently, their emphasis in explaining the emergence of experimental psychology is on the role of social rather than intellectual factors. They point out that, despite the widespread availability of those fruitful ideas which were necessary for the emergence of psychology, it was only in Germany that these ideas led to continuing growth in the number of adherents to the new discipline. They argue that at that time only in Germany were conditions suitable for the establishment of the new and differentiated scientific role of 'experimental psychologist'.

Ben-David and Collins suggest that German philosophers of the time enjoyed only low academic standing, while physiologists had relatively high prestige. On the other hand, the pursuit of philosophy offered much more favourable opportunities for career advancement than did physiology, where most routes for promotion had been blocked for some time. They argue that physiologists seeking advancement transferred their research to matters previously considered to be the subject matter of philosophy, while retaining the generally respected empirical methods which they had learned as physiologists. Moreover, philosophers seeking higher academic prestige learned these empirical methods and then applied them to their own problems. In this way, a new scientific identity, that of 'experimental psychologist', with favourable prestige and with opportunities for advancement was established. The psychologists then set up the research network which was to stimulate the future development of the new discipline. Finally, they recruited and trained students who, on completion of their training, moved elsewhere thus spreading the research network abroad.

This case study is taken by Ben-David and Collins to illustrate a general mechanism which they refer to as 'role hybridisation'. The process is a result of 'fitting the methods and techniques of an old role to the materials of a new one, with the deliberate purpose of creating a new role'.[9] They suggest that this will occur when both the chance of success in the old role is poorer than in the new one, and the academic standing of the old role is higher than that of the new one.

There is, however, a much more obvious factor which may account for the emergence of psychology at that time only in Germany. The failure of France, the United Kingdom and the United States to develop psychological research can easily be explained by comparing their relatively poorly developed procedures for recruiting students with the arrangements made in German universities. As Ben-David and Collins themselves point out, 'a major academic innovation has a chance of success only if it can attract a sizeable following'.[10] Following the reform of German universities after 1810, these universities had the dual functions of transmitting knowledge and providing opportunities for research. This was not yet the case with the academic systems of the other countries. In France, the first holder of a chair in experimental psychology, although at the prestigious Collège de France, was not required to train students. In Britain, both philosophy and physiology were still centred to a considerable extent outside the universities and consequently the recruitment of students was haphazard or non-existent. In the United States there were no facilities for research until the foundation of a graduate school in 1876; after this, 'a vigorous movement in experimental psychology, clearly derivative of the German movements, grew up'.[11]

However, the existence of institutionalised recruitment and training procedures in Germany does not, by itself, explain why psychology emerged at that particular time. Before completing the explanation, it is worth comparing the facts of Ben-David and Collins' study with my history of radar meteor research.

There are a number of clear resemblances. Firstly, it is possible to identify ideas which were precursors to the emergence of both fields. For instance, by the early 1930s, Appleton had suggested ionospheric investigations using radar-like apparatus and Skellett had suggested that meteors were affecting the ionosphere. Thus reference to the presence of 'fertile' ideas cannot be used as a complete explanation of the origin of either field. Secondly, the emergence of both areas of research is well characterised by the statement made by Ben-David and Collins of psychology, that the usual methods and techniques of one field were applied to achieve the goals of another field. For example, radar techniques developed for defence purposes were applied to solve problems in

ionospheric physics and to settle the astronomical controversy surrounding the origin of meteors. Indeed, the use of a technique developed
to solve one set of problems for the exploration of other problem areas is
a common pattern in the research I have described. Thirdly, the original
research workers in both fields had little difficulty in recruiting students.
Both research areas were established in growing university systems, with
institutionalised arrangements for first attracting students and then
guiding them towards a research career in the new field.

Nevertheless, there are a number of significant differences between the
two cases. The first and most obvious of these relates to the formation of a
new, differentiated, scientific identity as a result of the process of 'role-
hybridisation'. Ben-David and Collins argue that the new role is *deliberately created* in order to distinguish the new research from previous low
status work. But although their paper shows that the psychologists began
to engage in a new scientific activity, they present little evidence to show
that most of them saw themselves as consciously adopting a new role.

In the case of radar meteor research, it is clear that the research
workers did not deliberately try to differentiate themselves sharply either
from physicists or from meteor astronomers in order to confirm a new
scientific identity. On the contrary, they appeared to make every effort to
associate themselves with the astronomers by, for example, speaking at
meetings of the prestigious Royal Astronomical Society, by publishing in
astronomical journals and by inviting prominent meteor astronomers to
examine their apparatus. Indeed, this was to be expected, since for a
period of time the major part of the radar workers' research was directed
towards resolving the controversy about the origin of meteors. Consequently, the radar researchers were dependent upon the astronomers for
a definition of the controversy to be resolved, while the astronomers
depended on the radar researchers for the observations which might
eventually decide the issue. Nor did these researchers attempt to
differentiate themselves from other physicists. They recruited new members from graduates of physics, retained their membership in the Institute
of Physics, and the research groups located in universities continued to be
associated with the Physics Departments in which they had begun their
research.

There seems to be no evidence that those who began working on the
astronomical problem of the origin of meteors did so for reasons concerned with either a lack of career prospects in physics or with the relative
prestige of astronomy as compared with physics. During the late 1940s,
there was a dearth of university physicists in Britain and no reason to

suspect the existence of barriers to promotion. Moreover, in Britain at least, there was a sufficient supply of research funds to enable these men to pursue either physically or astronomically relevant topics. In fact, for the purposes of grant giving, little distinction was made between the two. Lastly, there is no reason to suggest that astronomy, as a discipline, was generally regarded as having a lower academic status than physics.

Thus the essential similarities between these two case studies are that both present evidence of a transfer of scientists, together with a set of techniques, to an area of research where it seemed possible that those techniques might provide solutions to problems on which little progress had previously been made. In addition, both areas had access to institutionalised procedures for recruiting students. Nevertheless, despite these similarities the notion of 'role-hybridisation' does not provide a satisfactory explanation of the reasons for radar researchers' early involvement with astronomical problems.

A theoretical scheme which would explain the emergence of *both* research areas might run as follows: like most scientists, the researchers involved in the emergence of a new research area were motivated partly by the hope that they could make worthwhile discoveries and partly by a desire to gain recognition (and possibly rewards associated with recognition such as promotion). In order to gain significant recognition the scientists would have to pursue research which was judged by at least a part of the research community to be both interesting and more than moderately successful. One way to do such successful research is to resolve long-standing problems by using a technique which has not been previously applied but with which one is familiar. This is exactly what some radar researchers achieved when they took up meteor astronomy. Similarly, some physiologists in Germany found that their techniques were of use when applied to problems which previously had been the concern of philosophers. Attempts to solve the problems raised by philosophers generated a continuing stream of further problems, leading eventually to the growth of a new discipline. But the possibility of achieving success in this way depends on the interaction of a number of social and intellectual factors. These include prior knowledge of the appropriate technique; the often accidental discovery that the technique might be appropriate in a new area; some contact with the existing practitioners in the field; the availability of recruits to the new discipline; and, for a major success such as that achieved by the 'founders' of psychology, the luck or judgment to find a problem whose solution has ramifications outside its immediate context.

In another case history, Mullins has studied the emergence and growth of phage research, a precursor of molecular biology.[12] For the purposes of his analysis he has divided the development of the phage research network into four stages, of which I shall examine only the first two: the 'paradigm group' and 'communication network' stages. His account can be briefly summarized as follows. The phage group's intellectual forebears were two physicists, Bohr and Schrödinger, both of whom speculated about the 'ultimate principle of life'. Their interest in this biological topic was matched by that of a number of physicists, who had concluded that physics would not provide interesting research until the construction of large and expensive apparatus had made further studies on nuclear particles possible, and that biology had the greatest number of unsolved problems which appeared to be open to fruitful investigation using physical methods.

As an outcome, during the period 1935-45, a number of physicists and bacteriologists began what became known as phage work. The decision by a central group of phage workers to take systematic steps to recruit scientists to phage work, principally by starting a summer school in 1945, marks the end of Mullins' 'paradigm group' stage and the beginning of the 'network' stage. During this latter stage, the problems tackled by the phage workers did not greatly change but the methods employed were gradually refined. The network stage culminated in a major success: Watson and Crick's publication of a model for DNA in 1953. As Mullins notes, the following nine years were chiefly spent in resolving further details of the structure and function of DNA.

Unfortunately, although Mullins states that he is concerned with the role of intellectual as well as social factors in explaining the development of phage work, he omits from his account almost all details of the problems with which the phage workers were concerned and of the techniques which they used to solve these problems. Nevertheless, Mullins does emphasise a number of interesting features. About half of the earlier phage workers had been trained to Ph.D. level in the physical sciences. The initial impetus to set up the group had come from physicists. But the central problem of phage work, the 'secret of life', was one which previously had been considered to be a topic in biology. However, it seems that the majority of biologists were unable to appreciate the significance of the phage experiments and had difficulty in understanding the methods used. Nevertheless, despite this apparent lack of biological interest, no one seems to have doubted the importance of discovering the 'secret of life', nor that this was a problem worthy of investigation for its own sake.

Some important themes run through both this case history and the two I have previously examined. As in the previous accounts, a body of scientists from one specialty (in this case, mainly physicists) applied their methods and techniques to the problems of another specialty (in this case biology and genetics). In contrast with the development of radar meteor research, the problem tackled by the phage workers — understanding the mechanism of the transmission of genetic information — had not been specifically posed by biologists. In general, biologists, though they presumably found the problem to be of some interest, did not particularly concern themselves with efforts to find its solution. Perhaps as a result, the early phage workers proceeded in some isolation from the rest of the biological community. This isolation was, in the main, broken down by the desire of the phage workers to use any technique they thought might prove useful, in combination with the physical methods they had originally applied to their problem. As their work progressed, they began to feel that biochemical techniques might be of some help to them, despite their initial distate for the research style of biochemists. The techniques of genetics had also been of use in phage work from the beginning. Consequently, the phage group began to form links with the genetic and biochemical research networks. Later, these were extended to include X-ray crystallographers and structural chemists.

From the evidence of this account, and the history of radar meteor research, one can conclude that communication links, taking the forms of friendships, attendance at meetings and reprint exchange among others, are established only when one or other party is doing research which is expected to yield useful information. Because initially the flow of information between biologists and phage workers was very restricted, the phage workers came to form a clearly defined and close-knit group, in contrast with the radar meteor researchers, who were not at any time self-consciously differentiated from either physicists or astronomers.

Fisher, in another interesting case study, has documented the decline of a mathematical specialty concerned with the theory of invariants.[13] During the second half of the nineteenth century, research on the theory became widespread throughout the Western academic world. At its peak, about one-third of the annual total of algebraic research papers were written in the field. Yet, by 1940, virtually all work on the theory had ceased. In retrospect, mathematicians have said that invariant theory was suddenly killed in 1893 by the work of Hibbert, who both solved one of the major problems and then introduced a new approach to mathematics which outmoded the whole field of enquiry. But, Fisher maintains, this explanation is false. Interest in the theory declined at varying rates in different countries, not because further work was unnecessary but because a variety of extrinsic factors prevented researchers passing on their interest in the theory to subsequent generations. Fisher argues that in Great Britain, the predominantly amateur mathematicians began to involve themselves in their professional careers; in America, students took up teaching rather than research; and in Germany, those involved either 'did not seem to want progeny . . . or did not have the opportunity to train them'.[14]

But this interpretation is unconvincing. As Edge and Mulkay have pointed out:

> It seems to be a remarkable coincidence that in Great Britain, Germany, and the United States, quite different external factors should entirely eliminate, within the duration of a single academic career, a specialty which had previously produced such a large proportion of algebraic research.[15]

A more plausible reason for the failure of a generation of invariant theorists to recruit scientific heirs is contained within Fisher's paper. He notes that Hibbert made a major contribution to mathematics in founding the 'modern algebraic' school. This school, which rapidly gained converts, laid emphasis on quite different kinds of problems and solutions from those considered important by the older mathematicians. In particular, a disregard of invariant theory was part of the ideology of the school. Work on the theory came to be considered 'old-fashioned, non-mathematical computation'.[16] As a result, those people who continued to work in the old area were not considered to be serious mathematicians. By the 1920s, the followers of the 'modern' school had come into ascendency, while there were few remaining invariant theorists still at work.

This evidence indicates that the demise of work on invariant theory was at least partly due to the relative success of the 'modern algebraic' school, who were able to show that their techniques could help solve not only the traditional problems of the invariant theorists, but also problems from other areas. Consequently, students were attracted to the modern algebraicists, in preference to the invariant theorists. The number of invariant theorists gradually declined as they were no longer able to attract recruits. At the same time, 'modern algebra' was being steadily developed to the point at which the methods and problems of invariant theory appeared to be quite outmoded by comparison. Interest in the theory then became confined to a small rearguard, which persisted until the 1930s.

I have reviewed the development of four scientific specialties in this paper. The growth of each was found to depend on an interaction between social and intellectual factors. In particular, I have suggested that scientists are most successful within the social structure of science when they solve 'interesting' scientific problems, an 'interesting' problem being one whose solution has significant consequences for the current and future work of other scientists. However, such 'interesting' problems are not easy to find. Most frequently, they arise by chance, revealed as a consequence of unexpected observations made with apparatus intended for other purposes. Sometimes, they arise because it is realised that techniques currently in use in one area of research are applicable to the unsolved problems troubling another area.[17] On occasion, the solution of such problems may generate additional, related problems, with the result that a new specialty or discipline may emerge to investigate them. The possibility of such a development requires, however, that recruits be available to join the new research area, and growth will continue only so long as a continuing supply of recruits is forthcoming. Eventually, as the research area's central problems are solved, and as techniques, theories and problems are incorporated from other specialties, the area may either decline in importance, gradually losing members to other more interesting fields, or it may become closely associated with other 'neighbouring' research areas. The bare outlines of these processes of development have been suggested by the case studies considered in this paper. However, the details still await further comparative research.[18]

G. Nigel Gilbert, Department of Sociology, University of York, Heslington, York YO1 5DD.

G. NIGEL GILBERT studied engineering at Cambridge and is now working for his Ph.D. there on the development of scientific specialties. He is currently lecturer in sociology at the University of York.

NOTES

1. This has been argued by M. D. King, 'Reason, Tradition and the Progressiveness of Science', *History and Theory* 10 (1971) 3-32; by R. D. Whitley, 'Black Boxism and the Sociology of Science' in P. Halmos (ed.), *Sociological Review Monograph* 18 (1972) 61-92; and by M. J. Mulkay, 'Some Aspects of Cultural Growth in the Natural Sciences', *Social Research* 35 (1969) 22-52.
2. The paper is a summary of some parts of a more detailed study of radar meteor research. The material on which the study is based is of four kinds. First, a literature

search yielded what is thought to be a complete list of papers published in the area between 1944 and 1960. These papers provide both an indication of the personnel who worked in the area and a record of the development of new knowledge. Second, contemporary research reports, records of meetings and conferences, and books written by the participants were consulted. Third, most of those involved in the emergence of radar meteor research in Britian were interviewed. (Most of the radar research on meteors was carried out in Britain, although there were also several centres involved in the research scattered throughout the world — in Canada, the USA, New Zealand, Australia, and Russia for example.) Fourth, several scientists currently working in closely related fields were interviewed in order to identify present day developments.

3. A. C. B. Lovell, *The Story of Jodrell Bank* (Oxford University Press, 1968) 9.

4. For details of Jodrell Bank's work on sources, see M. J. Mulkay/D. O. Edge 'A Preliminary Report on the Emergence of Radio Astronomy in Britain', University Department of Engineering, Cambridge, 1972; and 'Cognitive, Technical and Social Factors in the Growth of Radio Astronomy', pages 153-186 above.

5. G. Holton, 'Models for Understanding the Growth and Excellence of Scientific Research', pp. 94-131 in: S. R. Graubard/G. Holton (eds.), *Excellence and Leadership in a Democracy* (New York: Columbia University Press, 1962); D. J. de Solla Price, *Little Science, Big Science* (New York: Columbia University Press, 1963).

6. In contrast, W. O. Hagstrom, *The Scientific Community* (New York: Basic Books, 1965) and J. Gaston, 'Secretiveness and Competition for Priority of Discovery in Physics', *Minerva* 9 (1971) 472-92, emphasise the pervasiveness of competition within the scientific community.

7. Mulkay/Edge, 'The Growth of Radio Astronomy' also make this point, with respect to research on radio astronomy.

8. J. Ben-David/R. Collins, 'Social Factors in the Origins of a New Science: The Case of Psychology', *American Sociological Review* 31 (1966) 451-465.

9. *Ibid.,* 459.

10. *Ibid.,* 460.

11. *Ibid.,* 465.

12. N. C. Mullins, 'The Development of a Scientific Specialty: The Phage Group and the Origins of Molecular Biology', *Minerva* 10 (1972) 51-82.

13. C. S. Fisher, 'The Last Invariant Theorists', *European Journal of Sociology* 8 (1967) 216-44.

14. *Ibid.,* 242.

15. Mulkay/Edge, 'A Preliminary Report' II, chapter 11, 19.

16. Fisher, 'The Last Invariant Theorists', 218.

17. Michael Mulkay, 'Conceptual Displacement and Migration in Science', *Science Studies* 4 (1974) 205-234.

18. M. J. Mulkay/G. N. Gilbert/S. Woolgar, 'Problem Areas and Research Networks in Science', *Sociology* 9 (May 1975) 187-203.

Theory and Method in the Study of New Disciplines

M. J. MULKAY

Methodology in the Sociology of Science: Some Reflections on the Study of Radio Astronomy

The traditional view of methodology in sociology has been relatively simple. Its basic assumptions have been as follows: that empirical data relevant to sociological analysis exist independently of the investigator; that the fundamental task of the researcher is to 'gather' these data (the metaphor is revealing) whilst minimising any distorting effects that might arise from the investigator's intrusion into the social process; that adequate evidence for any one theoretical concept can usually be obtained by means of one single operational indicator; and that research method provides the link between theory and the collection of data, whilst remaining distinct from theory and independent of the data to be gathered. In recent years these assumptions have begun to be revised.[1] In the first place, it is argued that sociological research is a social act, an act in which those being studied usually participate with the investigator to produce the final observations. It follows that the sociologist must do more than simply take a few elementary precautions against distorting the results. He must begin instead to explore the social nature of the research act and he must begin to take his conclusions on this topic into account when interpreting his results. In the light of this argument, social facts begin to appear increasingly volatile and subject to variations due to the largely unexplored complexities of the research process. Thus it is necessary to view any one phenomenon from several perspectives. It is necessary to assume that there are likely to be several indicators for any single concept and on the assumption that the results given by different indicators will vary, to examine these variations, not only in relation to the phenomenon under study but also in the light of the social procedures which each indicator requires. Comparison between various indicators not only throws into relief the theoretical notions which are used or implied in interpreting empirical material; it also shows that theories about research techniques are involved.

For the rest of this paper I am going to accept these revised assumptions. I shall assume that sociological research is a social act; that the subjects under investigation are likely to be responding to a variety of definitions of the investigator and, through him, perhaps to other less obvious audiences; that any one sociologically defined phenomenon can be observed by means of several indicators; and that these indicators must be interpreted in relation to the specific social contexts created in the course of research. These assumptions raise difficult problems for those of us concerned with empirical research. In particular, they make exceedingly problematic the transition from observing social life to stating results. What I want to do now is to illustrate a few of these problems by reference to the study of the development of radio astronomy carried out by D. O. Edge and myself.[2]

My collaborator and I were interested, generally, in the nature of scientific development. We decided to study radio astronomy in particular, largely because my colleague had at one time been a radio astronomer and because it seemed possible that, by working together in the investigation of this field, we could produce a piece of research which would be unusual in giving equal weight to scientific and to social developments. Our initial definition of the problem reflected this concern with development and with the relations between social and scientific factors. Basically, we started with three fairly broad questions:

— How did radio astronomy emerge as an identifiable area of study?
— What was the sequence of scientific developments?
— Were scientific developments accompanied by discernable changes in social relationships?

These questions could be approached in several different ways. We could, for example, review the literature for relevant hypotheses and use the material on radio astronomy to test these hypotheses. There were, however, several good reasons for not proceeding in this fashion. There was in the first place scant literature on the emergence of scientific disciplines; and what literature there was seemed too piecemeal and its results too uncertain to provide convincing hypotheses. At the beginning, we knew very little about the development of radio astronomy. It was, therefore, impossible to judge without more exploratory study whether the few, questionable hypotheses available could in any way be tested against observations drawn from this field. Furthermore, hypothesis-testing requires uniform, controlled methodological procedures. Use of such procedures would perhaps have led us to miss just those things which were unexpected about radio astronomy and, therefore, especially interesting. In addition, whereas none of the existing sociological studies paid much attention to the development of scientific knowledge, we definitely wanted to use our unique chance of studying that in detail and in relation to social factors.

As a result of considerations such as these, we decided that our study should be frankly exploratory. In other words, we decided that we would not define in advance the detailed questions which were to be answered nor the precise research procedures which were to be adopted. We also decided that, given the scarcity of reliable studies in the area as well as the lack of convincing theoretical analysis, we would present our results with a minimal theoretical commitment. We would try to leave the theoretical interpretation of our material as open as possible until further comparable studies were available. Now it is likely that, in an exploratory study such as this, the difficulties of interpretation arising from the social nature of the research act will be fairly *obvious,* owing to the relative lack of control exercised by the investigators over the research process. Nevertheless, the kinds of problems which I shall now discuss are, I think, still present in sociological investigations of a more structured kind.

We began our research with a certain amount of information on the development of radio astronomy which my colleague had acquired whilst he was a radio astronomer and in the course of his subsequent irregular contacts with radio astronomers. We knew, for example, that radio astronomy started to expand rapidly during the 1940s and early 1950s. We knew that it required large-scale techniques, so that active radio astronomers must always be members of groups which have suitable equipment. We also knew who to go to for lists of publications and lists of group members. And we knew who had made major contributions to the field and who would, therefore, have to be interviewed. This kind of background knowledge and personal contact was invaluable in getting the research started and in helping us to overcome a whole series of practical difficulties. But the point I want to stress at the moment is that such knowledge is acquired whilst one is a comparatively uncritical participant, and that this knowledge is a social construct of doubtful validity. Let me give an example.

I can remember my partner's remarking right at the beginning of our study: 'We have chosen a very simple case. It all began when Jansky made this unexpected discovery in the early 1930s. This is shown by the way in which all graduate theses in the Cambridge radio astronomy group continued, until the 1950s, to cite Jansky's original contribution'. My colleague had formed this belief when he was a participant and it appears to be a belief which has become widely accepted by many radio astronomers who actually took no part in the early years. This view of the growth of the field has two main elements: it stresses the contribution of the 'great man'; and it sees scientific growth as a fairly straightforward development of intellectual opportunities revealed by the great man. Thus the development of radio astronomy is viewed by many participants as a simple, cumulative growth, having specifiable origins in the work of Jansky. This interpretation came, by way of 'background knowledge', to affect our initial perception of the kind of result we would probably obtain from our study. Yet it is almost entirely wrong. It was dispelled from our minds quite early in the research process, as we examined other sources of information. For example, when we interviewed those who had been members of the first radio astronomy groups in Britain, we found that they denied being greatly influenced by Jansky. And when we examined the citations they had made in those early days, we found that the references to Jansky in their published research reports were negligible. Reality was clearly more complex than the 'Jansky myth' implied.

I have given a very simple example of a participant's misconception which was taken over by the investigators (although in this case the notion was soon corrected). The point that I want to make is that it was only noticed because it appeared obviously incompatible with other information. Thus there may well be many other such erroneous assumptions, perhaps of a less obviously factual kind, which are taken over by the investigators, which are never noticed, and which help to determine the results. It might be suggested that this is the typical problem of the participant observer and that it can be avoided by using other research techniques in which participants have no part to play. I would answer this proposal in the following way. Firstly, if the sociological study of science involves a close examination of its *technical culture,* the active cooperation of technically competent participants must be gained in one way or another. Secondly, on many issues of sociological interest, members of a given research community are likely to have firm and agreed definitions of reality which are linked to their technical and scientific assumptions. It is often possible to regard such issues as problematic only if the investigator has enough technical knowledge to challenge these firm definitions.

The main thrust of my argument so far then is that if we are to study in detail the operation of scientific communities, we must have the active cooperation of participants or ex-participants; that including participants as investigators affects the nature of the research act and may lead to the investigators' taking over false, or incomplete, assumptions from the group under study; but the misleading assumptions can, at least sometimes, be corrected by the use of several sources of information or multiple indicators. This last point, however, raises a further question: how do we use these various kinds of partially conflicting information to reach a valid inference? In the case of the Jansky myth what we did was roughly as follows. On the basis of our background knowledge we put open-ended questions to participants in the course of interviews. The answers we received did not match our initial expectations about the contribution of Jansky. It was, of course, impossible to assess these conflicting data without some further, independent evidence. We used the relatively objective data provided by citations. These data are objective in the sense that they cannot be distorted by the selective perception of participants. However, the use of citation patterns in this way, as an index of lines of intellectual influence, clearly involves an implicit theory of citing. It may appear fairly obvious that, if British radio astronomers did not cite Jansky, they were not directly influenced by him. But in fact we know very little about who cites whom in science, and why. There has been no clear demonstration of the way in which citations reflect the processes of scientific influence. Thus our interpretation of the contribution of Jansky, although it seems at the commonsense level to be undeniable, appears upon closer examination to be based upon quite speculative theoretical notions about the nature of our research techniques, in this case, upon an implied theory of citing.

I have illustrated my themes so far in relation to the comparatively simple problem of establishing how far Jansky contributed to the emergence of radio astronomy.[3] The problem becomes considerably more complex when one attempts to describe the long term evolution of ideas in radio astronomy. In the first place, participants tend, in retrospect, to view much prior work simply as wrong. The current framework of knowledge provides their criteria for judging the significance of earlier research. Thus there is a tendency for scientists to dismiss much prior work, not as reasonable attempts to explore problems which were then scientifically ill-defined, but as errors. And, being errors, they are no longer scientifically interesting. This is the usual view taken by researchers *within* their professional community. Now it is very seldom that they talk of such matters to outsiders.[4] For most outsiders are both uninterested and technically incompetent. When interviewed therefore, they tend to gloss over their mistakes and wrong-turnings, not out of any deliberate intention to mislead, but because they regard such work as scientifically unimportant. There is a definite confusion in their accounts between *scientific* accuracy and *historical* accuracy. So, if the interviewer takes their accounts of intellectual development as complete, he is likely to get a misleading impression of steady, undeviating advance toward the state of knowledge which now exists. A similar pattern emerges when one examines participants' historical writings. On the whole, they miss out the slow, groping development which often occurs. Instead, they tend to take a fairly stereotyped form; they note the major discoveries which occurred early on, and then they skip quickly through to the current framework of knowledge — as if all that happened in between was part of an inevitable progression. Perhaps the only way of redressing this emphasis by participants on the contemporary scientific framework is by close, chronological study of research reports and, in particular, review articles and symposia. A careful examination of this material tends to reveal a continual series of false inferences, redefinitions of problems, and alterations of intellectual perspective on the part of scientists as their subject develops.

What I have just been saying implies the need, once again, to compare several kinds of information and to assess, or interpret, these kinds of information quite differently. In the study of radio astronomy, we regarded our reading of the original research reports as less subject to distortion, or 'selective emphasis', than participants' retrospective accounts. We regarded participants' special view of intellectual development as arising from their concern with scientific validity, a concern which was reinforced by their normal patterns of technical communication and which helped to determine the nature of their response to our investigations. Once more, then, our use of the data depended on an instrumentation theory; in this case an instrumentation theory which clearly took into consideration the social relationship between investigator and respondent. It might be objected that our interpretation of the various kinds of data was merely a plausible *ex post facto* assessment. There is, however, a partially independent check. The straightforward view of undeviating development proposed by many participants implies that major scientific advances will be perceived in advance and clearly predicted. In radio astronomy this has not been the case. Most of the major discoveries have, in fact, been totally unexpected.[5] This provides, I think, further support for the view of scientific development in this field as proceeding irregularly and involving continual reappraisals and redefinitions; a view which is supported by our interpretation of evidence drawn from the research literature but which is seldom volunteered by participants.

I have suggested that typical participants' accounts of intellectual development are incomplete and, to some extent, systematically biased. But I have *not* suggested that their accounts are essentially *inconsistent* with accounts which rely heavily on published research reports. These sources of information are normally different in emphasis rather than incompatible. This is borne out by the way in which participants reacted when we circulated our first draft through the post and asked them to comment on our historical reconstruction of scientific development. Our reconstruction was firmly based upon original research reports and contemporary discussions, where these were recorded, although it did take account of interview material and participants' historical writings as well. Our respondents reacted in the following way. They did not reject or heavily criticise our account of scientific development. Many of them concentrated on correcting fairly minor points of technical detail. A few made more substantial points which could be independently corroborated. Several expressed feelings of discomfort at seeing all their early 'mistakes' set down in detail. They clearly found it disheartening.

This relative lack of criticism from participants gave us increased confidence in our findings. Their concern with technical detail and with past errors offered some confirmation of our interpretation of the bias contained in participants' historical writings and in interview material. In making this last statement, I do not mean to imply that interview material is of no value in arriving at an understanding of intellectual development in science. Participants will not normally *volunteer* an account of scientific development which gives full recognition to discontinuity, misunderstanding, redefinition of problems, and so on. It is possible, however, as one's knowledge grows, to ask more probing questions, to challenge simplistic accounts, and to introduce into the discussion the views of other participants. These tactics usually lead participants to provide a more elaborate statement, which reflects more closely the actual historical complexities. Furthermore, certain kinds of relevant information can only be gathered by means of interviews. For example, it is very seldom that 'errors' are retracted in the official journals. We came across only one case in radio astronomy where an observational claim was later admitted in print to be wrong — and this admission was made in *Scientific American.* Now it is clear that many published observations do become widely suspect and generally ignored as unreliable. But this formation of scientific opinion occurs informally and is not recorded in the journals. Of course, to those who know the area well, the consequences of these changes in scientific opinion can be observed in the journals. But clearly, if we wish to understand in detail how these changes occur, we must try to explore the informal social processes, at least partly by means of interviews.

It is obvious that the research interview is a social act. It is, perhaps, equally obvious that the nature of this act will vary from one area of inquiry to another. In many areas, the investigator and the respondent will share a common framework of assumptions, a similar vocabulary and a similar background of experience, all of which will enable them to communicate fairly easily. This may be the case, for example, as regards research on the mass media, on the family, and so on. Even in these areas, of course, difficulties of interpretation arise. The most basic of these difficulties consists of knowing how far questions and answers mean the same thing to both parties and of discerning whether investigator and respondent are engaged in a particular role-set, which the investigator does not allow for but which nonetheless influences the results. The most common interview-set is that in which respondents regard the researcher as socially superior and, consequently, provide him with conventionally approved responses. Problems of these kinds are clearly evident in interviews with scientists. They do, however, take rather special forms.

In the study of radio astronomy we used three types of interview: where the respondent answered questions put by a sociologist alone; where questions were put by both a sociologist and an ex-participant; where the interview was conducted solely by an ex-scientist.[6] Each of these types of interview entails a different social context in which empirical material tends to be produced in different ways.

Interviews conducted by a sociologist alone tend to have a relatively low level of technical content. Even when the sociologist has a good layman's knowledge of the field, he is unable to discuss technical issues with the flexibility of a participant or ex-participant. Yet technical and social issues are intimately related. A scientist's typical account of why he took up a particular line of research at a particular time will stress technical considerations, e.g. 'the problems were scientifically interesting', 'suitable techniques were available'. Consequently, if one wants to know about the effect of competitive or other social pressures on the decision, it is helpful to be able to enter into a dialogue regarding technical factors in the course of which the respondent can be guided towards greater consideration of social factors. It is useful, therefore, to have a technically competent interviewer present. Perhaps the best arrangement is to have the scientist interviewed by both a sociologist and a participant/ex-participant. However, this social triangle does have its difficulties.

In order to gain the respondent's interest, allay his possible suspicions and establish rapport, it is usually necessary to open the,interview with questions from the ex-participant on technical/scientific developments. This exchange reassures the respondent because it resembles his everyday discussions with colleagues. Thus excellent rapport can quickly be established between respondent and ex-participant, and much information on social as well as technical issues can be elicited. If the sociologist continually intervenes in this process he is in danger of disrupting its flow and of preventing the respondent from elaborating his responses within this normal frame of reference. There is a tendency, therefore, for the sociologist to refrain from entering the dialogue as long as the respondent is providing new information. The only circumstances in which the sociologist feels obliged to enter the discussion is when the respondent's account of social events appears in some way problematic. Thus he tends to intervene when the respondent is inconsistent, when one respondent's account differs from that of others, or when issues are being examined about which the interviewee is reluctant to talk openly (such as secrecy or competition). In this situation, the sociologist becomes in an obvious sense (more obvious than when he is the sole interviewer) an outsider. And some respondents at least adapt by providing more guarded responses to those questions which the 'alien' sociologist appears to regard as specially important. If this is an accurate description of the triadic interview situation, some of the responses which it generates must be interpreted differently from those which occur when there is only one interviewer. This does not mean that the responses in a three-person interview are *more* problematic. They are simply different; and they require different treatment by the investigator.[7]

There are several other factors which affect the interview situation. For instance, those with the widest knowledge of the social and scientific development of research groups tend to be group leaders and other older members of the groups. These men are, therefore, particularly important sources of information and, when participants' accounts are inconsistent, one might be tempted to regard their views as more authoritative. However, they tend also to be most concerned with maintaining the group's reputation and, consequently, with preventing the passage of information which would reflect adversely on the group. Furthermore, group leaders are eminent members of disciplines which have much higher academic status than that of the investigators. It is, therefore, very difficult to break down the social barriers which support group leaders, in their tendency to present a favourable image of their group's activities.[8]

The general points, then, that I want to make are that even within this single study the social context in which interview responses were provided varied considerably; that the social context of the interview is, in fact, quite complex; and that the research context should at least be borne in mind when interpreting interview material.

In our study we tried to a limited extent to face some of the difficulties of using interview material. The procedure we adopted was roughly as follows: on the basis of the interview transcripts and other data, we identified a number of recurrent themes or issues, e.g. the relationship between the two main British groups or the way in which new lines of research came to be pursued.[9] We then extracted from the transcripts all statements bearing on each of these themes. This enabled us to judge the range of responses and the degree of agreement on particular issues. Continual reference was made to the interview transcripts in order to check that the material was being interpreted correctly in the light of the interview context. This material was combined with other data to provide the empirical foundation of the study. Quotations were used copiously to illustrate participants' views, to demonstrate the range of views and to give the reader as much direct contact as possible with the original data. Wherever it seemed particularly necessary we gave an indication of the interview context in which the respondent's view had been expressed. Because of the complexity of our subject matter and the imponderables involved in even the simplest kind of interpretation, we decided to check our work as far as possible by sending the first draft of our report for comment to all those we had interviewed, as well as to a number of participants we had been unable to interview.

We received a considerable response, much of which was useful in improving the historical and scientific accuracy of our study. Perhaps surprisingly, there were only two objections to the way in which we had used quotations from interviews. Certain aspects of our initial interpretation, however, received strongly negative comment, especially from group leaders. These comments concerned discussion of competition/cooperation, leadership and secrecy. Entering into a dialogue in this way with participants is, of course, quite unlike the traditional sociological approach, which advocates that the researcher should minimise social interaction with respondents. Our approach, in contrast, assumes that interaction is almost unavoidable and that the researcher, instead of trying to avoid interaction, should make explicit the social nature of the various research contexts in which he engages and should take these into account when stating his results. Thus participants' comments on our draft constitute additional data, no different in principle from the original interview material or from participants' historical writings. Nonetheless, these comments do require a somewhat different kind of interpretation, because they are the product of a distinctive type of social interaction. I shall discuss here only the comments on competition/cooperation.

In our preliminary report we stressed the prevalence of competition rather than cooperation among radio astronomy groups. This was based on the frequency of respondents' references to competition and rivalry, compared with the infrequency of accounts of cooperation. In addition, there was documentary and other evidence of one longstanding dispute as well as an almost complete absence of joint publication by members of different groups. A number of our interviewees, and especially the group leaders, reacted as follows. They made no complaint about the essential accuracy of our account of the one major dispute, between a British group and a group abroad. They claimed, however, that we had misrepresented the real relationship between the two major British groups. They pointed out that there had been much *technical* cooperation between the two British groups, which would not result in joint papers, and they gave examples of technical cooperation. They also suggested that joint publication was a poor index of scientific cooperation, for long term cooperative research might prove unproductive or produce disproportionately few results. Finally, they stated that the two large groups in Britain had adopted an explicit policy of avoiding research overlap and that this policy, which was itself a form of cooperation, significantly reduced the likelihood of outright competition.

This feedback from respondents clearly provided useful information. It drew attention to the existence of *technical* cooperation, which was not reflected in the number of joint publications. In other words, our assumptions (or our implicit theory) about the connection between joint publication and cooperation were shown to need revision. In addition, our notice was drawn to the policy of differentiation adopted by the two groups, for which there was independent evidence. Nevertheless, the response had to be treated cautiously. For several reasons, it could not be accepted entirely at face value. Firstly, there were *very* few joint publications. Secondly, there had been very few collaborative but unproductive ventures, and we had already noted them anyway. Thirdly, both the interviews and the background knowledge of my partner provided much evidence of inter-group rivalry.

This evidence, plus the very force and urgency with which respondents' criticisms were presented, led us to believe that their response was more than just a reasoned attempt to get the facts straight. The most likely interpretation, it seemed to us, was that we were seen by some respondents as putting in jeopardy the image of science as a cooperative and dispassionate pursuit of knowledge. From this perspective an account which threatened this image would be seen, particularly by scientists responsible for maintaining the groups' financial and social support, as endangering that support.[10] Thus when we stressed that radio astronomers were to a noticeable extent concerned with priority and professional repute, that such considerations influenced their research, that they led to competition and prevented active collaboration, we were seen by some participants to be undermining their whole professional life. Their response was to reassert vigorously the public image of science. The additional data gained by means of feedback led us, therefore, to extend our original analysis. We noted the occurrence of technical cooperation between groups. We placed more emphasis on the way in which groups avoided competition by concentrating on different lines of research. We also modified our assumptions about the ways in which figures on co-authorship can be used to indicate the extent of scientific cooperation. We did not, however, change our basic view of the relations between the two main groups, i.e. relations characterized more by rivalry than by cooperation, but a rivalry kept in check by the small degree of scientific and technical overlap.

The brief account given above of some of our research procedures in relation to competition and cooperation provides further illustration of my main themes, which may be summarised as follows:
— Even the simplest kind of sociological analysis involves a complex process of drawing inferences from partial evidence.
— When several kinds of evidence are brought to bear on a given problem, apparent biases and inconsistencies often arise.
— Attempts to resolve these inconsistencies draw attention to the methodological theories, either implicit or explicit, which underlie the use of every kind of evidence.
— Much sociological evidence is created in the course of various kinds of social interaction between investigator and subject.
— As it is impossible to eliminate such interaction, it seems necessary to have explicit theories of how evidence is generated within different research contexts.

— At present, formal theories of this kind are entirely lacking.[11]
— Thus methodological theories tend either to remain implicit, largely unnoticed and closed to critical appraisal, or they are introduced as speculative, *ex post facto* appendages.[12]
— Sometimes independent material gathered during the course of the study can be used to provide support for (or to modify) important methodological assumptions, e.g. the claim above that the nature of discovery in radio astronomy supported our greater reliance on research reports and review articles than on participants' retrospective accounts of scientific development.

The concluding paragraph of this paper could be written in at least two quite different ways. I can see no convincing grounds for preferring one rather than the other. *Ending one.* The sociological analysis of science, like other areas of sociological inquiry, is faced with an irresolveable dilemma. At present, in the study of any given social phenomenon, the interpretation of the results of available research techniques is as problematic as the phenomenon initially under investigation. Thus findings cannot be regarded as valid until we have satisfactory methodological theories. But satisfactory methodological theories are no different in principle from other sociological theories and they, too, need the support of firm methodological theories. We appear therefore to be caught in an infinite regression which effectively prevents any form of intellectual advance. *Ending two.* In the past the importance of methodological theories has not been properly recognised in sociology, nor has the extent to which methodological assumptions must vary from one research setting to another. In the sociology of scientific development, because it is a fairly new area of detailed inquiry, we have the opportunity of constructing explicit methodological theories more or less from the start and of conducting future research so as to improve these theories. For some time, of course, there will be a high degree of uncertainty, because it is at present impossible to assume that any research techniques produce results which can be reliably interpreted. In practice it will often be necessary to make 'reasonable assessments' of partially inconsistent data and to introduce speculative *ex post facto* methodological theories. But as long as the rationales behind these assessments and the nature of these methodological theories are made clear, they will be open to scrutiny and to improvement. This procedure appears directly analogous to 'pulling oneself up by the bootstraps'. The only indication that such a bootstrap operation can work is the likelihood that some of the most 'successful' areas of intellectual endeavour must have begun in a manner similar to this.[13]

M. J. Mulkay, Department of Sociology, University of York, Heslington, York YO1 5DD.

M. J. MULKAY took his B.A. at LSE, his M.A. at Simon Fraser University (Vancouver) and his Ph.D. in sociology at Aberdeen. He is now a reader in sociology at the University of York, where he is studying scientific elites and the sociology of knowledge.

NOTES

This article has already appeared in *Social Science Information* 13:2 (1974) 107-119.

1. Those unfamiliar with the revisions outlined below should consult the following sources, which will serve as an introduction to the current debate about methodology. A. Cicourel, *Method and Measurement in Sociology* (New York: Free Press, 1964); H. and A. Blalock, *Methodology in Social Research* (New York: McGraw-Hill, 1968); N. K. Denzin, *The Research Act in Sociology* (Chicago: Aldine, 1970); D. L. Phillips, *Abandoning Method* (London: Jossey-Bass, 1973).
2. See M. J. Mulkay/D. O. Edge, 'Cognitive, Technical and Social Factors in the Growth of Radio Astronomy', pages 153-186 in this volume; D. O. Edge/M. J. Mulkay, 'A Preliminary Report on the Emergence of Radio Astronomy in Britain', University Department of Engineering, Cambridge, vol. I (CUED/A-Mgt. Stud./TR7 1972) and vol. II (CUED/A-Mgt. Stud./TR8 1972) and *Astronomy Transformed: the Emergence of Radio Astronomy* (New York: Wiley-Interscience, 1976).
3. Problems of this kind are, of course, as much 'historical' as 'sociological'. Methodological difficulties similar to those discussed here must therefore be faced by historians as well as by sociologists.
4. Similar issues are discussed in another paper in this volume: see J. Law, 'Theories and Methods in the Sociology of Science: an Interpretative Approach', pages 221-231.
5. This is documented in detail in the sources given in note 2.
6. In distinguishing here between the 'sociologist' and the 'ex-participant' I have tried to reflect our respondents' perceptions as well as the initial division of labour between D. O. Edge and myself. As the research proceeded this division of labour became less distinct, so that I contributed to the analysis of intellectual development and, more notably, my partner contributed to the analysis of social processes.
7. It might be argued that the way in which an interviewer plays his part is determined mainly by personal characteristics. However, comparison of transcripts from the radio astronomy study shows that the same interviewers act quite differently in different interview contexts.
8. One must be very careful, therefore, before asking young graduate students to undertake research of this kind. They can easily become intellectually dominated by their subjects.
9. Some of these themes originated with our initial interview questions. Many of them, however, emerged as the study developed.
10. The study was carried out at a time when funds for basic research were being reduced.
11. This is largely due to the dominance of the methodological tradition which views research tools as, ideally, theoretically and socially neutral.
12. This is true for instance of our interpretation of group leaders' response to our treatment of cooperation/competition.
13. It could be argued therefore that sociologists of science have a unique opportunity of improving their own research by observing the similarities and differences between the disciplines they study, on the one hand, and their own discipline of sociology, on the other.

JOHN LAW

Theories and Methods in the Sociology of Science: an Interpretative Approach

In this paper I shall examine some aspects of the relationship between the conceptual categories and models which we make use of as sociologists of science, and the methods which we use to articulate, illustrate, and in a weak sense test those models and categories. I shall outline a theme, current in the literature of interpretative sociology and ethnomethodology, which stresses the interaction of methods and theories, and in applying the same approach to the sociology of science, I shall argue that our methodology, when combined with our theoretical orientations, has led to a particular and identifiable distortion in the type of theory we produce.

In the short time available, it is impossible to argue such a case fully. For this reason I shall assume a general familiarity on the part of the reader with the distinctions which interactionists and ethnomethodologists seek to make between their own *interpretative* enterprise and that of the so-called *normative* sociologists, and I shall limit my comments on these categories to a few initial assertions.[1] Again, rather than attempting an extremely sketchy analysis of the various theories of specialty and disciplinary development that are current, I shall confine my remarks to a discussion of my own recently published work.[2] I do this not because I believe that it is either especially good or bad, but rather because I believe that it, in its normative aspects, is typical of much work in the area. The special strengths and weaknesses of the writings of such authors as Mulkay, Mullins, Hagstrom, Crane and Whitley all merit attention, but this is quite beyond the scope of such a discussion paper, and I would want to argue, in any case, that the difficulties of normative theory which I shall raise in connection with my own model apply in general to most, if not all of the currently available models.

Specifically, the method that I shall use is to outline my previously developed 'mechanical specialty' model, and make some empirical criticisms of it. I shall then outline the methods used in constructing and supporting the model, and suggest that they interact with the theory in such a way that the latter, rather than being tested, is in broad outlines confirmed. I shall argue that such methods and theories are liable to do important violence to the scientist's own conceptual categories and that, specifically, the creation of the appearance of mechanical solidarity should be seen as a product of the methods employed. Lastly, I shall argue that it is only when we have fully analysed our methods that we will be able to avoid some of the difficulties that arise from premature prescription and normative theory.

Those aware of the general writings of Blumer, Garfinkel, Cicourel, and J. D. Douglas will recognise that this paper constitutes an application of some of their ideas to the sociology of science.[3] Those who have seen recent papers by Collins, McAlpine and Bitz, and Law and French, will realise that I lean very heavily on their writings in the sociology of science.[4] The reason that I am raising these issues again is because the implications of the interpretative approach for theory and methodology have not yet been fully assessed in the sociology of science. A second, and more specific reason, is that I want to argue that the oversocialised consensus theories towards which we have all leaned in greater or lesser degree constitute an artefact of our methods (and theories) rather than a fair representation of relevant data.

NORMATIVE AND INTERPRETATIVE THEORIES

T. P. Wilson has provided us with what is, perhaps, the neatest characterisation of the distinction between normative and interpretative theory.[5] In his view, normative theory possesses the following characteristics:
— Action is seen as rule-governed (because of internal and external pressures: *i.e.* dispositions and expectations).
— Explanation consists of identifying those rules.
— A rule is a consistent link between a situation and an action.
— Such a consistent link depends on *a)* the recognition of the situation by the actor, and *b)* the recognition of the actor by the audience.
— It follows that if social action is stable, there must be a substantial cognitive consensus in these two respects.

— This consensus is provided for by the fact that actors are socialised into a common culture, which provides symbols, meanings, etc.

It will be seen that most existing approaches to specialty development fall more or less within such a normative scheme.

Interpretative theory (which is found in some symbolic interactionist and ethnomethodological writing) argues along a quite different line:

— Interaction is seen as an interpretative process. It does not constitute the enacting of a prescribed role, but rather an attempt to devise a performance on the basis of an imputed (i.e. interpreted) other role.

— In this view a role is seen, from the actor's point of view, as a coherent pattern of behaviours which are organised in large measure around the alter's purposes or sentiments.

— The imputation of a role is always inferred, and thus tentative, and subject to change. The actor is thus engaged in the interpretation of an underlying pattern from particular instances of behaviour that are taken to reflect that pattern.

— It follows that from the actor's point of view, the particular action interacts with the underlying pattern in a mutually determining way, because he interprets particular instances in terms of the assumed pattern, but he imputes the underlying pattern from particular instances.

— From this it may be argued (and it is this that is most relevant from our point of view) that cognitive consensus is *not* assumed. The very stuff of interaction is about its negotiation. It also follows, and this is equally important that in order to explain action adequately, we must try to understand the situation from the actor's point of view. More specifically, we must attempt to understand his interpretations — that is, his changing cognitions. To do this, of course, we too are engaged in interpretative work, like every other actor.

While this may sound excessively theological, the practical implications of these contrasting points of view for the sociology of science will become clear in what follows. The point to remember in the meanwhile is that cognitive consensus, taken more or less for granted in the normative view, is at the very least empirically questionable from the interpretative standpoint.

MECHANICAL SOLIDARITY AND SPECIALTY DEVELOPMENT

The mechanical specialty model is an attempt to understand the factors that lead the scientist to work on one, paradigmatically bound problem rather than on another, and certainly this is an outstanding problem in a Kuhnian formulation of science. The model presupposes that scientists in many specialties have a high commitment to certain models of explanation, and the solidarity in such specialties may be understood as a special case of *mechanical solidarity.* Conversely, scientists in some research areas may be held in relationship by a commitment, less to certain models of explanation, than to a joint resolve to solve certain more or less well defined problems. These scientists, members of *subject matter specialties,* may be seen as being held in a relationship of *organic solidarity.* It was suggested that the development of a specialty may be seen as constituting a move from an organic to a mechanical basis of solidarity. This view, which was specifically developed to fit with Mullins' ideas of specialty development, is at least consonant with Kuhn's writings. I still believe that there may be some virtue in it, but I now want to argue that this can only be retrieved after a critical review of both the theory and the methods used to derive it.

CRITICISM OF METHODS

Without going into details, it may be argued that Kuhnian theory suggests that there are norms (or norm-like entities) which guide specialists in their work.[6] If one takes a broadly Kuhnian view, one seeks to establish the nature of these norms which are held to bind the scientists together in a specialty, research front, or invisible college. This is, in fact, the way in which I proceeded in my study of X-ray crystallography.

Thus, looking at the data which is used to support the model, it can be seen that the existence of mechanical solidarity is adduced from two main factors. First, it is argued that the fierce reaction to deviance in the specialty constitutes a partial proof of normative consensus. The empirical difficulty with this argument arises from the fact that only one case of serious controversy is to be found in the literature — that involving the unpopular theories of Wrinch. While it may reasonably be asserted that Wrinch was perceived by certain other (powerful) crystallographers as having transgressed *something,* and the form of the replies, especially that of W. L. Bragg, is very suggestive, it is a long jump from this to the argument that there therefore exists mechanical solidarity, and shared norms. The second line of argument is to suggest that the very lack of deviance is evidence for the existence of very strong norms — norms which refer to shared commitments to methods. Further, these methods can be identified through reading the literature. This line of argument, while clearly carrying some weight, is open to several rather fundamental objections. Firstly, the absence of perceived deviance can result from various factors: as suggested, it can result from the adherence to shared norms; but it can also result from the *absence* of shared norms, or from the failure of what the theorists of deviance would call labelling procedures. This lack of labelling might itself result from the invisibility of the deviant behaviour, from the unwillingness of powerful actors to label, or indeed from the absence of powerful actors. There is empirical work from other areas which suggests that some or all of these factors may be at work under certain conditions.

In addition, positive identification of shared norms (in this case shared attitudes to methods) presents difficulties. Thus, it cannot be argued easily that all actors have the same attitude to methods, for much of the paper consists of arguments to show exactly the opposite. If every actor innovates, and reacts to developments in a somewhat different way, then we have at the very least a considerable dilution of the 'sameness' implied by the notions of both mechanical solidarity, and shared norms. It is possible that a useful notion of 'sameness' may be retrieved via a Wittgensteinian notion of family resemblance, or indeed through Mulkay's notion of incompletely shared cognitive and technical norms, but at the present time the sociological implications of such a possibility have not been explored.

In this section I have argued that the evidence presented for the existence of mechanical solidarity in X-ray crystallography can bear other interpretations, and that there are good reasons for not dismissing these out of hand. Although this is an empirical argument, and one that refers to a particular case, I want to suggest that the methodological faults are not idiosyncratic, but are built into a particular, normative view of sociology and its methods.

NORMATIVE METHODS AND X-RAY CRYSTALLOGRAPHY

The first question to ask is what sorts of data are used in the construction of accounts of the type criticised above? The answer, at least in the case of the work on X-ray crystallography, is that such data comes from very limited sources — mostly from the published literature, for in writing such a conceptual history one reads many, if not all, of the papers published by the presumed specialists. In the case of X-ray crystallography, I used various important supplementary sources of data. I made considerable use of the *Festschrift* edited by P. P. Ewald: *Fifty Years of X-ray Diffraction*.[7] In addition, various review articles, accounts published in the popular press, a number of interviews, and an extremely small amount of private correspondence were used to try to fill out the picture.

McAlpine has described work of this sort as being equivalent to the 'writing of official histories of the Labour Party', and I think that though, perhaps, a little too cynical, this remark is not so far from the truth. I want to suggest that using data of the above type, given theoretical preconceptions of the sort that I took for granted at the time I was writing the study, leads, if not to specific conclusions about the nature and form of the norms, then at least to the discovery of norms of some sort. Let me elaborate.

Kuhnian theory of the sort here used directs the investigator to search and identify certain shared norms. In this respect, it may be noted that it differs little in principle from Mertonian work in the sociology of science.[8] The investigator is therefore directed in two ways. First, he tends to examine certain sets of data, rather than others. Some data are more relevant in the establishment of paradigm bound activity than others. Data about non-scientific action are seen as relevant only insofar as they tend to support or alternatively undermine scientific activity. Thus, non-scientific factors are seen as being of secondary importance only. Some data are more 'real' and useful in the search for scientific norms than others. It may therefore appear to be a fortunate coincidence that the 'purest' data — that from scientific papers — is at one and the same time the data that is most easily available.[9]

There is a second way in which the investigator is guided. Casting back to Wilson's observations about normative theory, you will remember that in assuming that actors orient themselves towards shared norms, the analyst necessarily makes the assumption of a high level of cognitive consensus. In the context of Kuhnian research, this means that when the analyst locates what appear to be shared methods or theories he tends to assume that these have a broadly similar meaning for all concerned. The existence of such norms is predicated on considerable cognitive consensus.

I therefore suggest that in organising our research around concepts such as norm, paradigm, mechanical solidarity, or for that matter specialty, or discipline, we are assuming that these or other similar terms are (or could be) consistently meaningful for the actors we are investigating. This means that they themselves share similar world views in the respects that we have investigated, and those world views are consistent with our conceptualisation of the area. The assumption is, therefore, that there is a reality that lies behind the data, a reality of which the actors themselves are more or less aware, and one which we are engaged in revealing through our methods. The corollary of this is that difficulties in methods that arise in the course of our investigations may be viewed as technical problems. If we can make our techniques sufficiently sophisticated, so runs the argument, then we will have a better access to the reality.

Note that this argument does not depend, for its strength, on the existence of *normative,* but rather on *cognitive* consensus. It is clear that normative dissensus is possible between actors who share common cognitions. However, with increasing cognitive dissensus, the identification of both role-playing, and the appropriate situations for appropriate role-play, becomes more and more problematic. A normative analysis becomes more or less impossible under such circumstances.

Finally, in this context, it strikes me that there is a case for arguing that in our normative and conceptual studies of scientific knowledge, we have gone some way to creating a self-validating methodological and theoretical system. We look for norms, we choose certain types of data — those where we expect to locate the norms — and we go on to interpret that data normatively. If we fail to find shared norms we take it either that our methods are not good enough or that the area has not been institutionalised properly. The idea that scientific action may be seen as an interpretative process is not consistently entertained, and as a result we find ourselves dealing with an oversocialised conception of the scientist.

INTERPRETATIVE SOCIOLOGY OF SCIENCE

The interpretative sociologist argues that a normative analysis is based upon a mistaken view of the nature of interaction. Rather than assuming cognitive consensus, the interpretative sociologist seeks to establish the degree to which it in fact exists. To do this he does not assume that actors structure their worlds in the way that he does. He rather attempts to do a good ethnography and to establish the nature of the actor's cognitions. His first aim, therefore, is to establish the various relevant scientific realities. (It may be objected at this point that this is what the normative sociologist attempts, too. In many cases this may be true, but the argument would be that he is hindered in his enterprise by his view of the nature of interaction, and his conceptions of rule-following.) From the interpretative point of view, there are several points to bear in mind.

The scientist, like all actors, is engaged in a process of definition — he is, in other words, involved in giving an account of himself which will be appropriately received by those with whom he interacts. The nature of this account varies with his own purposes and intentions on the one hand, and his view of the audience and the response he seeks to elicit from that audience, on the other. It follows that accounts provided will vary between different interactions. Now, in the work on X-ray crystallography I laid great stress on the importance of scientific papers as especially relevant accounts about scientific beliefs. However, looked at in this light, scientific papers may be seen as one *particular* sort of account, provided for a *particular* type of audience, in a *particular* type of interaction. Rather than being, of necessity, closer to an assumed normative scientific reality than (say) the backchat over a cup of coffee in the laboratory, we must now assume at the outset that these two types of accounts and all others are equally valid, equally important, and equally relevant in understanding the shifting world views, and hence the shifting scientific beliefs, of the actors concerned. We must not assign priority to certain sorts of interactions, even if we have been in the habit of doing so, and even if we normally think that they are really what science is all about. For to do so would be to impose our own world view, when what we are trying to do is to establish the scientists' world views. Only if we find that scientists in general assign especial importance and especial epistemological status to the accounts in scientific papers, should we ourselves assign their study greater importance. In practice it may well be the case that scientists do lay special emphasis on the accounts in scientific papers, but my hunch, based on my work in crystallography, is that there is immense (and nontrivial) variation between scientists on this count. For some, science is something you do in the laboratory, something you talk about, and something you get excited about. For others, science is what they write and what they read in the journals. I would even hypothesise (in conformity with the invisible college notion) that those who are generally felt to be of high status locate science less in the journals than in their own and other people's heads. Be this as it may, the status of scientific papers has to be assessed from the point of view of the scientist, and this is an empirical matter.

The second point is that an interpretative sociology involves careful study of the status of sociological methods. Thus we too interact with scientists and they provide us, wittingly or not, with accounts which we interpret in special ways because we are sociologists with special interests.

Now if we examine possible sets of role-taking pairs and note which types of accounts are easily observable, we find that these are very atypical from the point of view of the scientist. He only infrequently, for example, finds himself being interviewed by a sociologist or historian of science. This leads to two connected points. First, as McAlpine and Bitz have pointed out, if we use conceptual categories which the scientist does not normally employ in the accounts he provides in day to day interaction, then we can expect puzzlement or a meaningless answer. This is emphasised when one examines the role-taking pairs and asks oneself: how often are terms such as 'science' or 'specialty' likely to occur? In using such terms we may well be attempting to impose a version of the social order which scientists simply do not share. Secondly, there is a sense in which an interpretative ethnographic programme of the sort recommended is in fact unattainable. We cannot avoid our own interpretations of the actors' categories, even when we make an attempt to be sensitive in our methods, because we too are engaged in interpretation and our interpretations, organised as they are, are likely to do some violence to the actors' own categories. Thus, it follows that in principle our accounts have a status that is no different from those of the man in the street — except that we attempt to be sensitive and our interests, diverging from those of the man in the street, are somewhat specialised.

The third point concerns the possible nature of interpretative theory assuming, that is, that we want something to come out in the wash after we have done our ethnography. Here I have three main suggestions which are tentative in nature.

Noting that we have a different context of awareness to that of the scientist and that our interests are different, we may use as a paradigm case for the construction of theory, the case of the doctor and his patient. The doctor and patient talk and the doctor uses the patient's view of the circumstances, in order to create an account which attaches itself to different (and possibly wider) considerations. The disanalogy between our case and that of the doctor is that we are not normally in a position to argue that the scientists' interpretations are wrong, for our central concern is in fact the way that he structures his action. However, we may attempt to establish categories that are somewhat more general, categories which include their categories, but do not do violence to them. Thus, while the term 'specialty' may not be appropriate, other terms such as experiment, professor, or laboratory, may turn out to be acceptable.

The second suggestion is both more concise and more hopeful. Our context of awareness leads us to make connections between actors' categories which may not occur to the actors themselves. Thus we may find, as I suggested earlier, that there are systematic differences in the nature of accounts, and specifically in the importance attributed to scientific papers, between scientists who are held to be powerful and those who are not. In developing this and similar lines of argument I am implying that we may be at the beginning of a true sociology of scientific knowledge. However, there is a third point which limits what we can say.

This is that inasmuch as we must assume that actors are constantly remaking their worlds and providing new accounts with new categories, any theory that we make must be limited, as far as possible, to description and thus avoid prescription. While I realise that this is almost a contradiction in terms, it nonetheless seems to me that a theory which assumes the continuity of conceptual organisation over time is inimical to the programme outlined above, for the same reasons that led to the rejection of normative theory.

CONCLUSION

Some of you probably wonder where this leads us. The answer, as far as I can see, is that it leads us to an examination of our methods. It leads us to scrutinise and probably criticise previous theories that identify norm-like entities as structuring scientific action. And more positively it suggests that we study areas where we are able to do good ethnography — an obvious case being the participant observation study of laboratory working and account-making. If, however, in the study of disciplinary growth we are confined to historical studies, we must at least understand the manner in which our methods and theories structure our results.

John Law, Department of Sociology, University of Keele, Staffordshire ST5 5BG.

JOHN LAW read sociology at Cardiff and received his Ph.D. degree from the University of Edinburgh Science Studies Unit in 1972. Following a period as Simon Marks Research Fellow at the University of Manchester, he has since 1973 been a lecturer in sociology at the University of Keele. His current research includes work on the sociology of twentieth-century sedimentology.

NOTES

This article has already appeared in *Social Science Information* 13:4/5 (1974) 163-172.

1. These assertions are drawn from T. P. Wilson, 'Conceptions of Interaction and Forms of Sociological Explanation', *American Sociological Review* 35 (1970) 697-710.
2. J. Law, 'The Development of Specialties in Science: The Case of X-ray Protein Crystallography', pages 123-152 above.
3. H. Blumer, 'Sociological Implications of the Thought of George Herbert Mead', *American Journal of Sociology* 71 (1966) 535-544; H. Garfinkel, *Studies in Ethnomethodology* (Englewood Cliffs, NJ: Prentice-Hall, 1967); A. V. Cicourel, *Method and Measurement in Sociology* (New York: Free Press, 1964); J. D. Douglas, *The Social Meanings of Suicide* (Princeton University Press, 1967).
4. H. M. Collins, 'The Seven Sexes: A Study in the Sociology of a Phenomenon, or the Replication of Experiments in Physics', *Sociology* 9:2 (1975) 205-224; A. McAlpine / A. Bitz, 'Some Methodological Problems in the Comparative Sociology of Science' (mimeo, 1973); J. Law / D. French, 'Normative and Interpretive Sociologies of Science', *Sociological Review* 22 (1974) 581-595. Note also M. J. Mulkay, 'Methodology in the Sociology of Science: Some Reflections on the Study of Radio Astronomy', pages 207-220 above.
5. See note 1.
6. This is argued in some detail in Law / French, 'Normative and Interpretive Sociologies of Science' where, however, it is also suggested that there are important convergences between Kuhn's writing and the interpretative tradition in sociology, convergences which should be explored.
7. P. P. Ewald (ed.) *Fifty Years of X-ray Diffraction* (Utrecht: International Union of Crystallography, N. V. A. Oosthoek's Vitgeversmaatschappij, 1962).
8. This point is developed in Law / French, 'Normative and Interpretive Sociologies of Science'.
9. In fact, I feel sure that this is not a coincidence, and has to do with the reification of the public face of science.

S. W. WOOLGAR

The Identification and Definition of Scientific Collectivities

A basic preliminary task of many studies of science is the identification and definition of scientific collectivities. In this paper I intend to consider some problems of identification and definition, with reference to difficulties encountered in the course of my own study of the development of research on pulsars.[1]

The identification and definition of scientific collectivities first presented itself as a problem to me when I was engaged, with others, in trying to construct a preliminary theoretical account of some of the social and intellectual processes involved in the emergence and growth of research areas.[2] It was clear that the notion of 'scientific collectivity' was central, if not fundamental, to our theoretical statements about the processes of growth and development in science. Every proposition depended crucially on what actually constitutes a particular area of scientific endeavour. This led me to formulate three broad questions. Firstly, what is the precise meaning of the various terms commonly used to denote scientific research collectivities and intellectual groupings, such terms as discipline, specialty, field, problem area and so on? Secondly, since the analysis was intended as a possible guide for empirical work, how do particular concepts of scientific collectivities relate to techniques for identifying these collectivities? In short, how easy is it to operationalise the concepts embodied in our theoretical statement? Thirdly, what are the implications for our theoretical argument of particular ways of conceptualising scientific collectivities?

To approach the first question satisfactorily we must return to our basic ideas and perceptions of what goes on in a scientific community. In science as a whole, there appear to be many different processes of communication, of information exchange and of general contact between scientists. We assume that these give rise to a highly complex web of social relationships associated with the creation and dissemination of scientific knowledge. If we consider only those social relationships directly associated with the pursuit of specific research problems, there are a number of factors contributing to the formation of relatively small social groupings. Firstly, the intensive investigation required of most scientists means that their research activities tend to be highly specialised. Secondly, there is presumably a limit to the number of sources from which researchers can absorb technical material. Thirdly, it is likely that researchers choose mostly to communicate with those whom they see as concerned with problems similar to their own. Fourthly, researchers will be constrained to work in close proximity in cases where their projects involve the sharing of some costly component of basis apparatus. These factors together lead to a clustering of communication choices. Because these choices are made on the basis of participants' perceptions of common or related research interests, it is likely that many of the ties will be reciprocated and also that many of those not directly in contact will be 'linked' through a small number of intermediaries.

So if we start from the idea of communication choices between participants we can clarify our notion of a scientific collectivity by speaking in terms of a *research network*. A research network is a relatively intensive concentration of interest ties. At the same time, terms like 'problem area', 'research area' or 'field' can be used to refer to the established knowledge and current problems common to the members of a network. This way of describing a scientific collectivity implies that identification must be viewed as a two-stage procedure. Firstly, we have to use some technique of identification which reveals for us a web of interest ties. But precisely because a research network is defined in terms of a *relative* concentration of interest ties, it has no *inherent* boundary. So the second stage of identification is deciding where to draw a boundary. Inevitably, there will be a number of scientists whose membership is doubtful.

It is often assumed that concern with the membership of that minority of researchers who appear to be on 'the boundary' of a network is unnecessary. Because there is doubt about their membership these individuals are automatically classed as peripheral to the main area of inquiry and they are largely ignored. This view stems from the importance attached to 'core' members of the network. So long as the 'core' members are included, it is argued, the inclusion or otherwise of participants marginal to the field makes little difference to the analysis. In practical terms, we often read how researchers with less than (say) three publications in the area are not regarded as having made a significant contribution to the field and are therefore excluded from consideration as members of the network to be studied.

This assumption limits the analysis in several important ways. Firstly, although it is true that 'core' members often appear to demonstrate the widest knowledge of both social and scientific development, their accounts may be considerably affected by the central position they hold.[3] Although sociologists must recognise the importance of key members as sources of information, they should not be tempted to regard the accounts offered by such members as necessarily authoritative. Secondly, members seen as marginal may be important in a developmental context. Individuals with only a cursory interest in one area may be the source of a transfer of ideas to another area. Thirdly, participants may only be marginal to a research network at certain stages of its development. For example, in the early stages of work on pulsars, a number of researchers were involved in trying to interpret evidence provided by observations made with radio telescopes. These participants contributed by advancing candidate theoretical models for the pulsar mechanism. Subsequently, however, many theoretical suggestions were discredited in the light of fresh observational evidence. Some of the proponents of these suggestions then withdrew and maintained only a secondary interest in pulsars. Clearly, the relative position of participants in a research network may alter considerably as the network develops. Furthermore, different operational definitions of a network will lead to the identification of different groups of scientists as 'marginal' and, perhaps thereby, to divergent analyses of the social processes at work.

In the theoretical analysis mentioned above, it was assumed that the use of various techniques would not result in widely differing webs of interest ties nor, by implication, in the identification of widely differing research memberships. This is a crucial assumption. For if different techniques do produce significantly different network memberships, without our being aware of it we may well mistake instrumental effects for genuine empirical variation. Ideally, we should test this assumption by systematic examination of as many techniques as possible.

Traditionally, there are available a number of techniques for identification and definition of collectivities in science. These include:
— the use of comprehensive bibliographies to locate relevant publications and their authors
— the use of review articles to locate relevant publications and their authors

— the use of abstract services to locate relevant publications and their
   authors
— the cyclical search of references in scientific articles to find other articles dealing with the same scientific problem
— the use of citation analysis in recent computer clustering procedures[4]
— the cyclical naming of participants by other participants
— the decision of a 'panel' of participants as to what constitute the
   publications and members of a particular scientific collectivity
— the identification of scientists using particular types of equipment and
   apparatus.

This is a fairly simple statement of some techniques, each of which has its
variants and its own particular operational difficulties. I do not want to go
into the details of each technique. Instead I shall confine my discussion to
problems associated with one class of them.

The first five of these techniques relate to criteria of identification
based on the content of scientific literature; the next two relate to criteria
based on participants' own views of their professional contacts and of
their social and intellectual relations; and the last relates to criteria based
on the locational basis for social interaction between participants. Some
of the questions relating to the use of criteria based on participants' own
views have been raised elsewhere in this volume.[5] Here I shall consider
techniques relating to criteria based on the content of scientific literature.
This is for three reasons. Firstly, an observer having no previous contact
with a particular field of scientific enquiry is often obliged to utilise scientific literature simply in order to discover whom to contact and where to
ask preliminary questions. The content of the scientific literature thus
provides a convenient starting point to the research process. Secondly,
those techniques relating to criteria based on the content of scientific
literature appear to provide a relatively invariant technique in the sense
that almost any scientific area is amenable to a count of its publications
and authors. The use of scientific literature thus appears to be a tool providing some standardisation in the identification of research collectivities.
Thirdly, there is an attractive simplicity and apparent objectivity in
techniques involving head-counting. I shall now try to illustrate some of
the main difficulties which arise in use of techniques based on the content
of scientific literature by describing my own attempts to identify the
research collectivity associated with pulsars.

My initial objective was the straightforward one of locating all publications on pulsars. However, I quickly became aware of two major problems. Firstly, how was I to decide which types of publications should be

considered to make up the literature of the pulsar collectivity? Was there any justifiable way of distinguishing between the contribution made by an article in *Astrophysical Journal,* as opposed to a review in *Scientific American,* the historical memoirs of participants or even an inch of column in a national newspaper? Secondly, even if I decided on the relevance of different types of publications, I then had to decide which papers were associated with the collectivity on the basis of their scientific content. But many papers appeared to make only passing reference to the subject area under study. The main concern of such papers seemed to be elsewhere and their results appeared to bear only indirectly on the field to be investigated. Were the authors of such papers to be included or disregarded? How precisely should I decide which papers counted? In the light of such considerations I decided to make my collection as large and all-inclusive as possible in the first instance. Where any doubt occurred as to the inclusion or otherwise of a particular publication, it was included. Using a large number of sources in this way, a collection of 792 *items* was amassed.[6] I envisaged that various sub-sets of items, corresponding to different definitions of the field of research activity connected with pulsars, could be drawn from this basic file of items.

In relation to the first problem, it became clear that there was a large variety of types of contribution which made up the basic file of items. The following list was drawn up:

LIST 1. *Item Types*
1. articles and letters submitted to journals, excluding those items appearing under categories below
2. papers presented at meetings, symposia, conferences, colloquia
3. abstracts of items in category 2
4. reports of meetings, symposia, conferences, colloquia
5. reports issued by institutes, observatories or company journals
6. books, theses, reports of International Astronomical Commission
7. news articles, editorial articles, articles written by journal staff writers
8. published lectures.

This list thus represents the first set of criteria by which it appeared possible to delineate sub-sets of items. For example, it might be argued that analysis of the growth of a scientific field should only 'properly' be concerned with those items in category 1; that conference papers, abstracts, books, news articles and so forth are not, in some sense, representative of the growth of the field. It should be noted that this type of argument is seldom made explicit in sociological analyses of science. The particular selection of one or more of the above categories is usually not discussed and is based on the implicit assumption that the inclusion or exclusion of additional categories of item type will make no significant difference either to the membership of the field so defined or to the patterns of growth which are observed. D. Crane, for example, refers variously to 'publications' and to 'papers', but neither makes clear which categories of items she used to make up the field nor discusses the implications of her particular selection for the rest of her analysis.[7]

The second problem was to decide which items might be considered to deal with the particular topic of pulsars. When tackling this problem, there appeared to be two immediately obvious sets of criteria by which classification of 'pulsar items' could be made. One method relied directly on categories evolved by the compilers of Astronomy and Astrophysics Abstracts (AAA), an abstract catalogue published every six months. Items considered to be 'about pulsars' were listed in one particular section of the AAA. Using AAA, the following list of categories was drawn up:

LIST 2. *Abstract Categories*
1. items (from the basic file of 792 items) listed in section devoted to pulsars
2. items not listed in section devoted to pulsars, but listed as a cross-reference at the end of the section
3. items listed neither in 'pulsar' section, nor as cross-reference, but appearing somewhere in AAA
4. items excluded from AAA.

A second method of categorising items by topic relied on the occurrence of 'keywords' in either the title or abstract of each item. Thus the centrality of a particular item to the pulsar field might be assessed by noting the use of terms considered to indicate where its main concern lay. Two such terms are 'pulsar' (or 'pulsating radio source') and 'neutron star'. The following list of categories was devised:

LIST 3. *Keyword Categories*
1. both 'pulsar' and 'neutron star' appear in title of item
2. 'pulsar' appears in title, but 'neutron star' does not
3. only 'neutron star' appears in title, 'pulsar' appears in abstract
4. 'pulsar' appears neither in title nor abstract, 'neutron star' in title
5. 'pulsar' not in title, but in abstract, 'neutron star' not in title
6. 'neutron star' mentioned only, and appearing in abstract
7. no mention of 'pulsar' or 'neutron star' in either title or abstract.

Each item in the basic file of 792 was given a code corresponding to each of the above three lists of categories. Thus a thesis which appeared as a cross-reference entry at the end of the pulsar section of the AAA, and which had 'pulsar' in the title, (but not 'neutron star'), was given the codes 6,2,2. Having coded each item according to each of these sets of criteria, it was then possible to draw different sub-sets from the basic file by stipulating that each included item should meet certain requirements. In other words, it was possible to generate groupings of items according to requirements within each of the three sets of criteria. Groupings of items could have been generated merely by using the existing codes, in which case all those items which had the same three codes would have constituted a group. However, this would have produced a number of non-overlapping groupings of items. I have already noted that one of the most crucial and yet least explicated assumptions in many studies of science is that the use of various criteria of membership does not result in widely differing research collectivities. In order to test this I rearranged the original coding system. So as to examine the effect of incremental changes in the boundary or membership of the collectivity, rather than to compare memberships of distinctly different and mutually exclusive collections of items, a new scheme was devised whereby alternative definitions of the field were based on various combinations of categories within each of the above three lists. 'Combination numbers' each referred to that set of items having any of a particular selection of the codes given in lists 1-3. For example, keyword combination number 2 represents all those items having any of keyword codes 1, 2, 3 or 4 in list 3.[8] Six combination numbers represented item type, four abstract category, and five keyword coding. By choosing one of each of these combination numbers it was thus possible to define the collectivity associated with pulsar research in 120 ($= 6 \times 4 \times 5$) different ways. The combination numbers were so formulated that alternative definitions differed by the addition of a certain set of items to a basic core.

Figure 1 shows the extent of variation between different definitions. The smallest defined field, based on the most stringent criteria, contained 515 items, while the largest contained 792, corresponding to the total input of items. In some cases, a comparison of the membership of different definitions indicates the significance of including or excluding a certain set of items within the definition. However, this comparison can only be made in terms of numbers. It may also be the case that definitions resulting in fields of the same size have markedly different populations in addition to their common core. The precise extent and significance of

FIGURE 1. *The Number of Items Included in Different Definitions of the Pulsar Research Collectivity*

Keyword Combination Numbers	Item Type Combination Numbers																							
	1	2	3	4	5	6	1	2	3	4	5	6	1	2	3	4	5	6	1	2	3	4	5	6
1	**515**	607	608	610	625	**627**	547	645	646	648	663	667	563	663	664	669	684	688	**565**	667	668	674	690	**698**
2	518	611	612	614	629	631	556	655	656	658	673	677	577	679	680	685	700	704	579	683	684	690	706	714
3	535	628	629	631	646	648	597	696	697	699	714	718	628	730	731	736	751	755	631	735	736	742	758	767
4	535	628	629	631	646	648	598	698	699	701	716	720	634	737	738	743	758	762	637	742	743	749	765	774
5	**538**	631	632	634	650	**652**	603	703	704	706	722	726	650	753	754	759	775	779	**653**	758	759	765	782	**792**
	Abstract Combination Number 1						Abstract Combination Number 2						Abstract Combination Number 3						Abstract Combination Number 4					

Note

Example: definition (2,3,4) includes all those items with codes corresponding to item type combination no. 2, abstract combination no. 3 and keyword combination no. 4. Definition (2,3,4) thus contains 737 items.

'Combination numbers' represent various combinations of the original codes riven in lists 1-3. Combination numbers do not therefore correspond directly to the categories appearing in each of those lists. See text.

The numbers in bold are those eight definitions selected for subsequent analysis.

these further aspects of variation remain to be investigated. The main point to note is the large degree of variation evident in just one of the commonly used techniques for identification and definition of scientific collectivities.

It should be noted that the 120 definitions shown above is a vastly reduced set of a much larger number of possible alternatives. Firstly, the coding categories within each of the original three listings are not necessarily exhaustive. For example, we might decide to create extra categories corresponding to each of the sixteen permutations of the presence or absence of 'pulsar' or 'neutron star' in either the title or abstract of an item (list 3). Similarly, it might be thought necessary to distinguish between 'articles' and 'letters' or 'books' and 'theses' in list 1. Secondly, the various selections of category codes denoted by 'combination numbers' are not exhaustive. Even with the existing listing of codes (i.e. even with no additions to the categories in lists 1, 2 and 3) the use of all possible combinations of codes would lead to a phenomenal 485,775 alternative definitions of the field.[9] Thirdly, the sets of original coding categories themselves are by no means exhaustive. For example, we might decide that items should be coded according to the particular equipment or apparatus that was used to obtain the results presented in them. We could therefore set up an extra list of categories corresponding to the use of different sorts of equipment. Various combinations of these categories could then be used in conjunction with the combinations of other categories to produce further alternative definitions of the field. The addition of a single 'new dimension' to the coding system would quickly make the number of possible definitions become extremely large. In this event we might expect a still larger corresponding variation in the membership of fields.

It thus appears that my own attempts to set up various coding categories were themselves very selective. My purpose was to explore the possibilities of variation neglected by other authors, but it is likely that my choice of a particular range of definitions was affected by factors similar to those which guide the selection by some authors of a single definition. These factors relate, on the one hand, to the *practical constraints* involved in coding items and, on the other hand, to decisions about the *appropriateness* of particular criteria of definition. For example, searching for keywords in titles and abstracts is a relatively simple and practicable task. In addition, the choice of the particular keywords 'pulsar' and 'neutron star' is informed by the knowledge that these terms feature prominently in discussions relating to pulsar research activity. The choice of these particular terms is thus seen as appropriate to the task of definition of the field associated with pulsar research activity. Seen in this context, my attempt to explore a range of variation in definitions is equivalent to an examination of the range of practicality and appropriateness in terms of which the use of different criteria of definition can be variously assessed.

The largest of these definitions (6, 4, 5) with 792 items corresponds to the basic file of items, of which all other definitions are a sub-set. The use of this basic file is itself subject to a number of limitations. Firstly, my claim to the relative completeness of the initial collection of items is based on minimising the number of decisions I made with respect to the relevance of items which were collected. Where there was any doubt as to the inclusion of an item, I included it. Nevertheless, the choice of particular *sources* as relevant to my task and the perception that these sources would provide the information I required necessarily involved decisions as to the appropriateness of sources. These decisions were informed by my own knowledge of the nature of pulsar research. This would appear fairly obvious in the sense that I did not, for example, decide to consult *The Journal of Biochemistry*. It is perhaps less obvious, however, that a choice between two data sources, both of which might be considered rather more appropriate to the topic of pulsar research, may significantly affect the membership of the resulting field. Decisions as to the appropriateness of sources were also affected by an assessment of the likely practical difficulties involved. Thus, for example, I did not consider it practical to search for and use articles written in languages other than English.

In order to examine whether the differences in membership resulting from different field definitions significantly affected the observed pattern of growth, eight particular definitions were used to plot growth over the five year period 1968-72. Although it was not possible to compare and contrast the growth patterns of 120 definitions, these eight definitions were selected so as to include the maximum variation in combinations of characteristics. The eight definitions used are as follows (also in bold in figure 1):

Definition 1	(1, 1, 1)	Total no. of items 515
2	(6, 1, 1)	627
3	(1, 1, 5)	538
4	(6, 1, 5)	652
5	(1, 4, 1)	565
6	(6, 4, 1)	698
7	(1, 4, 5)	653
8	(6, 4, 5)	792

FIGURE 2. *The Cumulative Growth of Items for Eight Different Definitions of the Pulsar Research Collectivity 1968–1972*

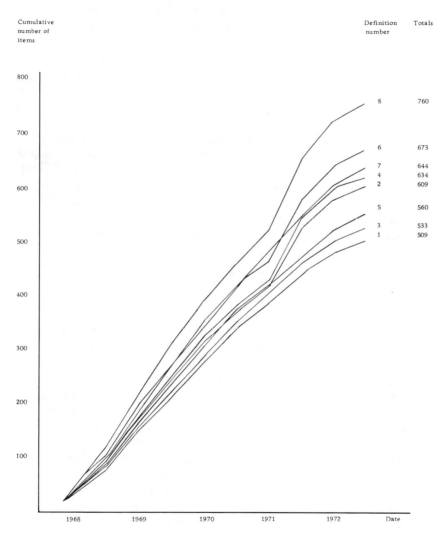

Note: The exclusion from this figure of a number of items for which publication dates could not be determined account for the difference between definition totals above and those given in the text.

Figure 2 shows the extent of differences in the cumulative growth patterns of the eight definitions.[10] It is likely that comparison of any other selection of definitions would exhibit marked differences of the kind shown here. In any case, the results in figure 2 demonstrate that the picture we obtain of the overall growth of the pulsar field depends to a considerable extent on the way in which we define that field. There is a distinct possibility, therefore, that our observation of other, more analytically interesting variables such as innovation, competition or migration will also be noticeably affected by variations in operational definition of the field and by variations in the definition of these variables themselves. On the other hand, the shapes of the growth curves shown in figure 2 appear roughly similar. Consequently, it may be that analysis of the social and intellectual dynamics of a field such as pulsars will not be significantly altered by the use of a limited range of different research procedures. Unfortunately, it is not clear on what basis we should choose one particular definition as the most appropriate for subsequent analysis. The extent to which different definitions of a research field influence subsequent sociological analysis must therefore be regarded as an important issue for further study.

By presenting some thoughts on the preliminary task of identification and definition of scientific collectivities, I have tried to highlight the complex interplay between our conceptualisations of these collectivities, the techniques for their location and the assumptions we make about practical difficulties likely to be encountered when these techniques are employed. In particular, by examining my own use of scientific literature, I have shown the extensive variation in the populations of the defined collectivities which can result. This throws considerable doubt on the commonly held assumption that the use of different techniques of identification and definition does not result in widely different research memberships. In addition, the extent of these differences poses major problems for subsequent analysis. To what extent does our use of techniques and the assumptions we make about them structure our studies? Do such factors determine our findings or do they merely influence them? In terms of the title of my discussion is there any significance in the subtle distinction between, on the one hand, *identifying* a scientific collectivity and, on the other, *defining* it? There is the likelihood of a definite connection between our research procedures and our subsequent findings. But the precise nature of this connection remains to be examined.

S. W. Woolgar, Department of Sociology, Brunel University, Uxbridge, Middlesex UB8 3PH.

S. W. WOOLGAR first studied at Cambridge. He is now working on a Ph.D. concerning the development of research on pulsars and has recently been appointed lecturer in sociology at Brunel University.

NOTES

1. Pulsars are an astrophysical phenomenon (the term is shorthand for rapidly pulsating radio sources) first discovered by radio astronomers in 1968. Since then pulsars have provided the stimulus for considerable scientific activity.
2. M. J. Mulkay / G. N. Gilbert / S. W. Woolgar, 'Problem Areas and Research Networks in Science', *Sociology* 9 (May 1975) 187-203.
3. See M. J. Mulkay, 'Methodology in the Sociology of Science: Some Reflections on the Study of Radio Astronomy', pages 207-220 above.
4. H. Small / B. C. Griffith, 'The Structure of Scientific Literatures I: Identifying and Graphing Specialities', *Science Studies* 4 (1974) 17-40; B. C. Griffith *et al.* 'The Structure of Scientific Literatures II: Towards a Macro- and Microstructure for Science', *Science Studies* 4 (1974) 339-365.
5. See note 3.
6. I use the term 'items' rather than 'articles' or 'publications' to denote any of the full range of types of contribution set out in list 1.
7. See D. Crane, *Invisible Colleges* (University of Chicago Press, 1972).
8. Due to limitations of space it is not possible to give a complete description of the selection of codes to which each combination number corresponds. A detailed discussion of this and other aspects of the same research is given in my Ph.D. thesis currently in preparation: 'The Growth and Development of Scientific Research Areas with Special Reference to Pulsar Research'.
9. See note 8.
10. The numbers of items under each definition in figure 2 differ from those given above. In each definition a number of items (a total of 32 of the basic file of 792) were excluded because their publication dates could not be determined.

WOLFGANG VAN DEN DAELE / PETER WEINGART

Resistance and Receptivity of Science to External Direction: the Emergence of New Disciplines under the Impact of Science Policy

INTRODUCTION

In the recent past there have been many attempts to regulate the development of scientific specialties according to politically defined goals. One may mention in this context policies concerning cancer research, peace research, space research, and environmental studies. In this paper we propose to discuss the conditions and limitations of such attempts which reside in the cognitive and social organization of the sciences themselves. Our purpose will be to discuss some factors which may determine the receptivity or resistance of science to external direction and which may provide insight into the possibility of controlling and regulating science *in line with political demands,* something which has hitherto largely been simply presupposed.

In examining this facet of the spectrum of governmental science policy, we shall consider those types of control which derive from a direct interest in the solution of specific problems (as, for instance, cancer therapy, the construction of a fusion reactor, and the provision of manned space flights). Such interests are focussed on a specific product value of science. They imply strong interference with the internal structure of scientific processes because they presuppose that the internal rules which determine problem selection and the orientation of intellectual development can be influenced extensively by political guidance.

This type of control must be distinguished from science policy objectives having to do with science for its own sake (e.g. the promotion of basic research by agencies of scientific self-administration), or aimed at the process value of science. The latter applies, for instance, when scientific development is viewed as a means of raising the qualification of manpower, or as a means for generating knowhow by which a society's problem solving capacity may in unforeseeable ways be augmented. The process value of scce is also paramount in policy considerations in those cases where the support of research is supposed to provide legitimation to the political system (which may be the case with peace research and with a good share of environmental research), or where the political inten- tion is merely to make available the indirect effects of science (such as improving the attractiveness of a certain region for industrial develop- ment). In all these cases the objective of political control does not imply an interference with the internal rules of development of the science con- cerned. Rather it links the internal dynamics of science to the utilization of knowledge for practical purposes. Consequently the receptivity of the sciences relative to such political demands is not as such problematic.[1] Problems of receptivity or resistance on the part of science arise in the first place vis-à-vis political demands bearing on a specific product value of science. In recent years this dimension of science policy interests has become more and more important.

The ends intended by such control are specific results, procedures, knowledge. We assume that these ends are not realizable by merely applying available science. Rather, a special form of scientific develop- ment is being institutionalized: a new type of scientific specialty which has, as its focus of development, political goals. We take the term 'spe- cialty' to signify an organizational unit of science which differs from the traditional disciplines by its lesser scope and from particular problem areas by a higher degree of cognitive and social institutionalization.[2] The specific criterion of differentiation lies in the self-sustained dynamics of research, in the development of a programme that both enables and guides the continuity of research.

The factors on which the possibility of 'institutionalizing by policy' depends, must be analyzed on three different levels: on the *policy* level, in which the objectives of science policy must be classified; on the *cognitive* level, in which the structures of science are defined as a cultural or intellectual enterprise; and on the *institutional* level, in which science is defined in terms of a system of social action. To reveal the conditions of resistance or receptivity of science requires an attempt to determine the interdependency among these three levels. In particular, it is necessary to identify the vital conditions and consequences on the cognitive and institutional levels which determine resistance or receptivity towards the objectives of science policy. By means of a dimensional analysis on the three levels indicated, we will first identify variables which are a condition for the demands, forms and possibilities of any intentional control of the development of science, then develop a model from which a series of interdependencies between the political demands, on the one side, and the cognitive and social structures of science, on the other, can be constructed.[3]

In most cases there is a lack of adequate theoretical and empirical analysis which would otherwise enable the formulation of hypotheses regarding the interdependency of particular factors. The catalogue of variables can be regarded as a sort of matrix for the design of case studies of the development of special fields. Thus the comparability of different case studies is ensured, and the danger that studies may often uncover questions which previous studies should have raised may be reduced.[4]

VARIABLES

Political Objectives of Control

A classification of the objectives of political control according to which scientific development is induced must achieve two things: it must provide characteristics of the underlying political problems which are independent of the scientific problems into which the latter are to be translated, and it must explain the selective impact of the political problem definition vis-à-vis science.

The political definition of a problem does not determine the way in which the science concerned defines the problem, nor the strategy of problem solution. The problem of cancer therapy, for instance, can be translated into various scientific tasks: into an experimental strategy designed to discover substances which have a particular therapeutic effect; or into a theoretical programme designed to clarify mechanisms of the inhibition of cellular growth. If it is assumed that science can be controlled by externally set goals, it follows that the reaction of science to such demands cannot be contingent. The selective impact of political problems upon science lies in the fact that it is binding, perhaps not for the structure, but for the function of scientific problem-solving. The demands of political control can be classified independently according to the technical functions of knowledge. We may distinguish four categories of these functions: assessment/description, systems control, construction and systems building. These functions correspond to various phases and levels of the strategic political utilization of science.

Demands for assessment or description correspond to the type of analytical politics. Here the goal is production of scientific information about the initial conditions and consequences of political action; the classical instruments for this are reports and social statistics. Such demands can be exemplified by surveys of the social, economic, and ecological *status quo* (regarding, for instance, the age structure of the population, the health systems of different societies, and the effect of thermal pollution of rivers), or by questions regarding the consequences and conditions of relevant events (e.g. an atomic war, or the development of smog over cities). In all these cases, scientific analysis is not an end in itself, but rather a means for further political action. On the level of analytical politics, however, this function remains a latent one; it does not become part of the scientific problem. The scientific analysis relates only to the initial conditions of political problem solving.

A more extensive scientification is implied in demands made on science to produce knowledge for systems control and for construction. Political action as such becomes a theme of scientific analysis — starting with the means of action. The demand is for knowledge to be implemented. The problem of action is translated into a technical problem. On this level, the utilization of science for policy-making, which corresponds to the type of 'means-ends rationalization', is distinguished by a kind of project approach. That is, a political goal is set beforehand and science is then expected to produce the instruments for its realization. The Manhattan Project for the construction of an atomic bomb and the manned space flight programme can serve as examples of this type of project initiation. The demand for systems control implies problems of the manipulation of complex systems, such as the demand for pharmacological control of diseases, for a means of obtaining a pure water supply, for a system of educational planning or for handling inflation. The knowledge required must assume the function of a lever engineered to control the effects and the output of the system, which is conceived as given. As against this, the demand for 'construction' relates to problems of the production of systems or objects. The prototype in this respect may be the construction of a machine, in the broadest sense (e.g. a fusion reactor or a process for desalting seawater).

Finally, the demands placed upon science with respect to systems formation are typical of a reflexive systems policy, that is for a level of policy formation which entails the integration of a number of areas of action. On this level, the political goals (or at least partial goals) themselves become an object of scientific analysis. What distinguishes the demand for the planning and formation of systems from the less complex problem of systems control is the 'reflexivity' of the approach. Scientific analysis may challenge the politically defined goal in the light of more general goals and principles to which politicians profess to be committed (which thus constitute the 'goals of the goal'). Systems policy may be exemplified by problems of maintaining an economic equilibrium (in the sense of coordinating the goals of full employment, monetary stability, economic growth, and a positive balance of trade), or by problems of urban renewal or educational reform. Thus far, however, this form of policy has rarely been realized. It has failed to materialize not only because of the unavailability of requisite knowledge, but also because of the limitations of policy-making. The situation results, however, not in the abandonment of demands on science for systematic policy formulation but in demands for the construction of even more complex systems involving, as additional marginal conditions, parameters which the process of policy-making must not violate (e.g. land-use regulations, private investment decisions, and resources of public finance). The effort to derive from the various forms of the utilization of science in politics specific functions of knowledge that science is expected to produce, does not allow an exclusive correlation. It is designed to explicate the typical forms of the demands placed upon science in different types of political decisions.

Cognitive Levels

On the level of analysis designated as 'cognitive', we may specify the epistemological and intellectual factors which, as they are to a relatively high degree technically binding, determine the structure and the development of a discipline or specialty. Since politically these factors are capable of being influenced within very narrow limits, they represent the central conditions for the resistance or receptivity of science in relation to external political control. Beyond this they affect a number of sociological elements of the dynamics of science as, for instance, cooperation or conflict between disciplines or specialties, the differentiation of specialties and evaluation processes within science.

It would be desirable to describe the cognitive factors exclusively in terms of the philosophy of science (in a broad sense of the term); however, this has not been achieved.[5] We shall not attempt to deal here with the more fundamental problem of whether a purely epistemological foundation of cognitive structures is possible at all, or whether such structures must, in the final analysis, be seen as socially constituted.[6] Indeed, the heuristic power of a sociological definition of scientific structures is itself subject to historical limitations. Only under the conditions of the institutionalization of science as 'a republic of science' — that is as a largely autonomous self-regulating social system — may the social and institutional dynamics of science (e.g. the community structure) have been a possible indicator for the dynamics of the cognitive structures. This, however, no longer applies to the conditions of the strategic development of science, of the politically motivated institutionalization of research in a wide variety of social contexts (in the universities, federal research centres, industrial laboratories, and so on). In order to decide whether such social dynamics are rooted in science, one needs independent indicators for the analysis both of the cognitive structures and of the potential of scientific progress in a specific research field.

The respective constituent cognitive elements of the structure which contain the intellectual conditions for the formation of specialties will be described in three dimensions: as methodological and technical factors, as theoretical factors, and as 'scientific relations'.

Methodological-technical Factors
The decisive cognitive criterion for the formation of a specialty can reside in the type of relation to the subject matter, in the use of a specific research technique or in the use of certain instruments.[7]

Conceptions of the subject matter reflect, on the one hand, different ontological designs of the subject (such as nature, meaning, ideal structures, norms) and on the other, different phases of theoretical development of the discipline. We may distinguish between the following modes of approach: description (classical biology); qualitative experiment (chemical elementary analysis); measurement (mechanics); interviewing (empirical sociology); and construction (mathematics, jurisprudence). The domains of X-ray crystallography, biometrics or electrophysiology may be taken as examples of specialties constituted by specific research techniques which are applicable to different object areas.

An example of specialty formation centering around a specific instrument is offered by radio astronomy. In each case, however, it must be asked to what extent the specific technique is in fact constitutive for the cognitive structure of a specialty. In high energy physics, for example, the theory determines the technical parameters of the instruments so unequivocally that the contrary relation is not conceivable.

Theoretical Factors

These factors concern the structures of concept formation and, in particular, the theoretical level of development achieved in a specialty at a given time. The latter determines the prevailing kind of research work done in a specialty (e.g. whether experimental 'trial and error' procedures or theory guided developments predominate). It is of significance for the development of a specialty and its potential for cooperation with other fields whether the definition of its subject matter entails normative implications (as, for instance, in peace research) or is purely descriptive (as, for instance, in physics). In view of the valuations they implicitly entail, normatively determined subject matters as a rule cannot be demarcated as clearly as can descriptively determined ones, and thus scarcely allow any sharp classification of research problems according to criteria of relevance. We can, however, distinguish between a minimal and a maximal normativity. According to the former, values are defined by the point of breakdown of a system (e.g. illness, death, the ecological 'death' of a river). According to the latter, the underlying values must be defined in terms of a continuum. Here the unity of the subject matter must be created by explicit consensus regarding the norms (e.g. in peace research, the definition of the concept of structural violence; in ecology, the transition from an analysis that identifies points of systematic crisis and breakdown to an analysis that examines desirable states of environmental welfare).

Another determinant of the structure and the potential for development of a specialty is its explanatory goal. This may be: causal-analytical (as in physics), functional (as in sociology and experimental pharmacology), historical-hermeneutical (as in archaeology), or formal inference (as in logic, mathematics, and statistics).

Finally, the dynamics of specialties can be characterized according to different degrees of openness to external influences or, contrarily, according to the degree of 'internal orientation' of their development. Its distinguishing feature may be:

— *experimental empiricism*: the priority of discovery over that of explanation
— *conceptualization strategies* of varying complexity: classification (early biology), model-building (cybernetics), theory development
— *theory dynamics*: for example the pursuit of a research programme on atomic theory, quantum theory or the revolutionary sequences of theories caused by anomalies[8]
— *normal science*: the exhaustion and occasional modification of a

paradigm, 'cleaning up' after the decisive breakthrough (e.g. molecular genetics today)
— *'finalization'*: a particular kind of theoretical development of externally determined problem areas on the basis of accepted general theories (plasma physics, metallurgy within the frame of solid state physics, agricultural chemistry).[9] Finalization must be distinguished from the mere application of theories to technical goals. The latter does not represent an independent pattern of development of a field of research. The application of theories can have at most indirect repercussions on theory formation.

Scientific Relations
This group of variables includes factors determining the cognitive relation of one specialty to other research fields, and in particular to the disciplines from which it originated. Here we are not only dealing with inter-theoretical relations or the 'meaning variance' of fundamental concepts, but also with the problem of the comparability and the transmission of practices of research, instruments, techniques and methods, the problem of the compatibility of the criteria of relevance in different sciences and of the reciprocal dependency and interaction of results.

   In the final analysis a definition, in terms of the philosophy of science, of the cognitive factors underlying the various types of specialty formation is needed — e.g. the differentiation of disciplines within a discipline (with or without organizational conflict), the emergence of interdisciplinary research, the labelling of 'outsider' areas — as well as a definition of the cognitive factors underlying the scientific status and prestige systems.[10] To characterize scientific relations we may, for instance, refer to:
— the theoretical and methodological background shared with other disciplines of special fields
— the specificity of the subject area in relation to the established classical disciplines. In this sense neurophysiology or biophysics are specific. It is possible to determine their relation to the different subject areas, theories and methods of physiology, physics, and biology. In these terms the subject matter of peace research or futurology is unspecific. It is not possible on the basis of the definition of the subject area to determine the relevance of the contributions of related disciplines such as, for instance, sociology, psychology, anthropology or physics.
— the interdisciplinarity of the claims and procedures of the specialty. Here we can distinguish between the *aggregative* approach within certain fields of inquiry (e.g. gerontology and urban research share the

focus of different disciplines) and a methodologically and theoretically *integrative* approach (as in the programme of human ecology as a
theory unifying human and natural conditions of reproduction)
— the dependence of the development of a specialty on results or upon
  discoveries in other fields of research (as is the case with pharmacology in relation to biochemistry) or, correspondingly, the relevance of a specialty for the potential development of other fields (as
  space research is relevant for geophysics)
— the presence of reductionist or anti-reductionist lines of development.
  Specialties can continue to follow the general tendency of physical
  reductionism (e.g. biochemistry in relation to traditional genetics).
  However, they can also define new and higher conceptual structural
  units as the basis of research programmes (e.g. Pasteur's biological
  theory of fermentation versus the chemical fermentation theory or
  early molecular genetics versus biochemistry).

Institutional Levels

The emergence of a specialty which can be described as a form of scientific change is to be analyzed sociologically as a process of institutionalization. What from the viewpoint of the philosophy of science constitutes
cumulative research, appears sociologically as a stable continuous social
activity. In these terms it is possible to indicate structures, conditions and
consequences of the formation of scientific specialties on the institutional
level.

We depart from a very general sociological characterization of specialties conceived as the institutionalization of a research area as an identifiable, stable and continuous activity. In the abstract dimension this entails
three things: a process of *differentiation*, which ensures the autonomy of
the specialty and demarcates it in relation to other research areas; a process of social integration, which creates the stable interrelationship of
scientific work and enables its 'social accumulation'; a process of
reproduction, which essentially ensures the recruitment of members of the
social community constituted within the specialty. The following description concentrates on features typical for the institutionalization of an
academic specialty. This is not to imply that there cannot be stable specialty formation in other social contexts, such as in governmental or
industrial laboratories with different mechanisms regarding the financing
and organization of research, the social control motivation.[11] The social
pattern of an academic specialty is, however, very close to that of a social

sub-system and may thus provide a model with respect to which the degree of autonomous institutionalization of a speciality can be judged.

The Process of Differentiation

It seems plausible that there exists a connection between the process of the formation of a specialty and its cognitive relations to other specialties and disciplines. Such relationships may be of interdependence, compatibility, or contradiction. In order to describe forms and degrees of differentiation sociologically, it will be necessary to describe the overlapping or the disjuncture of the interactions and institutions in related research areas. The variables relevant in this connection are:

— *the formation of an autonomous system of evaluation and reputation.* The differentiation on the cognitive level of epistemological goals, methods, and subject areas must have its analogy on the institutional level in the formation of specific evaluation criteria which are bound up with these cognitive contents. Peace research can serve as an example of an uncompleted process of differentiation. Its evaluation system is decentralized; peace researchers rely on the competent critique and on the ascription of reputation not primarily from a social community of peace research but from the respective related disciplines (psychology, sociology, political science, etc.).

— *the establishment of an autonomous communication system.* This may initially take the form of 'invisible colleges' but, when the process of differentiation is brought to completion, it takes the form of scientific professional associations, congresses and journals. Thereby a 'public' specific to the specialty comes into being.

— *the institutionalization of public relations,* that is, representation of the specialty in supporting institutions, in research reports, and the like.

— *the institutionalization of the expertise constituted by the specialty,* that is, the specialty's competence for problem-solving in a specific field is acknowledged by science as well as by politics and the general public.

— *institutionalization of transfer.* The contents of the special field are incorporated into curriculum planning and/or become a part of the formal standards of qualification for specific occupations.

— *institutionalization in fields of application.* The specialty is incorporated into industrial or governmental development programmes and may become, for example, the institutional link between data processing and industry, between electronics and strategic weapons and between medical specialties and medical clinics.

The Process of Social Integration

Here we specify certain variables which determine the form and degree of social cohesion within the specialty. These include:

— *structures of formal organization.* On the one hand it is necessary to identify the area of institutionalization of a specialty (e.g. the academic sphere, the Max-Planck Institutes, government-sponsored large-scale science research); on the other, to characterize resulting differences of degree in the bureaucratization of research and the social division of labour

— *informal structures acquired by the specialty,* such as the emergence of 'opinion leaders' and 'schools', the development of a functional division of labour, the formation of status systems due to the effect of reputation criteria and the emergence of social elites either as result of the self-perpetuation of established scientific reputation or of privileged access to important external resources.

Reproduction

Obviously, a scientific specialty is viable only when it is capable of attracting scientists who develop its research programme, and when resources are ensured. The factors which have particular relevance to the reproduction of scientists in a specialty are those which provide access to students and regulate the mobility of scientists from other fields. Here we have to consider:

— *the establishment of a separate training system,* that is the institutionalization of the specialty in the curriculum

— *the professionalization of the role of researcher* or teacher in the specialty, whereby the specialty comes to offer stable careers. The mobility of scientists to a 'professionalized' specialty is, as a rule, high. Work in the specialty may be considered a career in itself, not merely a transitional stage in a career, and the risk of going into the specialty is thus reduced.

— *the reversibility of a decision to work in a specialty.* The decision to join a field may, for cognitive or social reasons, be irreversible. The technical competence acquired may be so narrow that it is inapplicable outside the specialty itself. Work in a specialty may rank low in the scientific prestige system and even entail for the individual the stigma of being an outsider (as is the case of medical graduates who decide to work in anthropological medicine). These factors have a negative effect on mobility towards the specialty to the extent that they are not compensated by other factors (such as career security and the possibility of generous funding).

— *the problem of continuity in resource allocations.* The stability of a specialty may be influenced by the financial circumstances surrounding its development, in particular if the required resources are allocated by a centralized or a decentralized funding agency, if such allocations are made to depend on changeable political goals or on the agencies of scientific self-management, and if funding is made within the frame of a regular and formal system of allocations.

ON THE INTERDEPENDENCE OF COGNITIVE, INSTITUTIONAL AND POLITICAL VARIABLES IN THE DEFINITION OF RECEPTIVITY AND RESISTANCE

The political control of science is not a linear determination of scientific processes on the basis of independently defined political problems. Science itself shapes the social and political perception of problems and even more so their translation into problems to be solved by scientific strategies.

The 'Genetic' Dependence Between Political Problem Formulation and the State of Scientific Research

Anything that jeopardizes the existence or the functioning of the politico-social system may, in a general sense, be held to be a problem requiring political response. In a narrower sense, however, only that which lies within the scope of the system's capacity for action is viewed as 'problematic'. Whatever lies beyond this frame is perceived as a quasi-natural limitation or is ideologically presented that way in order to forestall criticism of the restrictions to which political action is subject. The more social and political processes are based on science, the more any increase in the system's capacity for action depends on analytical knowledge. Insights into the causes and conditions of their control make it possible to translate limitations into problems. This knowledge may serve as a point of departure for an effort to orientate science toward the development of a problem-solving strategy. On the other hand, however, this knowledge is generated not in terms of the imperatives of control but on the basis of the (relatively) internal and independent rules of development.

　　The dialectic underlying the relation between dependent and independent development of science within the frame of political control can be made explicit by the following example. For many years educational policy proceeded on the assumption that the raising of qualification standards made necessary by the dynamics of the economic system, and therefore the increase in the overall level of education, finds its limitation in the given natural distribution of talent. This conviction rested upon the premises of the openness of the educational system and the rationality of selection criteria, and embodied a concept of genetic intelligence and talent acknowledged by science. That talent is socially mediated was accepted only after statistical analyses had revealed regional differences in the distribution of talent and its correlation with factors of social stratification. From this point onwards the distribution of talent was no longer conceived as a limiting condition of social development but came to be a political problem for educational reform. The institutionalization of educational research was designed to mobilize science with a view to resolving this problem. If it can be said that the very perception of political problems is more and more influenced by science, this holds all the more for their translation into scientific strategies. What part of a political problem may be translated into a technical demand placed upon science depends (among other factors) on the capacity of the respective science. The competence of the disciplines to respond to political problems and the type of demands they may be able to fulfil vary according to their stage of development. The recourse of politics to science is in this respect a function of scientific progress. The transformation of political problems into technical demands will not, as a rule, be possible without the participation of scientists. Therefore, quite often the definition of the problem and of the demands will already be given in the categories and interpretative concepts of existing disciplines. This interdependence between science and policy formulation may serve to explain the fact that attempts to direct science towards the solution of 'external' problems only rarely extend much beyond the potentialities of science.

What problems are perceived in the concrete process of policy-making and what scientific problems these generate depend on, among other things, the institutional representation of science in the regulatory agencies, as well as on the administrators and the composition of scientific advisory staffs. It can be shown that the prevalence of physicists on the US President's Science Advisory Council had the effect of defining social problems predominantly in terms of the physical sciences.[12] In the field of urban renewal problems were often defined as relating to the development of new construction materials and new forms of housing construction.

We do not intend to consider in detail here the effects of the institutional structure of politics which may have a bearing on the scope of science policy. Our concern is to point out that the political intention to control science is itself not independent from science. The genetic dependence of policy formation on science does not, however, guarantee that the control of science will indeed be feasible. There always remains a critical difference between the technical demands placed upon science by politics and the problem-solving capacity of the respective science. It is this difference that constitutes the problematic character and risk of science policy. It is not only grounded in the inherent impossibility of making reliable prognoses of what is scientifically possible. A rational assessment of scientific potential is not the operative criterion in actual science policy. The definition of scientific feasibility given by the scientists, as well as the definition of demands given by politicians, follow from rules and interests, which will frequently preclude the intention of control being congruent with the development of science.

The Functional Dependence of the Political Direction of Science

Criteria for the Success of Control
It is important to ask when a policy designed to control science can be viewed as a success and when it must be said to be a failure; that is, when is a science receptive or resistant towards control? It would seem that in the case of product-oriented policies towards science, this can be decided according to whether the intended result (e.g. data, instruments, new materials, processes or machines) is obtained or not. However, this criterion is not as unambiguous as it appears to be. The direction of science is successful even when the result is a negative one, showing the desired goal to be impossible (e.g. the proof that a perpetuum mobile cannot be constructed). Furthermore, there is a question whether the time perspective of control should be made a criterion for success of direction. If it is assumed that almost every problem will be solved eventually, then one may be inclined to include the temporal perspective as a criteria of success. However, the length of time to the solution of the problem is not decisive here. Rather, the question is whether a solution is obtained as a result of a special development of science initiated by the external definition of problems, or from subsequently initiated developments in other disciplines, or whether it is due to progress in knowledge which, totally independent from the effects of political control, is achieved in fields of science which are developing according to their own

logic. Therefore, the receptivity of a science does not depend upon its producing a solution to the problem within the expected time span, but only upon the fact that political control initiates a development which proves to be constitutive for the problem solution.

Thus, it cannot be disputed that in the case of plasma physics, science is receptive with respect to the problem of developing a fusion reactor simply because this programme, on account of intrinsic difficulties, takes much longer to complete than expected. The orientation to the problem of the fusion reactor did create a scientific development — with special theories, methods, and instruments — which probably would not have occurred without external direction. It seems reasonable to speak of successful control if through this external direction a particular cumulative development of science is initiated which may be said to point to the solution of the problem. Thus, the evaluation of control, as the criterion for judging the success of the research process, is unconnected with its final result. This is important for the rationalization of science policy decisions as it allows an *ex ante* judgment. This requires criteria which allow one to determine under what conditions which scientific strategy promises success for a given objective.

We shall try to identify such criteria. Some fundamental definitions of resistance and receptivity can be stated if objectives of different complexity are related to specific levels of scientific potential which are characteristic for various phases of scientific development.

Levels of Political Definition of Problems and of Scientific Potential
Political problems and scientific achievement cannot be compared directly. How, then, can they be related to one another in an assessment of receptivity or resistance of science? The necessary link between them, the *tertium comparationis,* is provided by the technical demands we have classified above as correlates of the utilization of science in politics. The stages of description (assessment, systems control, construction and systems formation) are technical categories. They apply to any type of instrumental action, whether it is based on scientific explanation or not. These technical functions can be related to politics since in the process of increasingly 'science-based' politics problems of action are operationalized as technical problems. And they can be related to science as well, due to the operative character of the scientific explanation which is, in the last analysis, rooted in the experimentalistic concept of truth. Therefore, the various stages of scientific development imply various stages of technical capacity. We characterize the levels of cognitive

capacity by analogy to the stages of scientific explanation of natural systems. The problems occurring are arranged according to their complexity: the determination of relevant variables, the determination of the degree of their respective involvement or importance, the clarification of the system's conditions of stability (nominal values, threshold values), and the discovery of the system's mechanisms. The corresponding capacities of science may be described as analysis and measurement, functional explanation and causal explanation. They characterize the cognitive level of development of the scientific discipline in question. If this continuum is supplemented by the category of systems integration, which is to characterize the capability of science to integrate and transform results, theories, and methods of various research fields into more complex units, then a group of four levels of scientific capacity is obtained which can be contrasted with the four functions of political claims in regard to science. The ientral hypothesis for a determination of factors of receptivity and resistance is that these levels of capacity each characterize the respective cognitive level of development of science which must *at least* be attained if the correlative political demands are to be met.

Demands for assessment (defined above as describing status quo conditions, determining characteristics and sizes of objects, and identifying causal factors and concrete input-output relationships) can be met by disciplines which have developed few theoretical explanations for their subject area. Laboratories financed by the state were established as early as the eighteenth century, where minerals, water, and gun powder were successfully analyzed. The same is true for present empirical social research, which is carrying out effective surveys despite its diffuse theoretical condition. Description in science presupposes certain structuring theoretical concepts (the definition of variables, indicators, the construction of classifications, concepts of elements) and techniques (e.g. experimental processes in chemistry, polls and tests in social science). The potential of analysis is not tied to the ultimate validity of the theoretical concepts used (e.g. chemical analysis at the time of the phlogiston theory and national accounts in economics). The analytical questions which can actually be formulated in a problem area do, however, depend on the theoretical development of science. For instance, questions regarding the radioactive hazards of nuclear reactors presuppose nuclear physics, the concept of radiation injuries, and the Geiger counter. Demands for description, therefore, can contain many presuppositions on the part of science with respect to the definition of variables, their operationalization, and the instrumental techniques. As a rule, however, meeting them does not call for additional development of theory. They primarily presuppose in science an explorative (measuring, experimental) approach to the object, not its theoretical explanation.

Meeting demands for systems control requires more than the knowledge of input-output correlations by which the results of complex systems can be varied without clarifying their inner structure. It requires knowledge of the conditions and the degree of effectiveness of such regulations. Based on this insight, input-output correlations can then be sought systematically. As a rule, black-box theories and macromodels of the subject area will be sufficient. The history of medical therapy offers an example of the connection between demands for systems control and macrotheories. The attempt to cure diseases through drugs was, apart from some fortunate cases such as quinine, digitalis, and iodine, completely unsuccessful so long as it was carried out on the basis of purely non-deductive trial and error experiments. Only the discovery of causes of diseases and the knowledge of the importance of carrier and contact processes permitted successful control through vaccines, the illumination of carrier factors, and later through chemotherapy. The condition of success, therefore, was the development of adequate models of the process of disease, its causation and its mediating factors.

Demands for 'construction' presuppose the knowledge of the mechanisms predominant in the subject area, that is corroborated causal models and microtheories. The problem of increasing the efficiency of the steam engine may serve as an example. The task is to construct an artificial system and to economize its operation. The adequate level of the scientific problem approach was the structural explanation of the system. The problem remained unsolved as long as the engineers were handling it on the level of analysis and measurement, by systematically varying measure, weights and the assembly of engine parts. Only after an explanation of steam characteristics and of the heat process within the engine could there be real progress, beginning with James Watt's separate condenser. In the pertinent science this presupposed a cognitive level of development, on which the system's mechanisms can be understood with causal models.[13]

The specific cognitive competence of science necessary for the group of problems which we have characterized as implying claims for system building has so far hardly been investigated. These claims often imply the necessity for interdisciplinary research since the problem cannot clearly be assigned to any single discipline or research area. This is increasingly typical of the relationship between governmental science policy and the established organizational structures of science. It shows that political problems are translated into tasks for science, not only with respect to their technological aspect (hardware), but also insofar as they are problems of the social system. Whether these demands require a specific level of scientific capacity depends on whether the objective of control merely requires the aggregation of various sciences or their *integration*. In the first case, only institutional and organizational problems derived from the horizontal structure of the problem vis-à-vis the established cognitive organization of science will arise. An example of this is disaster research, which is research on psychological, sociological and technical causes. However, in the second case, the demand for interdisciplinarity often implies a theory of a complexity which science so far has not yet developed. This is the case in environmental research insofar as it has to develop its own theory of ecological or socio-ecological systems. Systems formation, as in curriculum development, requires a material, as well as a formal theory of higher systems. They imply a transcending of present disciplinary border lines in science and a certain fusion of natural and social sciences, whereby the latter will assume a leading part in providing the framework for the integration of the various bodies of knowledge.[14]

Determining Cognitive Resistance

The levels of the recourse of politics to science, that is the levels of its 'scientification' and the technical functions of the knowledge demanded, may now be structured in a table, together with the corresponding levels of scientific capacity which are deemed necessary for meeting such demands. (See opposite page.)

Attempting such a correlation contains many risks. There are examples which show that this correlation is not always a necessary or sufficient condition for success. Thus, classical engine technology (power engines and machine tools) proves that 'construction' does not always require causal theories but can be successful through empirical processes. The supposed technological superiority of the causal theory may fail due to its being tentative. Thus, for instance, the a-theoretical development of technology has succeeded in constructing amorphous semiconductors despite deductions from solid state physics that they could not exist. On the other hand, cancer research provides an example for systems control, which will probably be successful only when a causal theory has been developed. Finally it is not obvious that if empirical processes fail, only an improvement in theory and not an instrumental innovation for the experimental scanning process can lead to success.

TABLE: *Typology of Degrees of 'Scientification' of Political Problems, Functions of Knowledge and Levels of Development of Science*

Political objectives of control according to the degree of 'scientification' of political problems	Political objectives of control according to function of demanded knowledge	Scientific capacity (cognitive level of development)
'analytical' politics (rationalizing initial conditions of political problem-solving)	assessment (description)	basic structural concepts, operationalization, analysis and measurement
'means-end rationalization' (production of technical means of political intervention)	systems control	functional explanation, macro-theory of the subject matter
	construction	causal explanation, micro-theory of the subject matter
systems politics (reflexive process of goal definition for political intervention)	systems formation	integrated science, fusion of natural and social sciences theory of complex system

What, then, has been achieved with the correlation? Without denying the role of coincidence or intuition in scientific success and without excluding the risk this necessarily entails, it provides a definition of the 'normal', technological potential of different levels of development of science. Rational science policy must be based on such evaluation, rather than upon the unpredictable and surprising result (serendipity) or upon the perceived difficulty (anomaly). Within stated limitations, our model explicates some factors that have to be taken into consideration in determining the feasibility of science policy programmes. It represents an approximative model for the cognitive resistance or receptivity of different fields of science toward external control. In principle, receptivity is greater if the field's cognitive level of development guarantees at least the technological potential which is a normal prerequisite for the external problem: where data are demanded, the conceptual and instrumental conditions for developing measurements have to be available; where systems control is desired, functional theories must be available; and for demands implying system construction, causal theories must be at hand. Correspondingly, resistance may be considered a cognitive deficit which does not permit a scientific strategy of problem solution on the cognitive level appropriate to the complexity of the problem.

The cases cited above, such as the improvement of the steam engine and the development of medical therapy, are examples of cases of resistance to external direction. A more recent case is cancer research. Until recently, the experimental search for agents causing or curing cancer was carried out on an insufficient cognitive basis, essentially by means of drug screening. The cognitive resistance of science toward this strategy is due to the lack of theoretical knowledge of the function and structure of different substances and metabolic processes. Without such knowledge, the empirical search for a means of cancer control will remain an almost hopeless enterprise. Real progress can probably only be expected by the fusion of cancer research with molecular biology, a development which is now taking place. However, the feasibility of this fusion does not depend on the control of science through the cancer problem, but on basic research in molecular biology which was originally conducted without reference to external problems.

The cognitive receptivity or resistance of the social sciences may be illustrated by attempts to base educational policy on scientific analysis. As a rule, receptivity in the social sciences is given only with respect to demands for descriptive analysis. One may tace the surveys of Coleman *et al.* in the report on equality of educational opportunity as an example.[15] Findings concerning the uneven distribution of educational achievement among racial, ethnic and social classes are not questioned — despite some objections regarding the validity of the instruments.[16] Educational and social policy aiming at the reduction of the dependence of opportunities on the social origin of individuals may therefore successfully resort to science for reliable information on the status quo and on the extent of the problem. However, as soon as the demand is extended from the description of initial conditions to the development of means of intervention, the social sciences prove to be incompetent and hence resistent. In order to provide techniques for a strategic manipulation of the output of the educational system, corroborated black-box models of this system permitting distinctions between dependent and independent variables and identifying the functional significance of key variables would be necessary. The development of such models is, in general, greatly hampered by well-known difficulties of determining causal relations from non-experimental statistical data.[17]

The cognitive resistance of the social sciences becomes completely obvious when social sciences are confronted with demands for systems formation. With respect to the development of an integrated school system in the Federal Republic of Germany, for instance, the role of the social scientist is not to give the technical foundation and derivation of such systems, but rather to participate in political processes of planning and reform.

Obviously, the model developed so far has its limits. The question may arise whether the correlation between objectives of control and cognitive levels of science does not vary according to the internal complexity of the subject area. An indication of such a variation should be that the systems control problem of cancer therapy or prevention can only be solved on the basis of microtheories. A similar problem can be found in demands for description where the object's structure excludes a direct observation of the relevant size and characteristics. For such cases our assumption that demands for description in science as a rule merely presuppose an empirical progress and a relatively elementary methodological and conceptual development, obviously does not apply. Insofar as the exploration of an object presupposes technical innovation, such research will be dependent upon theoretical results with which indirect measurements and indicators can be corroborated. An example of this is the demand to specify how much oil is located beneath the North Sea. Such a question can only be answered indirectly, with the aid of assumptions about the speed at which pressure waves spread in different rock layers. If such theoretically-based indicators are not available, then science will be resistant toward external demands even though only a problem of description is involved.

A further limitation of the present model is its static character. Actually, receptivity and resistance are not defined by the statically defined level of a field's development but by the possible development which can be initiated by the intended control. The model must be enlarged by a dynamic dimension. It must be asked, therefore, whether the cognitive deficit of a discipline preventing an adequate strategy of problem-solving can be recovered — not simply through the general development of the relevant science but through a development which is oriented toward the external problem. The required steps of development are of different magnitude on different levels, for example the operationalization of concepts and the development of instruments, functional or causal theory formation. Correspondingly, the possibility of initiating them by the formulation of external problems decreases. This corresponds to the thesis that sciences are all the less controllable the 'harder' they are. Whereas the development of analysis and measurements as well as the design of experimental strategies may be linked relatively successfully to external goals (or at least be induced by an external problem), theory formation must, independent of all external goals, be left to the internal dynamics of science. Receptivity in regard to complex technological demands, then, can only reside in the application of available theories. An externally directed process of theory formation by which the required technological capacity of the discipline is produced *ad hoc* is unlikely, not to say impossible.

However, this thesis needs to be modified. It holds insofar as the 'open problems' of theory formation deal with fundamental, general research fronts. Thus, for instance, the *theoretical* solution to the problem of biological pesticides is excluded by the open problems of molecular biology. This gap cannot be closed by 'oriented' basic research. Therefore the problem cannot be treated by controlled theory formation but only by experimental empiricism, on the basis of already available functional and causal knowledge (e.g. from physiology and ethology). The situation is different, however, if the theoretical deficit concerns areas which can already build upon substantially completed or 'closed' theories. Here 'finalization' of science is possible: that is *strategic theory development,* according to externally set goals.[18] Examples of finalization include Liebig's theoretical solution of the problem of increasing agricultural yields through agricultural chemistry and the basic research directed towards solving general problems of the fusion reactor.[19] The receptivity of science to these tasks of systems control or construction lies in the capability of these fields to develop the required theoretical knowledge in an *ad hoc* manner.

Correlating the cognitive levels of scientific capacity with political objectives does not determine which scientific strategy — whether theory formation or experimental analysis — will lead to success. With the theoretical development of a scientific discipline, the possibility of providing additional theoretical explanation of fields of application will increase; in other cases the accuracy and efficiency of empirical processes is increased. Thus, the problem of producing a new material with specific characteristics (which is a problem of construction) can, in principle, be solved through theory formation in solid state physics (theoretical metallurgy). It can, however — and this is normally the case — also be solved through experimental analysis, by trial and error. The problem of controlling the development of pharmaceutics cannot be solved without a good functional theory; if such a theory is available, then it can be treated by qualitative analysis (experimental pharmacology). Therefore, no specific scientific strategies can be determined for the various objectives of control. Depending on the level of cognitive development, deductive and empirical processes can equally promise success. The level of cognitive development of a scientific field is the crucial reference point for judging its resistance and receptivity.

Determining Institutional Resistance
It does not seem altogether evident that, once cognitive receptivity is given, the success of policies in controlling scientific development can be frustrated by institutional resistance. The idea of control seems to imply that institutional factors of successful science (resources, manpower, work organization and so on) can principally be produced and employed as levers of control. Thus, institutional resistance would simply be a problem of degree. If the research aimed at by the control effort cannot be stabilized as a cumulative social activity within the established social system of science, then control cannot operate merely through incentives (money, mainly) and depend on the social mechanisms of the scientific system; instead, it must supplement and reconstruct this system by social planning, by establishing institutes, creating careers, and setting up training courses.

However, such freedom for the institutional manipulation of science cannot be assumed. First of all, there are external political limitations stemming from the integration of science into economic strategies of utilization and into political vested interests. There is, for instance, hardly an alternative to the institutionalization of product-related research in industrial laboratories of private business. Moreover, there are inherent limitations of complexity in the range of intervention. It is unthinkable that the planning of science can reconstruct intentionally all the essential social mechanisms of science, from creating motivation within the socialization process, to reorienting the status and prestige hierarchies of the established disciplines. Therefore, each external control of science must more or less utilize the given social structures of science and can replace them only in particular areas.

Generally speaking, these are limitations to the political direction of science which arise from the necessity to develop a field before it can be instrumentally employed. Thus, scientific socialization processes represent a crucial mechanism with respect to the continuous supply of manpower. At the same time, they structure motivations and orientations among scientists which complicate their manipulation and utilization. In particular they transmit a tendency towards general reflection and theorizing which is already a psychological factor of resistance towards an external control of research. Every control has to reckon with these factors, just as with those social processes (communication, group formation, work organization, social differentiation) which are essential prerequisites of productive science.

The variability of the social structures of science, above all, is limited by the relations between institutional and cognitive structures. Such correspondences between cognitive and institutional factors on various levels of disciplinary development have been described in several studies of the emergence of specialties.[20] Until now, however, it has not been clear whether these correspondences are coincidental or whether the institutional structures are functional prerequisites or necessary results of certain cognitive processes. It appears to be certain that cognitive processes of differentiation both require and promote a corresponding social differentiation within the system of science.[21]

The analysis of the institutional consequences of cognitive processes shows that there is quite a distinct relationship between a field's internal development and the development of a hierarchic system of reputation and evaluation. Cumulative theory developments and distinct research fronts permit a clear ordering of different scientific activities and results according to their relevance for the discipline's internal development. Given this connection, a stronger functional differentiation of specialties and problem areas is found in mature disciplines than in less developed ones. The internal system of status and prestige is tied to these differences.[22] Thus, the more a research field becomes cognitively hierarchical, the clearer are the differences of reputation and status in its social structure. This implies a lack of mobility among scientists towards research fields which are established under product oriented policies. With that we have identified a factor of 'institutional' resistance: insofar as scientists belong to disciplines which have obtained a cumulative theory development, externally oriented, 'applied' research will, as a rule, be ascribed a lower rank in the discipline's prestige system. This applies, for instance, to the diverse works on measurement and analyses which physicists could perform within the field of environmental research. Physicists, therefore, try to avoid such activities. However, corresponding barriers from the status system are missing in those disciplines which still proceed substantially in an experimental and untheoretical manner. This holds for physiology. Therefore physiology should not be institutionally resistant to external problems such as the experimental development of biological pesticides.

The effects of institutional factors operating independently from the cognitive structure of the discipline can be illustrated by the academic organization and professionalization of sociology. Sociology has been organized in the academic system in about the same way as the natural sciences, in faculties and departments with special chairs and institutes, with curricula and examinations — the latter marking its gradual professionalization. This is, of course, not a consequence of a particular paradigmatic stage of development of the discipline. The institutional differentiation of sociology does not, for instance, correspond to a hierarchy of status which relates different specialties to identifiable research fronts in sociology. It is, instead, the result of other factors, such as the external demand for sociological training (not necessarily specialized knowledge), and the dynamics of the university system which demand a certain degree of disciplinary organization for the administration of research and teaching — irrespective of the cognitive stage of development of the discipline or specialty.

This is the basis of institutional resistance. It promotes communication along the lines of discipline boundaries, preventing interdisciplinary work even in cases where this would be cognitively feasible. This kind of institutional resistance despite cognitive receptivity can be illustrated by the case of educational research in the Federal Republic of Germany. The initiative to establish educational research as an interdisciplinary specialty came from the scientific system, at about the same time that the educational situation became a political issue. The beginnings of research on the educational system were visible in economics and sociology. However, the establishment of an institute for educational research in the Max-Planck Society in 1963 had explicitly been justified by the almost complete lack of research on educational problems in the universities. This deficiency can be ascribed to the specialized organization of univer-

sities into disciplines. The foundation of a number of state institutes outside the academic system, dealing with special problems of education
research, is a further indicator that this kind of applied social research can
hardly be developed within the university. 'Numerous examples show
that attempts at educational research, whenever they have been
developed within traditional disciplines, became isolated as soon as they
transcended the borders of the established body of disciplinary knowledge.'[23] At the root of this type of institutional resistance there is apparently a conflict between the evolution of established disciplines and their
institutional structures, and the inherent criteria of relevance of the new
problem area.

It is true that disciplines oriented towards education as a focus of
research (psychology, sociology, economics, pedagogics) cannot easily be
integrated into a new genuine discipline developing a theoretical
dynamics of its own. It is, however, true that the demand for educational
research has met the institutional resistance of the academic system even
in those fields where, according to their cognitive stage of development,
the disciplines were indeed able to respond to the political demands —
and where they did respond, once the appropriate institutional setting
was provided.[24]

The case of institutional resistance of science despite cognitive receptivity is certainly not frequent or typical in science policy. Peace research
may serve as an example for the more familiar case where, due to cognitive resistance, even the provision of the most favourable institutional
circumstances will yield no results. Peace research has emerged as an
interdisciplinary field complementary to the field of international relations. It had been conceived as research based on the disciplines of political science, sociology, economics, geography and demography. In contrast to the field of international relations, where the orientations towards
the conditions of peace as an interdisciplinary subject could be achieved
at best by a long process of reorientation, the new field of peace research
promised results that might directly be translated into actual policies. It
thus received massive governmental support. Especially in Scandinavia,
and even more so in the Federal Republic, peace research became
organized in institutes outside the universities, with special foundations
designated for its support.

However, it became apparent with the foundation of the Deutsche
Gesellschaft für Friedens- und Konfliktforschung (DGFK) that despite
these efforts at institutionalization, it was not possible to integrate the
research of the various disciplines into a new field with a cognitive

dynamic of its own. Instead, disciplinary research projects were subsumed under the label of peace research and under the funding authority of the DGFK.[25]

Such consensual hierarchy of relevance is a prerequisite of an efficient interdisciplinary research strategy by which gaps in knowledge are identified and related to the competence of the various disciplines.[26] In fact, the problem of peace is conceived in such a way that it implies the global construction of political systems, a task which is not within the reach of any of the concerned disciplines, nor of their merely additive aggregation.

These examples show that institutional conditions may operate as factors of resistance irrespective of the cognitive stage of development of a discipline. They also show that the strategic variation of institutional factors designed to initiate or control scientific development may be frustrated by cognitive conditions. Science policy has to rely in every case on an assessment of both the cognitive and the institutional conditions of science relative to the objectives of political control.

Wolfgang van den Daele, Max-Planck-Institut zur Erforschung der Lebensbedingungen der wissenschaftlich-technischen Welt, 813 Starnberg, Riemerschmidstrasse 7, Postfach 1529, FRG.
Peter Weingart, Forschungsschwerpunkt Wissenschaftsforschung, Universität Bielefeld, 48 Bielefeld, Postfach 8640, FRG.

WOLFGANG VAN DEN DAELE received his doctoral degree from the University of Hamburg. He is a member of the Max-Planck Institute concerned with the preconditions of human life in the modern world and is currently working on a comparative analysis of science policy in the Federal German Republic.
PETER WEINGART received his *Diplom* and his doctorate from the Free University of Berlin. He is now Professor of Sociology of Science and Science Policy at the University of Bielefeld and is involved in studies on the interaction between scientific development and the articulation of public and political opinion.

NOTES

1. Compare the politically induced development of heavy ion research in the German Federal Republic, K. Prüss, *Kernforschungspolitik in der BRD* (Frankfurt: Suhrkamp, 1974).
2. See R. Whitley, 'Cognitive and Social Institutionalization of Scientific Specialities and Research Areas', pp. 69-95 in: R. Whitley (ed.), *Social Processes of Scientific Development* (London: Routledge and Kegan Paul, 1974).
3. H. L. Zetterberg, 'Theorie, Forschung und Praxis in der Soziologie', pp. 65-104 in: R. König (ed.), *Handbuch der empirischen Sozialforschung* (Stuttgart: F. Enke Verlag, 1967).

4. Comparative case studies of this kind are being prepared in a project on 'The Cognitive and Institutional Determinants of the Success or Failure of the Political Control of Scientific Development' at the Centre for Interdisciplinary Research, Bielefeld. This project will serve further to develop the theoretical concepts indicated here.

5. Compare, for instance, Kuhn's attempt to operationalize the paradigm concept in sociological terms by an underlying community structure or Polanyi's recourse to socialization for the transmission of inexplicable 'tacit knowledge' that is constitutive for any science. T. S. Kuhn, *The Structure of Scientific Revolutions* (University of Chicago Press, 1962); M. Polanyi, *Personal Knowledge: Towards a Post-Critical Philosophy* (University of Chicago Press, 1958; New York: Harper and Row, Harper Torchbooks, 1964).

6. This is a much discussed problem in the philosophy of science. Even if an analysis of the cognitive structures within the frame of sociology of knowledge were ultimately to prove fundamental, a line of separation would have to be drawn between cognitive structures and social structures. Thus, for instance, the compatibility of cognitive structures cannot be determined solely by relations of cooperation and communication, and the existence of a research front cannot be measured simply in terms of the concentration of scientists within specific object areas.

7. See also the distinction between 'technique', 'theory' and 'subject matter' specialties in J. Law, 'The Development of Specialties in Science: the Case of X-ray Protein Crystallography', pages 123-152 above.

8. I. Lakatos, 'Falsification and the Methodology of Scientific Research Programmes' pp. 91-196 in: I. Lakatos / A. Musgrave (eds.), *Criticism and the Growth of Knowledge* (Cambridge University Press, 1970).

9. See G. Böhme / W. van den Daele / W. Krohn, 'Die Finalisierung der Wissenschaft', *Zeitschrift für Soziologie* 2 (1973) 128-144.

10. On this conflict, see W. O. Hagstrom, *The Scientific Community* (New York/London: Basic Books, 1965) 159.

11. See R. Krohn, *The Social Shaping of Science: Institutions, Ideology and Careers in Science* (Westport, Conn: Greenwood, 1971).

12. P. Weingart, *Die amerikanische Wissenschaftslobby* (Düsseldorf: Bertelsmann Universitätsverlag, 1970) 100.

13. For example, in the case of Watt's discovery, it remains an open question whether Watt took the idea of latent heat from Black or whether he reproduced it himself.

14. The question remains whether in this field there are, in principle, limitations for prognostic theories resulting from the structure of the object.

15. J. Coleman *et al.*, *Equality of Educational Opportunity* (Washington: U.S. Office of Education, 1966).

16. On verbal ability as a measure of educational achievement, see G. Cain / H. Watt, 'Problems in Making Policy Inferences from the Coleman Report', *American Sociological Review* 35 (1970) 228-242.

17. W. van den Daele / P. Weingart, 'The Utilization of the Social Sciences in the Federal Republic of Germany: An Analysis of Factors of Resistance and Receptivity of Science to External Direction', *Report II, Wissenschaftsforschung* (University of Bielefeld, 1974).

18. See Böhme / van den Daele / Krohn, 'Die Finalisierung der Wissenschaft'.

19. On agricultural chemistry, see Wolfgang Krohn / Wolf Schäfer, 'The Origins and Structure of Agricultural Chemistry', pages 27-52 above.

20. Hagstrom, *The Scientific Community;* N. C. Mullins, 'The Development of a Scientific Specialty: The Phage Group and the Origins of Molecular Biology', *Minerva* 10 (1972) 51-82; D. L. Krantz, 'Schools and Systems: The Mutual Isolation of Operant and Non-operant Psychology as a Case-Study', *Journal of the History of the Behavioural Sciences* 8 (1972) 86-102; cf. P. Weingart (ed.), *Wissenschaftssoziologie*

II, Determinanten wissenschaftlicher Entwicklung (Frankfurt: Fischer / Athenäum, 1973).

21. In addition to references cited above, see B. C. Griffith / N. C. Mullins, 'Coherent Social Groups in Scientific Change: Invisible Colleges may be consistent throughout Science', *Science* 177 (1972) 959-964; and Kuhn, 'Postscript, 1969', in *The Structure of Scientific Revolutions* (University of Chicago Press, 2nd ed., 1970).
22. Hagstrom, *The Scientific Community.*
23. Deutscher Bildungsrat, *Aspekte für die Planung der Bildungsforschung,* (Bonn: Empfehlung der Bildungskommission, 1974) 71.
24. See van den Daele / Weingart, 'The Utilization of the Social Sciences', 104.
25. Compare E. O. Czempiel, 'Friedensforschung ist provokative Forschung', in *DGFK Informationen* 1-2; and C. Görk, 'Die Entstehung der Disziplin Friedensforschung', in *Zwischenbericht der Projektgruppe Fallstudien zur Wissenschaftsentwicklung* (manuscript, FU-Berlin, 1974). The reason that the identity of peace research has remained merely institutional (and we assume will continue to do so) lies in the normative character of its subject matter. 'Peace' as a reference point does not yield criteria to determine hierarchically the relative relevance of the contributions of the disciplines concerned.
26. This is illuminated by the debate over the so-called critical peace research; see P. Weingart, 'Bedingungen und Möglichkeiten einer kritischen Friedensforschung', pp. 186-200 in: D. Pforte / O. Schwenke (eds.), *Ansichten einer künftigen Futurologie* (Munich: Hanser, 1973).

Index of Persons